From Elim to Carmel

Aspects of Christian Doctrine and Experience

by
William Jones, M.D., D.D., LL.D.
Of the Saint Louis Conference

With an Introduction
by
Dougan Clark, A.M., M.D.
Of the Friends Church

SCHMUL PUBLISHING COMPANY
NICHOLASVILLE, KENTUCKY

Cover image Copyright: <a href='https://www.123rf.com/profile_marinakoven'>marinakoven / 123RF Stock Photo</a>

Published by Schmul Publishing Co.
PO Box 776
Nicholasville, KY USA

Printed in the United States of America

ISBN 10: 0-88019-602-5
ISBN 13: 978-0-88019-602-4

Visit us on the Internet at www.wesleyanbooks.com, or order direct from the publisher by calling 800-772-6657, or by writing to the above address.

Contents

AUTHOR'S PREFACE

THE RED SEA ROLLED its victorious waves above the chivalrous dead of Egypt's great army. It stood forever as a barrier between the taskmasters of Goshen and the shouting hosts of liberated Hebrew slaves. But wide and treeless stretches of blistering sand lay round them on every side. Although they were free, forever free, and the echoes of their independence anthem still lingered upon the desert air, or swept up the dry and sultry wadies on the hot wings of the wind, still the land of promise— the future home of the people and the nation— was ten days march westward across the trackless wastes of the desert.

Their inheritance lay on the other side of the Jordan. The clusters from Eshcol, the pomegranates, the rocks filled with honey and the valleys abounding in succulence, soil and climate, field, orchard, and vineyard, attest the divine veracity.

The possession of that inheritance could not add one jot to their freedom; that was perfect. But the land, their inheritance, could lay its wealth on their altars; it could open its resources for their sustentation, and give to them its facilities for growth and culture.

In that land was to be built the greatest nation the world had ever known; and from that centre was to go forth the influences that were to direct the thought of the world, and shape its history to the end of time. There in the fulness of time the Saviour was to be born, and the Book of Revelation completed.

But God's plan embraced much in detail. It involved man's obedience to law, and his fidelity to the divine purpose. The establishment of the nation was impossible without the development of a true manhood.

Bedouinism has its chivalry; but Jerusalem must have its prophets, its priesthood, and statesmen.

Ilderim, first among the Sheiks, was great in his tribal display; but when the world's most wealthy and cultured ruler stood before King Solomon, her verdict was: that "The half had not been told."

The unlettered and grimy slaves were free, and Egypt was forever spoiled; but the corner-stone of the great empire was not yet laid.

God brought the liberated company to the cooling fountains and the refreshing shades of Elim, that they might rest for a time and adjust matters; that they might at once enter upon their promised inheritance, and build the throne of David, and prepare for the wisdom and splendor of Solomon.

Between the place where the seventy royal palm-trees spread their foliage and flung their fragrance upon the air, and the place in the west where the fruits and spices of Carmel added their richness to Israel's store, the great events of all the ages have transpired. There arose the "Royal throne of David, the poet king of Israel;" and there in Oriental lustre was the brilliant career of Solomon. There the religious institutions and rites of divine worship were established; and there the Saviour was born.

There is a religious symbolism of great significance in

all of this. It typifies the freedom of the human soul from the bondage of sin; its purification and establishment in full salvation. It reveals to us the Solomonic splendors of a full-grown Christian manhood.

There were two distinct crises in the progress of Israel, and they were not alike, nor for the same purpose. There was the deliverance from bondage, with all that it implies. It embraces all that transpired from the time they ate the paschal lamb with the bitter herbs, until the refluent sea sang its funeral dirge above the Egyptian army. But there was a second crisis— a process as definite, a preparation as carefully planned and as authoritatively commanded, as that which pertained to the Passover. This was when they entered into their inheritance.

At the first it was the paschal lamb with the bitter herbs. At the second it was: "Sanctify yourselves; prepare yourselves victuals."

The second crisis was as definite and specific as the first, and corresponded in all things to that which was to be achieved.

The deliverance from bondage symbolizes the liberation of the sinner from the guilt of sin. The crossing of the Jordan and the possession of the land symbolizes full salvation, as taught by the Methodist Episcopal Church; and the glories of Solomon and the fragrance and fruitage of Carmel indicate the possibilities of growth and culture after the experience of full salvation.

—WILLIAM JONES

Publisher's Preface

THE PRECISE LOCATION of Elim is uncertain today, but biblical scholars agree on one point: the Israelites passed through on their way to the Promised Land. It was definitely encountered before they crossed the Jordan River. There is no question about the location of Mt. Carmel, above the current city of Haifa on the Mediterranean coast. Between the two locales lies the whole of historical Israel.

This is the vehicle Dr. Jones chose to convey his volume dealing with the Christian life, encompassing various points of interest between the moment of salvation and entire sanctification. He addresses several different areas that affect the Believer and his influence, and he does not shy away from controversy. Some of these spiritual debates have been laid to rest since the original publication of the book; some still boil strongly; but all of them he addresses with the eternal principles of God's Word. For instance, chapter thirteen alone is worth the price of the book. The author considers the effect of modern technology (for that day) on the Kingdom of God. He is ebullient with the tremendous possibilities such advances offer to spread the Gospel, and his joy shows through the whole chapter. It is no effort at all to employ the same standards of measure in today's world. If he could have seen the Internet, social media, the computer, satellite communications, mobile phones, he would not have been intimidated at all. Far from it—he would have been beside himself in considering the implications to spread the Good News.

These are timeless truths from God's Word, calling all to a holy life, whether in the first or the twenty-first century.

—D. Curtis Hale
Publisher, 2017

Introduction

THE WORD SERMON IS from the Latin *sermo*, a speech or discourse. But by common consent in the Church of Christ its use is limited to a discourse on some topic or theme connected with the Christian religion. Almost without exception also, the sermon is founded upon some text or passage of Holy Scripture. "The sermon," says the late Dr. Shedd, "is but the elongation of a text."

Dr. Austin Phelps insists also that in order to fulfil the true idea of a sermon the discourse must be *oral* and addressed to a heterogeneous — that is to say a *mixed* — audience. There is ground for both these positions. A written discourse which is read to a congregation is, strictly speaking, a lecture, from *lego*, to read; and the lecture is usually addressed to a class of minds who are interested in the particular subject treated of, such as science, or philosophy, or philanthropy. But a sermon is addressed to every class of minds, and its object is both to persuade and to instruct. Its aim is to reach the old and the young, the educated and the ignorant, the rich and the poor, the high and the low, the saint and the sinner. Sermons are given forth to the hearers, whether they be few or many, in that special form of public address which is called *preaching*. Essays are read, orations are committed to memory and spoken, lectures are delivered with or without the manuscript, but sermons are *preached*.

The importance of this mode of communicating divine truth, and persuading men to accept it, can scarcely be overestimated. It has always been God's favorite method of making known his will. A large part of the writings of Moses is in the form of sermons. The Lord spake unto Moses, and Moses spake unto the people. Many of the books of the Old Testament consist largely of sermons or sermon briefs. Psalms are full of topics for sermons, while Proverbs and Ecclesiastes, many chapters of Isaiah, of Jeremiah, of Ezekiel, and of all the minor prophets, are made up to a great extent of the word of the Lord communicated to his servants, and by them *preached* to Israelitish people. The prophets were the preachers of the Old Dispensation. The prophet, therefore, was not necessarily a predicter of future events, — though he often was such, — but any one whom Jehovah deputed and qualified to speak in his name. The etymology of the word prophet points to the thought of speaking *for*, or *on behalf of*, the Lord Almighty. And the utterances of the prophets were sermons.

And when we turn to the New Testament, we find still greater prominence attached to the art and method of convicting and persuading men by means of preaching; whether the object be to bring about the conversion of sinners, or the entire sanctification of believers. Evidently God's method of saving the world is by the preached Word, uttered in the power of the Holy Ghost. Jesus Christ, himself, was the greatest preacher that has ever been on earth; and his Sermon on the Mount was the greatest sermon that was ever preached. After him let us study Peter's glorious sermon on the Day of Pentecost, followed by three thousand conversions; the dying sermon of Stephen which probably prepared the heart of Paul to receive the gospel message a little later, and about which some one has written: "*Si Stephanus non orasset, Ecclesia Paulum non haberet,*" or, in English, if Stephen had not prayed, the church would never have had a Paul; then the inimitable sermons of Paul himself, adapted with wonderful tact to the audiences he was addressing, — always first to the Jews where Jews were to be found, but never neglecting the Gentiles after the Jews had rejected the message, — as at Antioch in Pisidia; at Lystra to heathen idolaters; at Athens to heathen philosophers; at Miletus to the elders of the Ephesian church; to the Jewish mob at Jerusalem; before Felix first, and afterwards before Festus and Agrippa at Caesarea.

Coming down to modern times, we may remark that much of the strong, sound theology of the Reformation has been preserved to us in the form of sermons. In the discourses of South, Barrow, Saurin, John Wesley, and many others, are to be found, as testified by those who have studied them with care, not only the "sincere milk," but the "strong meat," as well.

Nor does the present century, or the present generation, fall behind its predecessors in the matter of published sermons. Indeed, the reverse is true. Since the wonderful increase in power added to the art of printing by the use of the steam press and other inventions, there has been a correspondingly increased activity in the spread of this kind of literature. The weekly sermons of the late Charles Spurgeon were carried round the world and read in tens of thousands of homes. The same is true of those of Dr. Talmage. Not simply in the newspapers, however, but in many permanent volumes are embodied the best pulpit thought of the preachers of various denominations who are still living, or recently dead.

The discourses here presented to the reader are from the tongue and pen of Rev. William Jones, D.D., M.D.,

LL.D., of the Methodist Episcopal Church, whose present pastorate is at Sedalia, Mo. The thousands who have listened with delight to his able presentations of the truth and his masterly exegesis will be glad to know that these sermons are here offered to them in a permanent form. Dr. Jones is not only an able expositor, but also an original thinker; and over and above all his human wisdom and ability, he has the Holy Ghost, and his sermons are permeated by the fire and power of the Blessed Spirit.

As the Lord has blessed these sermons when preached may he abundantly bless them also as printed and read. We trust they may have a wide circulation, and that they may promote the cause and kingdom of our Lord Jesus Christ. To him be the glory forever. Amen.

—Dougan Clark, A.M., M.D.
Richmond, Ind.

I

EASTER SERMON

"And if Christ be not raised, your faith is vain. But now is Christ risen from the dead, and become the firstfruits of them that slept." —I CORINTHIANS XV. 17, 20.

THE FACT OF THE RESURRECTION of Christ from the dead and the *bona fide* restoration of his body to life is the one great fact of Christianity. The apostle predicates all the other truths of the Christian system upon this one basal fact. If this is true— if this can be proved— all the incidental and collateral truths are secure; and while this remains unimpeached the whole fabric is safe— no difference about the mistakes of Moses nor of Ingersoll. If Christ be risen from the dead the entire superstructure must stand, and the apostle concedes all, if this is successfully controverted.

Here is a central point— a fact stated that may be proved, or if it is false it can be easily shown. The resurrection of Jesus, therefore, has been the vital point of attack throughout the entire history of the church. The resurrection of Christ has been assailed and defended as the very citadel of truth. The apostle graciously concedes as a fact that "if Christ be not risen" all the rest is useless. So vital is this fact that it would be impossible to let the resurrection of Jesus go, and save any part, of the Christian system from the general ruin. His resurrection is the climax of his miraculous power.

This fundamental fact is the most carefully guarded, the most accurately stated, and the most thoroughly attested of any other fact of the gospel narrative, because its truthfulness establishes all the rest, and its invalidation would impeach both Jesus and the apostles.

If Christ did not rise from the dead, Jesus is an impostor, and the Bible is a fabrication. But if he did rise from the dead, the truth of the Bible is sustained, the honesty of the disciples is vindicated, and the fact of the redemption of humanity by the priestly sacrifice of Christ, is established beyond all disputation.

Jesus appreciated the importance of this event, and made his resurrection the one grand crowning fact of all history.

His resurrection is, therefore, as thoroughly established as any other fact in the world, and the efforts that have been made to discredit it serve only to show how impregnably the truth is fortified at this point. Infidelity has always been sorely perplexed with the stern array of facts that lie grouped about the tomb of Jesus, and many ingenious theories have been invented to explain them away.

In regard to the facts of the crucifixion, the death and burial, there has never been any controversy, and in regard to his absence from the grave all agree.

The old story that he was stolen by the disciples, has been abandoned, and the assumption that he was not dead, that he was only in a swoon, was too absurd to obtain credence in this critical age.

The idea that a band of Roman soldiers acting under

the solemnities of a military oath, with the severe penalty of military law hanging over their heads should *all* fall asleep at one time, and sleep so soundly that the rolling away of the stone and the removal of the body of Christ should not arouse them, is more incredible than the resurrection.

So great was the stone that one or two could not remove it, and the movement was so free from haste and confusion that the grave-clothes were carefully removed and deposited in the tomb, and the linen cloth that bound his head was folded and laid in a place by itself.

That this bold and skilful feat, worthy of the courage and acumen of the most accomplished burglars of any age or land, should have been achieved by a band of timid and discomfited disciples of the Nazarene who were trembling from fear at their own peril, is impossible.

That they should have kept their secret through all those years of investigation, and then after having conceived and executed such a deception should have taught the world the sublime morality of the New Testament, and sealed it with their own blood, is far more miraculous than the facts of the gospel.

That the weak and fainting sufferer who sank beneath the cross before he was nailed to it, should have endured the crucifixion for so many hours, who appeared to be dead, and who then received a spear wound in the side that not only opened the sac that contained the heart, but that actually pierced that vital organ, who was pronounced dead by the Jewish and Roman officers of the law, was laid in the grave and remained there until the morning of the third day; that he should then suddenly revive, and without any supernatural aid, push away the stone, whose weight was such that it required the strength of several men to move it, and come forth alone and walk away from the guard, is a fabulous conception.

In order to obviate the force of the facts that support

the resurrection of Jesus, the renowned and scholastic Renan invented a theory of romance. He assumed that the whole matter was an hallucination, the product of a vivid and excited imagination.

He says, "It is the peculiarity of a fine organization to conceive the image promptly and justly, and with an intuitive sense of the end. The glory of the resurrection belongs to Mary Magdalene. Next to Jesus, it is Mary who has done most for the establishment of Christianity. Queen and patron of idealists, Magdalene knew better than any one else how to assert her dream, and impose upon the world the vision of her passionate soul.

"Her great womanly affirmation 'He is risen,' has been the basis of the faith of humanity. The strong imagination of Mary Magdalene enacted the principal part. Divine power of love. Sacred moment when the imagination of an hallucinated woman gave to the world a resurrected God."

We know it as a scientific fact that persons of a peculiar and poetic temperament, under the influence of strong excitement, appear to themselves to see the objects their minds have conceived as if they were externally before them; but it is reserved for the scepticism of this age to transform the resurrection of Jesus into a romance.

The realm of speculation is a safe region for theorizers, it affords ample opportunity for oratorical gymnasts. But when once these rhetorical gladiators enter the arena of logic, when they come within the realm of evidence, when they stand face to face with the great facts that challenge the ages as they go by, we quickly perceive the weakness of their defences.

If the story of the resurrection were a freak of the imagination instead of a recorded fact, we should expect to find the style in which it was told florid and extravagant. Creations of a pure fancy are easily detected. They are always unnatural, unreasonable, and extravagant or exaggerated; they are usually without purpose, and marked with the weakness of their origin.

In the Herculean effort of Mahomet, he parades before the world angelic beings whose very greatness is puerile, and whose performances are absurd without being impressive.

And if the angelic appearances described by those holy women that testify of Jesus had been the productions of their own minds, they would not have been true to life; there would doubtless have been multitudes of the heavenly visitors, they would have been of astonishing form and of remarkable brilliancy, and each one would have exhibited his personal genius in the performance of wonderful feats of power.

But the style of their narrative is severely simple. We are told of the angels, whose appearance, number, and proceedings are exactly in harmony with the facts in the case, and worthy of having been ordered by the highest intelligence of the universe.

So far from trying to make the most of them, they describe them as men; it was only on subsequent reflection that they decided that the beings they saw could not have been men.

Furthermore the honor does not belong to Mary at all. If Renan is as honest as he is intelligent, he knows that it was the Roman soldiery that guarded the tomb who first said, "The angel of the Lord descended from heaven, having a countenance like lightning, and his raiment was white as snow; and for fear of him the keepers did shake, and became as dead men." There is not much romance in the scene at the tomb as first described by the soldiers, and which the world believes to-day. The tinge of romance that has recently adorned that story was born of the genius of a French poet of this wonderful century.

It was not the women who were affrighted on this occasion, it was the soldiers, who fled terrified to the city, and first told the story of the risen Christ. I have no doubt as to the truthfulness of the first statement of the guard. They saw just such a being as they described.

We cannot account for the mortal terror that over-whelmed them on that occasion upon any other theory, nor can we account for their flight and the removal of the stone. But these are the facts; and the women found the keepers fled, and the stone rolled away, and the tomb empty. It is not only reasonable that God should send an angel to roll away the stone, but it was emi-nently proper, that he should convince the guard of the supernaturalness of the whole transaction. It is on the same principle that the circumstances at the cross, wrung from the centurion the reluctant confession, "Surely this is the Son of God."

But when the disciples came, the angel sat over on the terrace of rock where the Saviour had lain, looking like a young man dressed in clean linen clothes, and he said, "Behold the place where they laid him." It is every way proper that inasmuch as the angels sang the advent of Jesus in the glad acclaim of "Peace on earth and goodwill to men," and watched about the tomb during the hours of his slumber, that they also should have some conspicu-ous part in the heraldry of his resurrection.

If we examine the particulars of what Magdalene saw and did, and if we carefully analyze her statements, we shall not find any occasion to ascribe to her the glory of an imaginary resurrection. Hers was a humble part, but a great joy, in a real resurrection.

Mary was not in a mental state to dream of a living Jesus. The novelist has misapplied his own philosophy. His scientific hypothesis is correct; but Mary was not in an imaginative mood. She was overwhelmed with a great sorrow at the death of her dear friend. She had witnessed his death on the cross; she had seen him buried in Joseph's tomb. If she had formed any mental picture then, it would have been of the mutilated and mangled form of her dead friend. It is doubtful if Mary had ever heard the suggestion of a resurrection. The prophetic declaration of Jesus, which he made to his disciples concerning this fact, they neither understood themselves nor repeated to others. The only thought of these devoted women was to have the precious remains properly embalmed, that they might in this manner preserve the object of their love. The very fact that they had come with their spices for that purpose, proves that they had not dreamed of a resurrection. The hallucinated party is the novelist, who attempts to turn the facts that had survived the criticism of the centuries into a romance.

As these sorrowing women came near the tomb, not anticipating any change, they inquired, "Who shall roll us away the stone from the door of the sepulchre?" But when they came in sight the stone was already rolled away.

At the discovery of this fact, Mary turned back to tell Peter and John what she had seen. But she did not report a vision. She did not report a resurrection. Her sorrows were intensified; a burglary had been committed, and the tomb was robbed. That was the scope and trend of her imagination as her sorrowing heart cried out, "They have taken away my Lord, and I know not where they have laid him!"

Instead of taking on the form of a romance, her thought was that the tomb had been robbed of its sacred treasure; her cup of sorrow, already full, was embittered by outrage and indignity. The last sad rite, the only remaining expression of affection, was now entirely prohibited, and some malicious design was to be perpetrated upon the mangled form of her dead friend.

Such was the effect of these thoughts on her mind that she seemed almost unconscious of what was transpiring about her; even the appearance of a supernatural being, made but a slight impression on her dejected spirit.

The women whom she left at the sepulchre were frightened by the angelic vision which they saw, and fled, too much alarmed for a time to report the message received from the celestial visitor.

But when Magdalene returned to the tomb, and stooping down saw, through her tears, two persons in white, sitting one at the head, and the other at the feet, where the body of Jesus had lain, she was not startled; she conversed with them without fear. When the angel asked her why she wept, the burden of her sorrow was still the same, "They have taken away my Lord, and I know not where they have laid him."

After this, the Lord himself appeared, and asked the cause of her sorrow and tears; and so far was she from the dreamy and visionary state attributed to her by the French novelist, that she mistook him for the gardener, and said, "Sir, if thou hast borne him hence, tell me where thou hast laid him, and I will take him away."

In this state of mind, if Mary had created a vision, if she had given to the world an imaginary being, it would have been a perfect likeness of the mangled and mutilated body of her dead friend. The ideal formed in her imagination at this time would necessarily be like that which she sought, that she might moisten the rigid features with her tears, and embalm them with her offering of costly perfume.

It could have been none other than the living Christ whose familiar voice thrilled through her stupor of grief, and reversed the whole current of her life, changed all her theories in a moment, and drew from her confiding though sorrowing heart, the glad confession, "Raboni, My Master." And, as if to authenticate her testimony and put to shame the romancing sceptics of all ages, Jesus gave her a message to the disciples which no person could have fabricated. "I am not yet ascended to my Father, but go to my brethren, and say to them, I ascend unto my Father, and to your Father, and to my God, and to your God." This message refers to that which passed between Jesus and his disciples the night of his betrayal. "A little while, and ye shall not see me: and again, a little while, and ye shall see me, because I go to the Father." Inasmuch as Mary could not by any means have known what Jesus said to the disciples in that last interview before the betrayal, this message would be strong proof of his restoration to life; while all the facts combine to show the entire absence of the imaginative element in the story of the resurrection of Jesus.

The sceptical and imaginative biographer of Jesus, the one whose florid rhetoric and sophistical statements now control millions of infidels, and harass and perplex many thousands of people in the church, declares that the resurrection of Jesus is purely a figment of the imagination. Paul says, "If Christ be not risen," all the rest is vain.

There is nothing imaginary nor speculative in the gospel system. It is composed of a stern array of facts which appeal to the consciousness and reason of humanity; and the apostle, instead of appealing to the passions in gorgeous rhetoric and romantic legends, applies his resistless logic to the central position, and declares that if the resurrection of Jesus from the grave is not true, the whole story is a fabrication. There could not be anything fairer than this proposition. If this can be established, everything else is secured; if this fails, all is not only lost, but is manfully surrendered.

If Jesus had been an adventurer he would have prepared the disciples for this event beforehand; he would have planned it all, and given them the outline of his procedure before his death.

But Jesus purposely chose to establish this fact after its occurrence, and the jury, before whom this case was brought, was of the most intelligent and stubborn character, and the apostles were among the very last to receive the fact. It was not until the last gossamer vestige of doubt was swept away that they gave full credence to the fact.

The very intensity of their love made them suspicious. They had too much at stake to be willing to be deceived; it would only add to the severity of their disappointment.

At the crucifixion the disciples were thrown into a state of utter confusion. They still thought the Messiah was to be a temporal king; whether they journeyed to Emmaus or returned to their fishing-grounds on Tiberias, their thought was, "We trusted that it had been he which should have redeemed Israel."

The entire college of apostles was in that state of mind which required such proof as could not be invalidated.

The disciples had not seen the sepulchre. It was not a safe place for them. The tomb that concealed the lifeless form of their Master had no special attractions for the disappointed and sorrowing followers of the Nazarene. Even after the affrighted guard fled from the empty tomb, only Peter and John had the love or the courage to go near the place. The women were in less peril; and anxious to embalm the body, they sought the sepulchre early, only to find it empty. They reported the fact to Peter and John, who came in haste, and found the linen clothes and the napkin disposed of in the most orderly manner, proving that there had been no robbery of the tomb.

The stone was rolled away, the body was gone, the affrighted guard was fled, and the disciples were confronted with the Lord's promise that "he would rise the third day;" and to this day, neither Jew nor pagan, higher critic nor scholastic infidel, has been able to explain away the facts.

The fact that no other solution of the case has been given

must satisfy the world that no other reasonable one can be given.

The disciples slowly took in the fact of his resurrection; they returned to the city, they assembled their scattered brethren and told them the thrilling story, they talked over the statements of Jesus before his crucifixion, which he had made about his rising from the dead.

At this time the women, accompanied by Joanna, joined the disciples, and reported having seen two angels, who commanded them to remind the disciples what Jesus had said before his crucifixion, and that these things were written of him in the Scriptures. Then they remembered his words. They recalled the fact that it was the third day, but instead of exciting their imagination it aroused their sluggish reason; and instead of calling troops of mysterious figures from the peopled shades of fancy, they began to ask, "Ought not he to arise?"

Then the impetuous Peter became excited about the angels at the sepulchre, and visited it again. He did not rush in, as at the first, but stooping down he carefully peered into the empty tomb and saw only the linen clothes lying as before.

If we collate the evidence, we find that Mary Magdalene was the first witness. Then the Lord appeared unto Peter. Then came the other Mary and Salome. They told of the message of the angels. They told of Jesus, said they had touched his feet, and that he would go before them into Galilee. Then came the brethren from Emmaus, who said, "The Lord was made known to them in the breaking of bread."

After this Jesus appeared unto them in a place of social worship. He let them examine his wounds, and on another occasion, that they might know that there was no deception practised upon them, he ate before them. And for the sake of Thomas, who was not present on the former occasion, he repeated this test, vitalized and fortified his

faith by incontrovertible evidence, and thoroughly satisfied his logical mind and won from him the glad confession, "My Lord and my God." And for forty days Jesus
lingered about the scenes of his earthly life, and appeared
to them eleven distinct times, under such varied circumstances that no important fact in the chain of evidence
could be omitted.

Then, after all of this, came the Apostle to the Gentiles.
He is above suspicion. He is not a poet nor a sophist; he is
not a novelist nor a romancer; he is not a theorist. He is a
lawyer and a logician from the school of Gamaliel; he is
an enemy of Jesus, hunting the disciples to the death.

Paul was not won by fancy, he was not subjugated
by fear, he was not convinced by argument. The
stricken apostle was convinced by evidence, — by ir-
refutable evidence, by evidence clear and strong,
which swept like a cyclone through his soul, and authorized him to say to the world, for all ages, "But
now is Christ risen from the dead, and become the
firstfruits of them that slept."

The fact of Christ's resurrection does not rest on the
visionary statement of an hallucinated woman, it is supported by testimony that has not been impeached because it cannot be impeached.

If anything may be stigmatized as a figment of the
imagination, it is the infidel theory of the resurrection
of Jesus.

But the facts of the gospel since its inauguration cannot be accounted for except on the basis of a risen Christ.

Why do not infidels account for the marvellous
spread of the gospel? why do they not account for its
revolutionary power on purely philosophical principles? From whence comes that invisible force that is
now transforming the world? Was all of this produced
by a woman's dream?

The history of the world, since the beginning of the

gospel dispensation, cannot be accounted for on visionary theories.

History strikes its roots down deep into the actual and the real. The great movements of the gospel in the world, like the movements of the solar system, are in accordance with the principles of divine law.

It is not the nature of a lie to live two thousand years and exert a beneficent influence on humanity that increases in majesty and power as the years go by.

The disciples that fled from Calvary under the influence of fear could never have been transformed into heroes by a phantom or a lie.

We turn away from all speculative theories with a sense of pity for those who are so credulous as to receive those unreasonable statements. We open the divine record that challenges the most critical investigation, — a record that for two thousand years has survived the severest scrutiny, and has never receded from any published statement, and never abandoned a single position taken.

Since the champion of Christian faith hurled the challenge of the text into the midst of the Philistine camp, no mailed warrior has come upon the scene to break a lance with him. Out in the realm of speculation they have gathered in great numbers; they have rehearsed marvellous stories sitting around their campfires to encourage each other; they have skirmished with imaginary giants in the land of shadows— but the testimony of God's word still remains, "That Christ being raised from the dead, dieth no more." That "he is the Son of God with power by his resurrection from the dead."

The glory of this manifestation does not belong to Mary, but to him who said of himself, "I am the resurrection and the life."

This, the greatest of all acts, the crowning miracle of Jesus Christ, being thus firmly established, the other facts and doctrines array themselves in their natural order.

The whole gospel system is divine. It is supernatural. The incarnation, the vicarious death, and the resurrection, are underneath and lie back of the "new birth" and communion with God.

These fundamental facts are inseparable from spiritual life, — heart purity, the resurrection of the body, and everlasting life in heaven.

The apostle knew that there was neither delusion nor deception in the matter, and he could say without doubt or fear, "But now is Christ risen from the dead, and become the firstfruits of them that slept."

Not only is the grave cleft through, and the prey delivered, and the body restored to life, but spiritual death is swallowed up in victory; and in the consciousness of this fact on this beautiful Easter Sunday we call upon the church to shake off the stupor of fear, and arm itself for the battle; and we call upon the bending heavens to join us in one triumphant song: —

"Lift, lift your glad voices in triumph on high,
For Jesus hath risen, and man shall not die.
Vain were the terrors that gathered about him,
And short the dominion of death and the grave;
He burst from the fetters of darkness that bound him,
Resplendent in glory, to live and to save.
Loud, loud was the chorus of angels on high,
The Saviour hath risen, and man shall not die.
Glory to God! in full anthems of joy;
The being he gave us death cannot destroy.
Sad were the life we part with to-morrow
If tears were our birthright and death were our end;
But Jesus hath cheered the dark valley of sorrow.
And bade us immortal to heaven ascend.
Lift, lift, then, your voices in triumph on high,
For Jesus is risen, and man need not die."

II
CHRIST THE LIFE

"In him was life; and the life was the light of
men." — JOHN i. 4.

IN EVERY SYSTEM of truth there are some fundamental principles, certain central ideas, that are as
essential to the completeness of the structure
as the hub is to the formation of the wheel, — a given
centre from which all the other parts radiate, as the
other parts of the wheel diverge from the centre.

The Bible is the central book of the world. It is the inspiration and origin of literary effort; and for the overthrow or defence of the Bible a large majority of all the
other books in the world have been written.

The truth of the Bible is the central truth of the universe. The first ray of light that broke through the gloom
which settled upon the world after the fall was the promise of a Saviour; and the complete development of the
New Testament revelation presents Jesus to the world, as
the central fountain of all good.

The text teaches us that the intellectual, social, civil,
and religious life of the world, is in him, and that the

impulse to all progress is from him. The history of the world reveals the fact that where the light that is inherent in Jesus Christ as the manifestation of God does not shine upon the pathway of man, there is no advancement, no progress, in any department of society.

There are two channels of communication between God and man, two methods by which the Father can reveal himself to his children,— to their consciousness and to their senses. We see the realm of nature about us, and we know it is a reality. The eye sees the objects of beauty and grandeur, and the ear hears the sounds of melody and harmony that fill the air. These, with the other organs of communication, transmit to the soul convictions of the reality of these different objects.

The different organs of the body speak of what they know; and the soul of every man, without hesitancy or doubt, receives the testimony of these different organs.

It is through these organs of sense that God does manifest himself to us in a written revelation. In regard to man's consciousness, the spirit of man testifieth of itself. In its own secret cognizance and intercommunion, the soul asserts certain things to be true. The soul's own existence, independent of and superior to the body, is perhaps the most conspicuous and emphatic one of the entire list of spiritual truths.

This soul-power, which we call consciousness, is the sum total of all the faculties. It is the ability of the soul to know its own existence and its own individual relationships. Consciousness is the perception of a person or thing or event in its relation to its environments or parts. Conscience is the perception of a thing, or an act or event in its relation to some authoritative standard of right. They are not the same. Man is a unit; he is tripartite,— soul, body, and spirit,— one man, inseparable. The consciousness declares its relationships, cognizes its relationship to the past and to the future, to the visible and to the invisible, to the transient things of this life, and to the eternal verities of the life to come.

This quality of individualism through the consciousness apprehends the relation of each person in the human family to all the other members of the same family, and to a personal God. It recognizes him in his different manifestations, as creator, redeemer, saviour and preserver. But beyond the mere recognition of the fact, there is a more sublime height to which man may attain. He may not only know God, but he may converse with him.

The intimacy which existed between Adam and his creator in the Edenic life, and which was interrupted by sin, is renewed in Jesus Christ. The Spirit of God beareth witness with the spirit of man. The human spirit sees God, hears the voice of God, and talks with him. The only possible meaning we can attach to prayer is based on this fact. Prayer would be the most odious deception, and the most insane delusion, if God and the petitioner did not meet in Jesus Christ and there converse as friend with friend.

The fact therefore of man's inner selfhood, his spiritual and intellectual existence, the movements and manifestations of the spiritual man, is as well established as any fact in the material universe.

The soul knows its own actions, as well as it knows the movements of the body. The spirit apprehends God as its father as clearly as the eye sees the earth and sky, and that which is demonstrated to the consciousness is as well established as that which is demonstrated to the senses.

Christianity is the manifestation of the God who created man and made the heavens and the earth, it is established on the same foundation on which the universe rests, it cannot go into a state of decay until the eternal Father becomes bankrupt.

Christianity was made for man, and is in a special manner adapted to his nature and condition. Christianity has an inward and an outward being, it has a twofold revelation. It is revealed to the consciousness without any connection with the organs of sense. God the Father does, in Christ Jesus, put himself directly in contact with the human heart.

The way is so plain that a penitent soul, without reading a book, or hearing a voice, or seeing a priest, may draw nigh to God and be conscious of his justifying grace; he may receive the divine testimony to his sonship, and be filled with "that peace which passeth all understanding."

This inward life of Christianity far surpasses the outward form and manifestation, and is as indestructible as the throne of God.

Persecution may suppress all worship, the written word may be proscribed or shrouded in an unknown tongue, and thus concealed from the believer, it may be burned or banished, by a despotic sovereign; but without regard for the edicts of tyrants, spirit will blend with spirit around the blood-bought mercy-seat, the creature will converse with the creator, and God in Christ Jesus will live and reign in human hearts.

Although the fountain of Christianity should be sealed by the edicts of kings, it cannot be dried up; and when the seal is broken it bursts forth fresh and strong in streams of life and gladness, and the earth wherever it flows is vitalized by its presence, buds and blooms, and fills the land with its fragrance and fruitage. But God has not chosen to confine himself to this mode of revelation. He has put his religion into a form that addresses itself to the intellectual nature of man into a form that challenges his reasoning powers.

God reveals himself to man in a written and authoritative word, and he exhibits his love in the gift of his Son; and these revelations and manifestations are as distinctly visible to the consciousness and sense, as the fact and phenomena of the material universe, and we can as successfully disprove the works of God in nature, as we can disprove the revolutionary and saving power of his grace, and whoever denies the divinity of the Christian religion in its revealed form, denies also the inward revelations to his own spiritual nature.

The written word is the essential outward expression of the Christian system. It is the body of the truth; it is the anatomy of doctrine, the bony structure which gives uprightness and stability to Christianity, and makes the outward form and inward life always harmonize in their general facts. It is the visible organism of spiritual life. It is the authoritative outward testimony to the world of that experience which every truly renewed man receives directly from God. The written word in its doctrinal statements, in its propositions and promises, in its admonitions and encouragements, is as *essential* to the proper regulation of man's outward life as the sun is to the proper regulation of the solar system.

As the world of humanity was separated from God by transgression, and now lies in the slough of pollution paralyzed with crime and helpless of self-recovery, it would perish forever did not some life-giving power reach it from without.

The history of humanity for six thousand years proves that no society of civilized men can be organized, possessing the elements of improvement, without religion in some form.

All nations, ancient and modern, have recognized this fact, and religion in some form, either true or false, has entered into and become an essential factor in all their governmental institutions.

In the civilization of the past, atheism proved itself so destructive in its influence on national life, that ancient Rome and Greece were anxious to maintain the public religion as a judicious restraint upon the people; for without it they could not secure public peace and order.

From these fundamental facts we perceive that man without the true religion cannot exist in that state of civilization and culture that becomes him as an intellectual and moral being, and because of this fact, he must have the manifestation of the divine person, and the revelation of the divine will.

It has also been demonstrated by history that no nation ever made any permanent advancement without the light and impulse of the Bible.

It is true that they have had some temporary prosperity, and for a brief period have seemed to progress, but they have soon given way to anarchy and confusion; and in those countries where they have forgotten God or defied him, adversity has swept away their possessions, and ignorance and squalid poverty stalk unrebuked in the centres of ancient learning and wealth, thus verifying the fact that there is no intellectual, social, civil, or religious life for the world outside of the person and merit of the Lord Jesus Christ.

Look abroad over all the world to-day, — Christianity flings down the gauntlet to the world, — behold those nations where the highest civilization exists, where the greatest number of influences centre that are calculated to elevate and ennoble the race, where science, culture, and social life exist in the highest and purest sense; then look into those nationalities where there are none of these things; then compare these with those fragmentary and wandering tribes scattered up and down the earth; arrange these nations and tribes according to their civilization and culture, and you will find without one single exception that their advancement has been just in proportion to the light the word of God has shed upon their pathway — those who have no light being most sunken and debased.

This being true we appeal to the world, to philosophers, to statesmen and reformers, who reject Christianity, to give us some solution of this mystery, some reason for this strange phenomenon.

There are seven hundred millions of the human family now in the world that have no knowledge of the Bible, and we put the question fairly to every rejecter of Christianity: Is there anything in their character or condition that would induce you to change places with them?

A careful analysis of the situation reveals to us the fact, that at the time Jesus made his appearance among men, at the time when the star of Bethlehem shed its radiance upon the darkness of this world, there was not one nation on the face of the earth in a state of healthful advancement, there was no moral improvement in any department of society; social life was everywhere in a state of incipient decay. The sceptre of power, was wrested from the hand of justice, and righteousness wandered solitary and alone in the hiding-places of the earth. Cruelty and oppression, dwelt openly among men, and red-handed crime stood unrebuked in public places.

Egypt, the seat of ancient learning, had already in the fulfillment of prophecy become "the basest of kingdoms," and there was not on the face of the earth one single nation, except where the light of the Jewish Scriptures had quickened their dormant faculties into a new life, but what was growing worse continually, and with rapid strides hastening to destruction.

Who arrested this tide of death? who lifted the darkness that lay like a pall upon the moral world? It was He, in whom is "that life which is the light of men."

Reasoning upon these facts, we find it to be true as a general principle that men now without the light and influence of Christianity are constantly growing worse.

There are now seven hundred millions of human beings in the world dwelling in those lands that are under the influence of the Bible. Upon their pathway its holy light has been more or less perfectly diffused, and without exception, whenever the light of the Bible reaches a man, whenever its lucid rays, enter his mind, it inspires him with hope, he at once rises up from the slough of degradation and begins to advance in the scale of intellectual and moral improvement, he falls into line, and keeps step with the advancing column in the grand march of human progress. In the struggles of this life those who have the light of Christianity are the only ones that improve. If the survival of the fittest is the law, then only those who walk in the halo of this divine light are the titled classes; for they alone progress. Where did the great inventions of this century originate? Who applied steam to navigation? Who covered the earth with railroads? Who bridged the ocean with a wire over which thought travels unperceived? Who invented the telephone, the heliograph, and the phonograph. Without one exception all these marvellous inventions have been given to the world by men who live in the radiance of the gospel light, which quickens the whole man into a new life.

Did any pagan ever invent anything for the permanent benefit of the race? Has any invention for the purpose of lessening man's burdens and quickening his progress been given to the world except by some person whose intellect had been baptized by the light of Christianity? An appeal to history presents such an array of facts as should silence forever every enemy of the gospel.

The barbarous state of man is not his natural state. He was not created a savage and left to the influence of his environment for the development of his Intellectual and moral nature, and for the cultivation of his reason. The first man was made perfect. He commenced his career at the head of the column. He was crowned, and sceptred and had dominion, at the first. No child of the Edenic pair, no scion of the fallen head, ever equalled Adam in intellectual greatness. No fallen being could equal in brilliancy and force the qualities which Adam possessed, which were his by creative act, and which he retained after the fall, although they were blurred by passion, and subordinated to new and narrow limitations under the environments of the new probation. Barbarians are the degenerate children of those who have forgotten God.

But wherever the word of God is proclaimed, in whatever language or dialect it is communicated, there the light of a Christian civilization, and the impulse of a Christian education, open their treasures alike to all.

Who introduced into the world this transforming power? From whence come those revolutionary forces? From what centre goes forth those potencies that create the new order of things."

This power proceeds from Him who is "the life," and whose life "is the light of men."

When the world "by wisdom knew not God," when the car of human progress stood still, Jesus bade it move forward. He came and stood by the bier on which lay the hope of the world, but for him forever dead; he breathed upon it, he bade it arise, and straightway it revived.

Jesus poured his life-blood into the veins of an expiring world; he breathed upon the widespread ruin, and the arid wastes of sin became redolent of a luxuriant foliage; he stirred the smouldering fires of expiring intellect, and infused new life and new energy into a degenerating race.

The true principles of philanthropy were never known till Jesus said, "Blessed are the poor in spirit;" and when he gathered the apostolic leaders together just before the ascension and commissioned them to go forth and teach in his name, he was careful to incorporate that sentiment into the great commission. We hear his voice as in majestic tones it runs through the ages, "Go ye into all the world, and preach the gospel to every creature. Lo, I am with you, even unto the end of the world."

These sublime words constitute the great centre of moral power so far as the gospel can be formulated. We learn from this authoritative teacher that all raised distinctions of nations or race, of language, color, or caste, are nothing in the sight of God.

The gospel of Jesus Christ was the first message of good news that ever fell upon the ears of the poor. When Jesus said to the Baptist, "The poor have the gospel preached to them," more than ninety per cent of all the inhabitants of all the world were poor. They dwelt in poor houses or in huts, or lived in the open air, as climate and convenience dictated. They were poorly clothed and poorly fed. They had no social or civil or moral advantages, squalor and wretchedness was the heritage of the poor in all lands. There was no man on the earth to plead their cause, or interest himself in their improvement. The masses were so low in the scale of being that they were not enumerated in the census.

But Jesus gathered these poor forsaken outcasts around him, — his heart was touched with sorrow for them, — and with a voice thrilling with tenderest sympathy he said, "Come unto me all ye that are weary and heavy laden, and I will give you rest." I make no distinctions in favor of the rich, you are all alike, you have immortal spirits, you were created equal, your capabilities for happiness and progress are the same. "In my father's house there are many mansions." I come to you as your Saviour. I reveal these great truths to you, and then I lay down my life for you, to deliver you from the bondage of ignorance and sin, and whosoever receiveth me shall be saved.

And under the inspiration of his doctrine, and his presence, these degraded beings abandoned their idolatrous rites, and turned away from their pagan altars, and commenced a career of moral and intellectual advancement.

And from that date until the present moment, in all

lands wherever these truths have been proclaimed, the same results have followed, demonstrating the truth of the text, that Jesus is the life and light of the world.

Jesus Christ demonstrates the divinity of his religion: First, to the individual; second, through the individual to the world. He makes the individual holy, and purifies society by making each individual pure. By the enthronement of himself within the heart, by the impartation of his life and purity, he makes his disciples like himself. This is the *Deus Hominem*, the God in man, process of salvation and growth. This feature of Christianity differentiates it from every other system of worship or philosophy. It is said Socrates died like a philosopher; but it must also be admitted that he lived like a philosopher, the best heathen philosopher the world ever saw. But he was accused of crime and cast into prison; a court was organized, the testimony was taken *ex parte*, he was convicted, and sentence of death was pronounced upon him.

While waiting for the executioner a friend went to his cell and informed him that his door was unbolted, and that he might then escape. But the philosopher said, "No; I am too proud to fly. I am going to abide the laws of my country. I will die for the belief in which I have lived. I will die for the principles I have advocated for so many years."

And when the hour of his execution arrived, he drank the poisonous lotion [*sic*], exclaiming, "I drink the hemlock to-day, but whether I shall be better off tomorrow God knows." It was the sublimity of philosophy that inspired that thought and prompted such heroic action.

But let us contemplate another scene. Within the gloomy walls of that prison standing at the end of the street, is an aged man; his massive brow is wrinkled by care, his long white locks fall dishevelled upon his shoulders. That man had mastered every science known to the schools. By the severe processes of Jewish logic he had tested every principle of philosophy, and had passed up to the sublime heights of religious experience; and from the time when he met the Nazarene on the way leading to Damascus, down to the time of his imprisonment, under all the circumstances of his eventful life, the fire of a true Christian heroism had burned on without abatement.

"In perils by land and by sea, in peril by the heathen, in peril of his own countrymen, in peril of robbers, and in peril of false brethren. In conflict with wild beasts at Ephesus, or contending with men more fierce than the beasts of prey, he counted not his own life dear unto him," if he could but finish his course with joy. And when years of toil had worn him down, and the care of the churches had consumed his strength, as he lay in his dungeon at Rome awaiting the sentence of the law, he looked back over more than a quarter of a century of sacrifice and toil in the Master's vineyard. He looked forward to the prepared home and the reward for faithful labor, his soul kindled with religious fervor at the prospect, and he exclaimed with rapture, "I am now ready to be offered, and the time of my departure is at hand. I have fought a good fight, I have kept the faith, I have finished my course, henceforth there is laid up for me a crown of righteousness which the Lord, the righteous judge, will give unto me at that day."

Socrates died like a philosopher— Paul died like a Christian; and from that time to the present moment, in the cell or at the stake, in foreign lands or surrounded by friends in luxurious homes, the aged pilgrim and the Sabbath-school child in the supreme moment exclaim, "I have finished my course, henceforth there is laid up for me a crown!"

III

THE TRANSFER OF THE AARONIC
PRIESTHOOD TO CHRIST

"Then cometh Jesus from Galilee to Jordan unto John,
to be baptized of him." —MATTHEW iii. 13.

JUDAISM WAS A typical service. The high priest was
the official type of Christ, who is high priest of
humanity forever.

The Aaronic priesthood was established by divine
authority as a symbol of Christ's priesthood, and it
must of necessity continue until he came, and when
the antitype came and was officially proclaimed, all
that was typical ceased.

It is universally accepted that all the symbols of Judaism were fulfilled in Christ, and the Aaronic priesthood
and the prophetic office were merged in him, and that
both ceased at once and forever. If this is not true there
seems to be no significance to the apostles' statements to
the Hebrew Christians, for that is the burden of that epistle.

It is unwise, and does violence to all the symbolism of
the Bible, to force the scenes at the Jordan, into the new
dispensation. The new dispensation could not ensue until

after Christ be risen from the dead; "Salvation was to come out of Zion."

It mangles all history and all chronology to connect the life of Jesus with the ordinances of the Christian church, and the scholarship that cannot discriminate between the events that close the old dispensation and those that open the new is too obtuse for the present age.

The fact is clearly stated that Jesus submitted to a ceremonial washing or ablution practised in the Jewish church. He accepted it, rather "he sought and obtained," at the hands of his herald, the administration of an official rite for a specific purpose, and the forceful connection of this act and its adjuncts with the new dispensation has given rise to a great deal of controversy and confusion during the later centuries of the Christian era.

This discourse is a careful consideration of the nature and significance of this rite, and of the necessity of its administration to the world's Redeemer. What did the Baptist do to Jesus? How was the water applied? and what was the object of this public administration?

The assumption that Jesus received Christian baptism, and that the mode of its administration was by immersion, is not supported by the facts in the case. This entire class of teachers continue to ring the changes on the prepositions εκ and εις, and on the word "baptizo" as a modal verb.

But the New Testament use of the prepositions alone is sufficient to extinguish the theory of exclusive immersion, while the advocates of that system seem to be almost entirely dependent upon the arbitrary use of those terms for the support of their views. John preached a baptism into the remission of sins. The candidate, by penitence and the reception of this ordinance, *passed into* a new condition, a state of personal salvation. He experienced a change of life embracing the pardon of all past offences and a complete purification of the moral nature, and this change was wrought by the Holy Ghost because of the faith the penitent exercised in the Messiah, the coming one, "the Lamb of God that taketh away the sins of the world" by the priestly merit of his death.

The assumption that the prepositions decide the question in favor of immersion in any instance is without support by any evidence.

The Greek preposition which is translated "in," as it is applied to the Jordan, is the same word which is used to indicate the approach of Jesus to John, and if we insist that εις always expresses the idea of withinness or envelopment, then Jesus must have been placed in that relation to the Baptist. Such an assumption is so manifestly absurd that no one who cares for his standing among scholars would be found in that attitude.

Furthermore, this term is correctly rendered by more than a score of English words, the existing facts enabling the discriminating speaker to select the proper one.

It is translated "upon." "Then cometh Jesus to John upon the Jordan." This is the classical use of the term, as illustrated in Exodus vii. I5, "Get thee out unto Pharoah [*sic*]... So he goeth out upon the water." The king walked upon the banks of the Nile. There is a parallel passage in Tobit vi. I, "They came upon the river Tigris, and lodged there." The historian does not say whether the angel and Tobias went into camp on the bank of the stream or slept in the water. He leaves that to the discriminating sense of the reader.

The baptism of Jesus did not partake of the nature of John's baptism, I. John baptized his converts into or unto repentance. Their reception of this rite was a public testimony to the fact of their change of life. Therefore, if the baptism of Jesus partook of the nature of John's baptism, he must have previously repented of sin. 2. John required of his converts faith in the expected Messiah. Therefore, if Jesus received John's baptism, he must have professed his belief in a coming Saviour, and John must have encouraged him in this belief. This is too glaring to need exposure. Jesus knew himself, consequently could not believe in himself.

The baptism of Jesus did not possess the nature of Christian baptism. This ordinance of the Christian church was not instituted until after the resurrection of Jesus from the grave. At the mountain conference in Galilee, Jesus met the eleven apostles by appointment, and said, "All power is given unto me in heaven and in earth; go ye therefore, and teach all nations, baptizing them in the name of the Father, and of the Son and of the Holy Ghost." — Matthew xxviii. 18, 19.

John's baptism was not the same as Christian baptism. There is no account of the administration of Christian baptism until the day of Pentecost.

Christian baptism is administered to the candidate in the name of the Father and the Son and the Holy Ghost. It is the outward symbol of the faith the candidate has in the existence of the Holy Trinity, and the public dedication to his service, and Jesus could not have been baptized in that faith. There is a great absurdity in the very suggestion of Jesus being baptized in his own name, and in profession of his fidelity to his own cause and person; and yet all of this is true if Jesus ever received Christian baptism.

3. The import of Christian baptism is absolutely inapplicable to the person and character of Jesus Christ. As a sign, baptism is the symbol of the Holy Ghost, and is the external witness of the internal cleansing which pertains to all truly regenerate persons; and as all unregenerate persons are defiled by sin, the idea of former pollution and present cleansing is inseparable from the fact of baptism as a public profession of Christianity.

As a covenant seal, baptism is the pledge (*a*) of our fidelity to God, (*b*) of the divine faithfulness to us. God thus enters into covenant relations with his children under the solemn seal of this ordinance. And if the candidate fulfils his contract and walks in the fellowship of God, the divine Father fulfils his promise of pardon, regeneration, and sanctification of comfort, strength, victory, and eternal reward beyond the grave.

This being the true import of Christian baptism, that sacrament could not be applicable to the Saviour of men.

There is another class of teachers who affirm that he was baptized to furnish an example to his people. But we think this could not be so. The example would be essentially defective in one of its most prominent features. Jesus was not baptized until he became thirty years of age. Does the putting off of this rite until that age harmonize with the early and continuous piety of Jesus? Would it be walking in all the commandments of God blameless, for pious young men now to defer their baptism until they become thirty years of age, after the example of Jesus?

(b) But his example is defective in another important feature. He was not baptized until after all the people had received that ordinance at the hands of his official proclaimer. At least three of the evangelists relate the baptism of Jesus as taking place after all the people had been baptized. If he was baptized for an example, why was he not baptized in his youth, that he might furnish an example for the young?

Having thus briefly cleared away these specious errors, we formulate one simple question. For what purpose was Jesus baptized, and what is the true significance of the rite administered to him by his herald? A correct answer to this question will solve the problem of the mode of its administration.

We state as an antecedent fact, a fundamental fact in redemption, that the work of Jesus, in a primary sense, was not exemplary. There is a wide difference between a redeemer and an exampler. A redeemer ransoms the embarrassed party, delivers him from whatever embargo is upon him. An exampler shows the embarrassed party how to deliver himself. Jesus is the Redeemer. By priestly rite he sacrificed himself for the redemption of the world. He came into the world to preach a pure morality and make an atonement for sin. Everything he did was subordinate to that one royal purpose, and his baptism by John had reference to his qualifications as a teacher and as an atoning priest. The thoughtful reader will bear in mind that there are two orders in the Aaronic priesthood; the priest of the first order could teach in the synagogue and administer in the temple, but none but an high priest could make atonement for sin. (Hebrews ix. 7.) "But into the second went the high priest alone once every year, not without blood, which he offered for himself, and the errors of the people."

The baptism of Jesus was a part of the public preparation he was to receive. It was the ceremonial consecration by which he was inducted into the first order of the Aaronic priesthood. Zacharias, the father of John, was a priest, and John was a priest by descent and according to the Jewish ritual.

Christ was to become a priest by ordination, as he was not of the tribe of Levi. John did not inaugurate a new order of things. Salvation was to come out of Zion. Jesus was to come to the world through all the ordinances of the Jewish church. He came through the long line of priesthood reaching from Aaron to Calvary. He did not disregard any claim of the church; he met completely every obligation of the Mosaic ritual; he was circumcised the eighth day; inducted into the priest's office at the age of thirty, and for three years taught publicly in the synagogues; kept the passover; and finally, through the eternal spirit, offered himself, a "Lamb without spot or blemish," and opened the portals of salvation to the entire world.

Having conformed to the requirements of the ceremonial law in all things, and waited until he was thirty years of age, the period fixed by law for a priest to enter his sacred office, Jesus sought at the hands of his herald that which the church now calls ordination, as it was necessary, not only that the church should recognize his official relation, but that it also should give him its authority.

But when he came to John, the Baptist, knowing who Jesus was, and realizing the fact that his baptism into repentance was not applicable to the spotless Redeemer, forbade him. But Jesus explained to John that he did not want the baptism of repentance which he was administering to the penitent Jews who had come out to his ministry, but that which he wanted was the priestly ablution inducting him into the Aaronic priesthood, in order that he might open his mission to the world. "Thus it becometh us," "You and me, for in this we fulfil one important part of the ceremonial law which is essential to the completeness of my righteous record."

Jesus assured the Baptist that he was the proper person to inaugurate him into the priestly office, and as every other part of the ritual had been observed, it was now in order for John to sprinkle upon him the water of purification according to the Jewish ritual, and make him a priest of the first order, that he might thus be prepared for all that was to follow.

There were two orders of the priesthood, and Jesus was to become the "High Priest of humanity." He must therefore of necessity become a priest of the lower order first, it being preparatory to the high priesthood. If you turn to the eighth chapter of Numbers you will find recorded there that part of the Jewish ritual— that specific ordinance which John administered to Jesus. It is this, "And the Lord spake unto Moses, saying, Take the Levites from among the children of Israel, and cleanse them... And thus shall ye do unto them: Sprinkle water of purification on them, and they shall be clean; and after that they shall go in to do the service of the tabernacle."

There can be nothing more clearly stated than that John did induct Jesus into the first order of the Aaronic priesthood by sprinkling upon him the water of separation according to the Jewish law.

That Jesus received his authority to teach in the Jewish synagogue from John is clearly established by his own testimony. In the twenty-first chapter of Matthew in the thirty-third verse it is recorded, "And when he was come into the temple, the chief priests and the elders came unto him where he was *teaching,* and asked him, by what authority doest thou these things? and who gave thee this authority? And Jesus answered and said unto them, I also will ask you one thing, which, if ye will tell me, I also will in like manner tell you by what authority I do these things. The baptism of John, whence was it? from heaven, or of men? And they answered and said, We cannot tell. And he said unto them. Neither tell I you by what authority I do these things."

This testimony of Jesus is the key to this subject. It explains in the most satisfactory manner the object and design of Christ's baptism.

The chief priests and the elders find Jesus in the temple instructing the people; they, being responsible for the honor of the church and for the purity of its worship, impelled by a sense of duty, did as they should have done. They asked him for his credentials. They inquired of him by what authority he, being of the tribe of Judah, exercised the office of a priest by teaching in the temple; and also who gave him that authority?

Jesus replied by asking them the question whether they believed John to be a divinely authorized teacher or not? And he assured them if they would answer his question he would then tell them who gave him authority as a priest. And they denied John rather than indorse Jesus. If they had acknowledged John's authority as a priest, Jesus would have called their attention to the fact that John had publicly consecrated him to that office by sprinkling upon him the water of separation at the Jordan, according to their own law, which we have cited. Jesus was not of the tribe of Levi, and there was no way by which he could enter the first order of the priesthood but by the law of the church. If that is not the true meaning of the Saviour's question we cannot see any significance to it.

But viewed in this light the whole subject is clear; "suffer it [permit it] to be so now;" for by this act it becometh us to fulfil all righteousness, present and future. It is as if Jesus had said to John, "I am the Messiah; I am to become the High Priest of humanity forever; but I cannot enter the office of an high priest except by the priesthood of the first order. I am of the tribe of Judah; by descent I am a king, but I must become a priest. You are of the tribe of Levi; you are a priest by descent and a prophet by divine recognition; this triune office and authority belong to me as the Messiah; but I can neither teach in the temple nor become a high priest to offer sacrifices until after I am made a priest of the first order. Therefore, that I may be blameless before the law, and fulfil all ceremonial and ecclesiastical righteousness, make me a priest of the first order by sprinkling upon me the watery ablution; then when the scribes ask for my credentials I will show them that my authority is of thee, and as I cannot go on with my mission until this is accomplished, it becomes you, it is your duty as my official proclaimer, to do this for me; therefore 'sprinkle upon me the water of consecration, for thus it becometh us to fulfil all righteousness.'"

On the supposition that Jesus was immersed, the friends of that system must show what he meant by fulfilling all righteousness, for no Aaronic priest had ever been immersed; but for fifteen hundred years, without one exception, every priest had been sprinkled with clean water before he was permitted to enter upon the duties and exercise the authority of a priest.

And as Jesus was a priest, and did exercise that office in the Jewish church, carefully observing all the minutiae of the passover feast, we must either accept this statement of the case as correct, or show where, when, and by whom he received the ceremonial washing that made him a priest according to the law of the church.

Furthermore, inasmuch as Jesus could not receive the baptism of repentance which John administered to the penitent Jews that waited upon his ministry, and could not be baptized in his own name, and become a member of his own church, for he was the head, and could not be baptized for an example at the age of thirty years, we are compelled by the force of overwhelming testimony to acknowledge the fact that the baptism of Jesus, administered by John, was nothing more nor less than his public consecration to the office of Aaronic priesthood, a rite which was always performed by sprinkling the water upon the candidate, and always when the candidate was thirty years of age.

For the perfect confirmation of these facts, we only need to follow the history a little farther. The record says, "Straightway, when he was come up out of the water." Just as soon as the law pertaining to the first order of the priesthood had been complied with, God anointed him with the Holy Ghost, and with divine authority made him a high priest forever, after the order of Melchisedec, saying, "This is my beloved Son, in whom I am well pleased."

Aaron was a high priest. He was a type of Christ. After he had been made a priest of the first order, he was consecrated high priest, according to the formulary of that office, Leviticus viii. 10-12, "And Moses took the anointing oil, and anointed the tabernacle, and all that was therein, and sanctified them; and he anointed the altar and all his vessels, both the laver and his foot, to sanctify them; and he poured of the anointing oil on Aaron's head, and anointed him, to sanctify him."

This holy oil with which the high priest was consecrated to his office was a symbol of the Holy Ghost, which was poured upon Jesus when God made him a high priest forever, after the order of Melchisedec, and merged the Aaronic priesthood in him into his eternal priesthood. Immediately after this, when Jesus had opened his ministry, as we read in Luke iv. 16-21, "Jesus went into the synagogue on the sabbath day, and stood up to read. And there was delivered unto him the book of the prophet Esaias, and when he had opened the book, he found the place where it was written [he knew what he was looking for, as prophesied of him]. The Spirit of the Lord God is upon me, because he hath anointed me to preach the gospel to the poor; to heal the broken-hearted, and to preach deliverance to the captives; to set at liberty them that are bruised, and to preach the acceptable year of the Lord." He then closed the book, and sat down and said, "This day is this Scripture fulfilled in your ears."

When at any other time was Jesus anointed to preach the gospel to the poor? When did he receive an official commission from the Father? When was the power and authority of the Aaronic priesthood transferred to Jesus? We read in Hebrews vii. 12, "For the priesthood being changed, there is, of necessity, also a change of the law."

When, besides this instance, was the priesthood changed from the tribe of Levi to the tribe of Judah? When did the temporary and symbolic priesthood of Aaron cease, and the perpetual priesthood of Jesus begin? When was the initiatory service removed from before the tabernacle, and performed in the open wilderness, and in the presence of millions of people, to show that the new dispensation would not be circum-scribed by the narrow limits which were necessary to preserve the purity of the other.

Paul's testimony is, as stated in Hebrews vii. 24, "But this man, because he continueth ever, hath an unchange-able priesthood." Again he says, in Hebrews x. 9, "God taketh away the first, that he may establish the second."

If these changes did not take place when Jesus was anointed high priest at the Jordan, they have not yet transpired.

But we find strong collateral proof of this position re-corded in the prophecy of Daniel ix. 24, "Seventy weeks are determined upon thy people and upon thy holy city, to finish the transgression, and to make an end of sins, and to make reconciliation for iniquity, and to bring in everlasting righteousness, and to seal up the vision and prophecy, and to anoint the Most Holy."

The prophet by the Holy Ghost fixed the date and the formulary of this service six hundred years before it oc-curred, and it transpired at the appointed time. John was the last in the line of prophets. He was both prophet and priest; vision ceased with him; vision and prophecy were sealed, and remain sealed forever. Christ was inducted into the priestly office by John, and anointed high priest by God himself. The temporary priesthood of Aaron passed away, and the everlasting priesthood of Jesus Christ was established. God said, "This one, whom I have anointed with the Holy Ghost, and made an high priest forever, over the household of God, is my beloved Son."

God established the Aaronic priesthood. He preserved and kept it in force for fifteen hundred years, and then, in the presence of an assembled nation, while the priests still served at Jewish altars, and the last one of his holy prophets lingered upon the threshold of the new dispen-sation, God merged the prophetic office and the Aaronic priesthood, with the kingship of Judah, in the person of his Son, Jesus Christ, in whom "all power and all authority" are now vested, both in heaven and in earth.

We learn from these historical and doctrinal facts that: (*a*) Christ's mission was not primarily to set us an example, but to redeem us from the thraldom of sin. If we consent that any part of salvation is by example, we must see that instantaneous salvation is not only impossible, but the wildest delusion. We are subject to his law, under the operations of grace, while *his* obedience and *example* had reference to a law that had been violated by our federal head. Jesus must vindicate the divine government in its Adamic administration before he could redeem its guilty subjects. So we perceive that humanity is delivered from the guilt and corruption of sin by virtue of the sacrificial merit of his death.

(*b*) As none but a high priest could make atonement, Jesus must of necessity become a high priest before he could offer himself, and as none could become a high priest who had not served in the first order of the priesthood, it is apparent that the baptism of Jesus by John the Baptist was the administration of the law by which he was inducted into the first order of the priesthood in the Jewish church.

(*c*) God having instituted the Aaronic priesthood, and clothed it with divine authority, it must of necessity continue until God should officially terminate its existence.

(*d*) The high priest being a type of Christ, and the entire Mosaic economy being a typical service, it would have to continue until the person typified should come and be officially proclaimed.

(*e*) The Aaronic priesthood terminated in Christ, so when he was ready to enter upon his work, John the Baptist, who was his official proclaimer, called the millions of expectant Jews together to receive him. Up and down the valleys, from city to hamlet, rang out the voice of John, "Prepare ye the way of the Lord."

John the Baptist did not open the Christian era and inaugurate the Christian dispensation. He was the last of the prophets. He closed the old dispensation. As an evangelical prophet he preached repentance, and the scribes and Pharisees came to him, confessing their departure from Judaism; and after the way was prepared, "Then cometh Jesus to John," on the Jordan, "to be baptized of him."

John knew Jesus, and was conscious that the baptism of repentance was not applicable to the world's Redeemer, and declined to baptize him. Jesus then explained to him "that salvation was to come out of Zion." He assured John that he was not an innovator; that no jot or tittle should pass from the ceremonial law till all be fulfilled. He assured John that what he wanted was the ceremonial ablution of the Levitical law; that he might thus on his part fulfil all righteousness, and that he could not proceed with his work until this was accomplished. He assured him that he must receive the watery ablution of the first order of the priesthood before he could be anointed high priest forever over the household of God. And so soon as John understood the import of this service, he complied with the divine request. Then, just so soon as that was done, "Straightway," the record says, immediately, for these baptisms were the different parts of the same service. For, according to the prophetic statements of Isaiah and Daniel, and according to the after statement of Jesus himself, God the Father anointed him high priest forever, by pouring upon him the Holy Ghost. "So Christ glorified not himself to be made a high priest; but he that said unto him. Thou art my Son, this day have I begotten thee; said also in another place, Thou art a priest forever after the order of Melchisedec." "And this man, after he had offered one sacrifice for sins forever, sat down at the right hand of God." "For, by one offering, he hath perfected forever, them that are sanctified."

One way of escape is open for humanity, — through the priestly merit and intercession of Jesus Christ. One thing is essential for all, — to accept Christ in his priestly office and service, and let him save them.

IV
THE TRANSFIGURATION OF JESUS
[Preached at the Pitman Grove Camp-meeting]

"And as they came down from the mountain, Jesus charged them, saying, Tell the vision to no man, until the Son of man be risen again from the dead."
—MATTHEW xvii. 9.

THERE ARE NO FACTS more potent than the facts of history, and perhaps no single fact or event in the life of Jesus is more fruitful in doctrinal thought and brilliant suggestion than the sublime scene upon this mountain of wonders.

I used to ponder much what all of this signified. No words of the man of Galilee ever touched my youthful heart like the incident of the transfiguration. In my imagination I would follow this illustrious group to their solitary retreat. I would stand a little apart from them, and gaze entranced upon the amazing occurrence, while God wrapped the mountain in a garment of light, and bathed the heavens in celestial brightness, and from within the sacred precincts of the excellent glory bade the ends of the earth hear and obey his Son.

The injunction of secrecy which the master placed upon this transaction has been dissolved by the court of heaven, and the fact with all that relates to it is given to the world.

The traditions of the church gather about Tabor as the place of this miraculous transaction; but the facts point to Hermon, or to some timbered seclusion among the Judean hills, as the more probable selection. Tabor was, at that time, and had been for years, a military post, and was then occupied by a portion of the Roman army.

It was after the miraculous feeding of the multitude in the wilderness that this event occurred, and in the early morning, after a whole night spent in prayer.

Jesus never did anything for the simple purpose of displaying his power. He multiplied the bread to supply the wants of the famishing thousands that waited upon his ministry. He healed the sick and raised the dead because that was a legitimate part of his mission. But the transfiguration was a unique manifestation, and was given for a specific end. It was for the purpose of establishing the disciples in the fact of his messiahship, and to officially transfer the sceptre from Judah's hand to the person of "David's royal Son," the sovereign head of the new dispensation.

One primary fact must be observed; only three of the disciples were with him on this occasion; and the same three were with him in Gethsemane. There is apparent here the presence of that principle that is universal in the divine government, — that exalted privilege implies increased responsibility, and that glorious manifestations cannot prevent the coming of sorrow to those who are still subject to the environment of law.

These three men are typical men: they are the representatives of classes. They hold the fundamental truths of the gospel in common; but they are distinct and divergent in manner and style. Like three great mountain peaks in the same range, they overlap and interlace each other in the adjustment of their rocky roots, but separate as they rise, and become isolated and sublime in their solitude as they approach the summit.

Peter was hasty; he was the embodiment of impetuosity; he was cyclonic; by nature he was surcharged with spiritual dynamite. He occasionally made a mistake or perpetrated an unfortunate indiscretion; but he was always true to his convictions.

When he cut off the ear of the high priest's servant, Jesus healed it at once, showing how he can correct the blunders of the willing workers, while there is no antidote in the divine magazine for stupidity and indifference.

James was entirely different. He was a careful, practical man. He gathered up the fragments "that there be nothing lost." But James was an orator and a logician. He was the most expert in forensic skill of any one of the original band. He was an organizer also, and a wise administrator. He was the John Wesley of the apostolic college. He touched material and spiritual elements, and they crystallized into permanent form to remain forever.

John was not like James nor Peter. John was preeminently a man of love. He was the bravest, most heroic, and chivalrous of the group. John was a theologian and philosopher, the teacher in the fundamental doctrines of the new religion.

John speaks of the Logos, the Logic of God, "the Giver of life," "the Word," at whose command the universe arose. But John spoke also of the life, not the βιος, the manner of the life revealing the delicate processes of life, but the ζοε, the life itself, that infinite fountain from whence issues all good. John's courage and fidelity never failed him. He leaned on the bosom of Jesus at the last supper, and went with him to the judgment hall. He awaited patiently the issue of the trial, and lingered within the shadow of the cross to catch the last pulsation of infinite love that gave eternal life to a lost race.

Each one of these three men had a special line of work, a special mission to humanity. Vistas of divergent possibility opened to them; highways of unlimited achievement invited their adventurous feet.

These three men represent the three large classes of active workers who are now doing most for the advancement of the kingdom of God. These men have their followers among those who are the leaders in the great religious movements of the world. Jesus gave these men this vision; but its doctrines and practical lessons are the heritage of the church through all the ages.

It was important that the disciples should be well established in all the fundamental facts of Christ's kingdom. It is essential that those who lead in any great movement must first know, in themselves, the nature and significance of the truths they are to promulgate.

The events that group themselves about the closing days of the old dispensation, and become tributary to the setting up of that "kingdom that shall never be destroyed," could not be ambiguous. It was important that no uncertainty should obscure their relation to the things that were passing away, nor to the new institutions that should be established when the typical and transient should pass away forever.

To this end John summoned the multitude to the Jordan to witness the transfer of the prophetic office and the Aaronic priesthood to the person of our Lord Jesus Christ. Since the Holy Ghost descended upon him there, no high priest has stood in Aaron's place, and the prophetic office is closed forever.

So now on the heights of this sacred mountain God calls the chosen few; and with the pomp and splendor of a divine sovereign, beneath the overwhelming glories of the opened heavens, and in the presence of all the interested parties, God the Father turned over the sceptre of authority to David's royal Son.

There are two facts distinctly stated in this Scripture:—

1. "Jesus was transfigured before them."

To transfigure signifies "to change the form of." It is a term used only in a spiritual sense, and is applied strictly to the scenes of the mountain, and it signifies to "become elevated and glorious."

This change in Jesus was the outshining of his innate glory. It was the unveiling of his divinity. It was a normal object-lesson, showing how the two natures lived together in one person.

This manifestation on the mountain was not, as some expositors assume, an optical illusion serving a momentary purpose. It was not a mountain mirage woven from the misty shroud of the morning. It was a great spiritual fact. It was the divine nature of Jesus in its regal robes, shining out through the thin veil of flesh.

Jesus must demonstrate himself to his disciples in his official and authoritative capacity, or they could not demonstrate him to the world. Jesus must perfectly win them, if they would succeed in winning others.

These three men, chosen as leaders of the new movement, were Jews. They were familiar with all the facts of tradition and history. They had followed Moses from the burning bush on the Midian plain to the thunder-split summit of Nebo's awful height. They had heard the voice of God amid the pealing thunders and clanging trumpets of Sinai; and they had seen the gleaming shechinah flashing forth the divine presence in the temple. They had looked upon the pillar of fire and of cloud that continually guarded and guided the wilderness march, and they had seen the obedient waters leap from the smitten rock; and before they could surrender Moses and the prophets for the Nazarene, they must be thoroughly satisfied that he was the legal successor of these distinguished worthies, — the Messiah of God.

It was for the purpose of demonstrating his

messiahship, and making the official transfer of the sceptre and kingdom of Judah, that this delegated conference was appointed. For this purpose alone he was "transfigured before them."

As they stood on the stony slopes of that sacred mountain in the gray light of that memorable morning, his garments seemed to be caught in a shower of radiance, and became "white as no fuller on earth can whiten them." The mountain scenery caught the inspiration, and like as the trembling dewdrop reflects the perfect image of the sun, the yielding hilltops, bathed in the divine effulgence, mirrored back the glory of their Maker.

This radiance passed away, as a red cloud at sunset fades into twilight or deepens into darkness; but the demonstration was complete. It crystallized in their thought and affection, to remain in its sublime beauty forever. It became a part of their being. It was incorporated into their selfhood. It was a religious experience, fused forever into the soul; and years afterward, when Peter would confirm the truths he had preached with his dying testimony, he declared that he had not followed the cunning and fabulous devices of men when he made known the power and coming of the Lord Jesus Christ. The apostle affirmed that he was an eyewitness of his majesty; that he was with him in the holy mount, and that he heard the voice from within the excellent glory which clothed him with kingly authority, and proclaimed him the Son of God with power.

And that sublime figure which John saw in his vision on Patmos was only a colossal copy of what he had seen on the mountain of glory, vibrating for a moment between dust and deity, warm and lifelike as a man, but vast and glorious as the eternal God.

These men saw him from before whose face the heavens and the earth shall flee away, and they were forever afterward satisfied.

2. The second fact of this lesson involves the future life of humanity.

What emotions throng us, and what anxieties oppress us, as we gather about the graves of our loved ones. How we have thought on death, on the future, on the life and the home that await us there. But the scenes of the transfiguration sweep away the mists, and leave the fact standing out clear and distinct in Heaven's own holy light.

"There appeared unto him Moses and Elias talking with him." These ancient worthies were not there at that early morning hour purely by accident. They were not looking for a mountain solitude in which to locate a summer resort. They were there to confer with Jesus, and to encourage him in the work of redemption, and to establish the disciples, and to witness to the transfer of the kingdom. The law and the prophets, with the priesthood of the past, met there with the gospel and its agencies; one system of redemption, with a diversity of methods. Moses was the great lawgiver of the Jews. For nearly two thousand years the nation had been under his authority; and his ritual was the standard of their morals, and the formulary of their worship.

Moses had seen God face to face on Sinai and on Pisgah; and had passed from that place to the inner court. This mountain conference was a delegated assembly. Moses appears on this occasion as the representative of a great company; his constituency were the countless dead of all the ages.

Moses died on the mountain height, on the east side of Jordan. God buried him in an unmarked grave in the land of Moab. The angels were his pallbearers; the winds that swept in fitful gusts about the rocky peaks of this sacred mountain sang his requiem. There were no mourners present. This was the triumphal hour of a great soul, — a unique experience, never repeated in any age or land. Isolated from his birth, spending his infantile days in seclusion, or solitary and alone amid the splendors of the Egyptian court, or in the gloomy solitudes of mountain and desert, Moses had lived apart from the world; and his death on the stony heights of Nebo was a proper climax of a life so perfectly isolated from society. There never was such a funeral. No such splendid *cortege* ever assembled within the marble halls of the great, or with measured tread and uncovered brow marched to the silent city of the dead. It was—

> "On Nebo's lonely mountain,
> On the east side Jordan's wave,
> In a vale in the land of Moab,
> They made his lonely grave.
> And no man dug his sepulchre,
> And no man breathed a prayer;
> For the angel of God upturned the sod.
> And laid the dead man there."

The other illustrious delegate to this select convention was Elijah, the hoary-headed and bearded prophet of Israel. He did not die; "God translated him that he should not see death."

Elijah has a large constituency. He represents the countless multitude of those who shall not die; those who shall be alive at the coming of the Lord. "For we shall not all sleep, but we shall all be changed. In a moment, in the twinkling of an eye, at the last trumpet; for the trumpet shall sound, and the dead shall be raised incorruptible, and we shall be changed." "Then we which are alive and remain shall be caught up together with them to meet the Lord in the air." These are the constituency of him who, whether on Carmel or in the presence of Ahab, compelling the fire to descend upon the altar or the floods to irrigate the parched land, dividing the Jordan or mounting the celestial chariot, was perfect in the fellowship of his God.

On that eventful day, as the weary prophet, full of labor and of years, journeyed beyond the Jordan, amid the foothills that border the eastern plain, not far from the base of Nebo, God sent his messenger for him. His chariot was of the purest amber, through which the electric brilliance shone like burning naphtha. The lightnings were his steeds; the whirlwind was his charioteer; and mounted on this celestial equipage he swept up the luminous pathway of the skies to the presence of the eternal God.

But now after the roll of centuries these two men, representing the entire human family, stepped out from the shadows upon the stage of life, and are seen and known of men.

Moses and Elias talk with Jesus. Doubtless there was very much transpired, incidentally, that is not recorded; but the purpose of the meeting is not lost sight of for a single moment. "They confer with him about his death." "They appeared in glory, and spake of his decease which he should accomplish at Jerusalem."

Moses and Elijah were interested parties. They had much at stake. They had prophesied of his coming and of his death. The time of fulfilment was drawing near, and they would know how he was getting on with his work. Moses had made the record that "the sceptre should not depart from Judah, nor a lawgiver from between his feet, until the Shiloh should come; and unto him should the gathering of the people be;" and even now the sceptre trembled in the princes' hand, and the crumbling throne of Israel's shepherd king was ready to fall into perpetual ruin.

But while these celestial visitors lingered in the brightness of this divine manifestation, Peter wanted to build tabernacles. He would make one for Jesus, and one for each of the heavenly visitors.

The dignity and majesty of this occasion overwhelmed Peter. He could not tell which of the trio was supreme, neither could he keep still under such intense excitement. But while the apostles were planning for the recognition of true leadership, God settled it forever. He spake with an audible voice. From the sacred precinct of the excellent glory came forth the authoritative declaration: "This Jesus whom ye have seen this day foreshadowed in his coronation robes is my beloved Son. Hear him. Hitherto ye have heard Moses and the prophets. The mandates of Moses have been authoritative and final; his manual has been recognized in the synagogue and in the temple; and the voice of his conscience has been the standard of your morality in all lands. But to-day, in the presence of Moses and Elias, and with their full knowledge and consent, and in the presence of these three men who are to represent me in my church to the end of time, I transfer all power and all authority, in heaven and in earth, to my beloved Son; and this authoritative commission embraces everything in the church and in the state, in the departments of salvation and of culture. Hear him. To-day the sceptre departs from Judah's hand; no prince will ever again sit on David's throne. The priesthood of Aaron, and the prophetic office which were merged into him at the Jordan by his herald and proclaimed from heaven by God himself, are this day by divine authority augmented by the kingship of Judah. Moses is not abrogated, the prophets are not abolished, the law is not annulled; but all power and all authority are this day merged into the eternal priesthood and kingship of my beloved Son; and henceforth whoever officiates at my altars must receive his credentials from his hands. Hear him."

The cloud immediately disappeared; the voice was hushed. Moses and Elijah returned to their invisible pursuits; but Jesus remained alone with his awe-stricken and trembling disciples.

This sublime occurrence in the history of Jesus suggests some very important truths:—

(*a*) That earnest, believing prayer always precedes special manifestations of the Divine Presence. The labor and the waiting of these chosen ones were amply rewarded. The pearly drops of sweat, the product of their climbing toil, were transmuted into a coronet of glory for the brow of Jesus. And it is only in this way that Christians ascend the heights of glorious revelation. None but those who absolutely surrender all, utterly abandon all expedients, and trust the *priestly merit* of Jesus alone, can have the fulness of Christ revealed within by the Holy Ghost.

Religiously, man must go down in order that he may rise. It is only those who humble themselves that shall be exalted.

(*b*) It teaches also the distinct individuality of the dead.

Men are not transformed into angels by death. No man can escape himself. No person was ever any better, or morally worse, after death than he was while living. Death is not a factor in the formation of character nor in the process of salvation. Death never determines the destiny of any being.

Dives in Hades, was as respectable and as pure, as he was in his palace. It is probable that he behaved better in hell, than he did at home. He was the same man, but the environments were different, and things were to some extent reversed. There was in the elementary furnishing of his habitation the entire absence of ice and wine; and the service was exceedingly limited. But he was not changed; it was the same selfish man, wailing out his piteous prayer to Abraham for a single drop of water to relieve his pain, that when on the earth left his duty to be performed by the compassionate servants, and the merciful dogs, while he with gay companions, with splendid equipage and liveried attendants, sought his own pleasure.

Death does not change anything but positions and personal relationships. Death is the result of antecedent moral action, and cannot affect moral character. Your loved ones that sleep in the rural churchyard, or lie uncoffined in the deep blue sea, are not affected in their moral nature by the incidental circumstances surrounding their death. Their individuality and identity are as enduring as the eternal throne.

(*c*) It reveals to us the fact, also, that the saints in heaven are interested in the salvation of men. While we worship here, they applaud before the throne. They cannot participate in this service because of their changed environment; but, doubtless, they look out from their spirit home with supreme delight upon the achievements of the church. While we surround this altar, Cookman, who went "sweeping through the gates," washed in the blood of the lamb, and Coleman, whose white plume leads the van far up the shining way, and Palmer and Inskip, with Bishop Simpson, and the sainted Wiley, whose mouldering dust rests in the flowery kingdom, — with spirit fingers sweep the immortal lyre.

(*d*) But we learn further that special manifestations of God to the human soul are essential preparations for successful work.

The excited apostle would build tabernacles, and remain upon the mountain. He would have a time of perpetual exultation. But Jesus said, "Arise, let us go." There was important work even then awaiting them on their return, which their less favored brethren were unable to perform.

There are those who imagine that religion is a personal luxury to be enjoyed without regard to the needs of others, or that it is at the best a preparation for death. To that class of persons, the name of Jesus is only an amulet or a charm; while another class, in the very ecstasy of selfishness, sing, —

"My willing soul would stay
In such a frame as this,
And sit and sing herself away
To everlasting bliss."

But true fellowship with God prepares its possessor for a noble and useful life, for glorious achievements, for victory and reward.

(*e*) It teaches us that none but those who have been in the transfiguring presence of Jesus are really and truly prepared to live, to labor, or to die.

Pentecost was the reproduction of some of the features of the transfiguration. It was the official enthronement of the Holy Ghost as the administrator of this dispensation; and when he had interpreted and applied this vision in the upper room, the disciples were prepared for labor or for death. Jesus went from this mountain conference with the Father, from within the pavilion of the excellent glory, to Gethsemane, to Pilate's judgment hall, to Calvary, and to Joseph's tomb; but the tomb could not hold him, and he went from there to Olivet, and to the throne of power.

In the same manner all true Christians go out from the transfiguring presence of God, to labor and to sorrow, to serve at the bedside of the dying, or minister consolation to the bereaved. They go from the mountain heights of religious privilege, which are the essential places of divine preparation, to work in the vineyard of the Master; to endure hardness, as good soldiers, for Jesus Christ; to suffering and to death; to glory, honor, and eternal reward.

(*f*) But, finally, it reveals to us the fact that Jesus is the central figure of the universe, the abiding one of all the ages.

When the heavenly pageant had passed by, "They saw no man, save Jesus only." Moses and Elijah had returned to their place. The Father had withdrawn his glorious presence, the bright cloud and the "excellent glory" no longer enveloped the mountain; but Jesus remained with his disciples. The dwelling-place of God is with men, and the divine tabernacle remains to the end of the ages.

Fables and philosophies all fail, they disappoint us in life and desert us in emergencies; but the divine Redeemer is a satisfying portion to the soul. Wealth may be turned into smoke and ashes in a single hour, health and friends and honors may disappear together, the waves of sorrow may dash over our trembling bark; but Jesus walks above the threatening billow, he comes to bring deliverance to the stricken soul, and anchor the storm-tossed vessel in the haven of eternal rest. Death may claim the body as its own lawful prey, but Jesus is the "Resurrection and the Life."

The light of infidelity goes only to the grave, and goes out in endless night; but Christianity throws the rainbow of promise over the tomb, scatters all the darkness from the valley of death, and throws out its scintillations until they mingle with the effulgent beams from the eternal shore, irradiating and illuminating, with a halo of glory, our pathway to the throne.

V

THE PERPETUITY OF CHRIST'S KINGDOM AND THE UNIVERSALITY OF HIS REIGN

[Baccalaureate Sermon, Preached before the Faculty and Students of Baker University, June, 1894]

"And in the days of these kings shall the God of heaven set up a kingdom, which shall never be destroyed: and the kingdom shall not be left to other people, but it shall break in pieces and consume all those kingdoms, and it shall stand for ever." — DANIEL ii. 44.

"And his dominion shall be from sea even to sea, and from the river even to the ends of the earth." — ZECHARIAH ix. 10.

THERE ARE TWO KINGDOMS in this world,— the kingdom of satan and the kingdom of Christ; the kingdom of darkness and the kingdom of light; the kingdom of evil and the kingdom of good; the kingdom of antichrist and the kingdom of Christ.

There are two distinct personalities, each with a following, who are now contending for the supremacy, —

contending for the possession and control of the material and moral forces of this world, — Jesus and Apollyon.

These antagonistic characters and forces are not the necessary parts of the same kingdom. Satan is not a co-adjutor of Jesus Christ; he is a usurper and an assailant. These prophetic declarations of Scripture which we have read refer to the gracious kingdom of God, to Jesus Christ and his spiritual kingdom which he has set up in the earth, to his church which he has purchased with his own blood. As prophet, priest, and king, Jesus cannot be separated from his church.

The Scripture we have read is a divine assurance of the universal dominion of the gospel kingdom. It is to extend from sea even to sea, and from the river even to the ends of the earth.

The text also indicates the forces by which this is to be accomplished. It emphasizes the fact that the gospel itself is the generic agency of this achievement. If this text has any significance, it teaches us that the Lord Jesus Christ is to subjugate, possess, and rule this revolted world.

I think it must be apparent to all in the light of this Scripture that God did not build this earth with all its varied and sublime possibilities only for a stage on which Satanic power might play its fantastic freaks for a season. I think it is equally clear to every thoughtful mind that the church which the Saviour purchased at such fearful cost should own the material and moral world, and direct all their forces, not by arbitrary edict, not by ecclesiastical manifesto, but by the persuasive power of intelligent love, by the nature and force of Christian thought.

We believe that the resources of the gospel are equal to the accomplishment of this result, and that the gospel will secure this end whenever it is fully apprehended and properly directed. The fact that the gospel has not already accomplished this end is a perpetual testimony that the ultimate resources of the gospel have not yet been developed, nor its agencies fully appreciated nor rightly directed.

We dare not concede that sin is a necessary factor in the government of God, neither can we affirm that the sequences of sin, in the form of moral and physical evil, under the divine blessing become the essential forces in character-building, and the indispensable agencies in the disciplinary processes of probational life. If we concede these points, we have accepted all that is embraced in the necessitarian philosophy.

Sin is never a helper. Nothing that God has condemned can ever become a working force in his kingdom. God cannot share his glory with another, nor divide the honor of his throne with his arrogant foe. Sin never becomes a blessing to the perpetrator, therefore it cannot be a benefit to the community.

No sequence of sin was ever transformed into a gospel agent. By the very being and nature of sin it is always a curse; and God cannot make it a blessing to any for the simple reason that he cannot change its nature. Sin is a gangrene upon the human heart, and affects society as it does the individual.

Neither do we sympathize with that popular and prevalent error of this period, — that sin is stronger than the gospel, and that it will remain in the ascendency until Christ comes the second time. In the ultimate victory of the gospel, sin and all its sequences in the form of moral and physical evil, and all its adherents of men and devils, will go down in the abyss.

It was for this victory over evil that Christ came into the world. This is the supreme mission of the church; and for the achievement of this purpose it has flung its banner to the breeze.

But the church can never accomplish this result until it does legitimately control the thought and commerce of the world; and whenever Christianity is supreme in the domain of commerce, and in the realm of human thought, and thought and commerce harmonize with the genius of the gospel, the work on the human side will be complete, and the victory won. The church must control the thought of the world, or utterly fail in its mission.

Christian experience is a potent factor in the influence of the church; but however bright and ecstatic it may be, it always finds its level in the thought- channels of the individual Christian. This is what the Saviour taught us when he said no man could keep new wine in old bottles; for by a law of psychology which is universal in its application, experience is always subordinated to the thought.

We have seen a friend of our earlier years thrilling with ecstatic emotion, revelling in the very sublimity of poetic conception; and when the excitement was at white heat, we have heard him exclaim in the raptures of holy song: —

"Were the whole realm of nature mine,
That were a present far too small;
Love so amazing, so divine,
Demands my soul, my life, my all."

But this ecstasy subsided, that intense enthusiasm abated, and his experience hastily conformed to another train of thought; and as he placed a mutilated dime in the treasury of the Lord, he sang in doleful strain: —

"When we asunder part,
It gives me inward pain;
But we shall still be joined in heart,
And hope to meet again."

Every effort to separate the Christian religion from the fundamental thought of humanity, or to carry forward the enterprises of the gospel on any other line beyond the highwater mark of Christian thought, has been a failure.

It must always fail, because Christianity is more than a sentiment; it is more than a delightsome experience. It is a life, a divine force operating through humanity. It is a vital, spiritual force permeating the individual, and affecting and controlling society by the aggregate thought-force of the church.

Christianity touches and controls humanity by the agency of thought. The weapons of Christian warfare are not carnal; they are thought and spirit. Baptized thought; thought on fire with divine love; thought refined and sublimated; thought molten and flowing heavenward, bearing on its translucent bosom the renewed affections of a saved and progressive manhood.

By the force of universal law, the march of humanity is always along the highway of thought. Nations follow, but cannot go in advance of their leading thinkers. Nations are exalted and refined, cultured and perpetuated, or they are barbarous, sensual, and debased, according to the tone of thought given to them by their schools and priesthood, by the secular press, scientists, and statesmen.

The strength of a nation is only equal to the consensus of its religious thought. No nation ever arose or fell, advanced or retrograded, except as it followed in the footsteps of its controlling thinkers. The activities of a nation are the creations of its thought and the enterprises of all peoples cluster about their systems of thought.

The Olympics and circus of the East were the expression of national thought as surely as baseball, the prizering, the grain-pit, and the race-course represent the thought of the Western world to-day.

We go back along the highway that authentic history has cast up across the centuries, to the beginning of national life, and we behold their dominant thought taking form in the monumental piles, that record their folly. We stand amid the perpetual desolations of Egypt, and we perceive that Egypt arose and flourished and fell, following the evolutions of her thought.

Four thousand years ago, Egypt was the seat of learning for the whole world. Out from her universities, her schools of philosophy and law, of art and music and medicine, went forth those thoughts and principles and those trained thinkers, that gave to Rome her system of laws, and to Greece her sculpture and philosophy, that made Homer first among the poets, and enabled Hippocrates to become the father of the healing art. But we discover that the thought and commerce of Egypt were inseparable in their progress and undivided in their destiny.

Take down your ancient map; follow the pathway traversed by the caravans that went out from Cairo and Alexandria; behold the cargoes of wheat and rice, of spices and sugar, the productions of the loom and the shop, that went up the coast or across the country to Capernaum and Damascus, to Tyre and Sidon and Antioch, where they met the impetuous stream from the East; and these united currents turned and flowed westward to Ephesus and Corinth, to Athens and Rome, even as far as the British Isles.

Thought and commerce always travel together. They are the handmaids of virtue and religion, of life and progress, or they become the nemesis of sensuality and death.

Along the common highway of thought and commerce the old civilizations marched steadily onward until Roman law reached its zenith and Grecian art was perfect. But when the golden sceptre of wisdom was exchanged for the bacchanalian thyrsis, thought became sensualized and commerce was debauched, and the glory of those old civilizations departed forever. History, that faithful chronicler of human events, reveals the fact that no nation ever rose above the upper margin of its best thought; and we are persuaded that a semi-Christian thought, a feeble type of Christian life, is no defence for this nation against the encroachments of paganism from the East, against the sensuality of materialism, against the putrid flow of licentiousness and anarchism now flooding the land.

The chief obstacle to the speedy consummation of the prophecy of this text is the robbery, the bold, high-handed robbery that emasculated Christian thought has committed on the resources of the gospel. It is no matter whether this felony, be embraced in the weakness of a numerical atonement, or couched in that mischievous formulary, that makes sin a necessary factor as a training force in the divine government. If the atonement is complete, if the embargo of the fall is removed from humanity, then whoever limits God in the realm of his grace smites in his puerile effort, the cross on which the Saviour died, and stamps upon the blood that was shed for man's redemption, and with burglarious intent, enters the tomb of Jesus and despoils the conquering Christ of his victory, wrung from the jaws of death, and from the devouring mouth of hell. In his thought, therefore in his purpose, he flings aside the chaplet of his triumph, and sullies the royal diadem which the Saviour was to wear, when, in the supreme moment of his victory and man's exaltation, we should crown him Lord of all.

The church was divinely organized and equipped to be the light of the world, to eliminate by its divine alchemy every evil force, and vitalize, invigorate, and build society according to the divine ideal; and the marvellous achievements of the past are but the faint prelude to the grand enterprises yet to be accomplished.

Pentecost did not impoverish the magazines of spiritual power; and the church is now putting on its complete armor, and preparing for the final victory. Standing on the gilded heights of this the most marvellous of all the sixty centuries of human history, we see the cimeter of Christian thought flashing above the heads of God's most arrogant foes.

Christ is King by divine right. He has conquered, and is crowned. Redemption is no longer a contingency of his kingdom; the work of redemption is perfect and completed.

When Pilate wrote the superscription in Hebrew, Latin, and Greek, "This is Jesus, the King of the Jews," and put it upon the cross, he wrote better than he knew. He gave to the world a fulfilment of prophecy; he gave to humanity a great truth; and beneath that superscription, Hebrew sentiment and theology, and Grecian intellect, with its art and philosophy, and Roman law and authority, surrendered to Christ. At his cross the three departments of the kingdom of tripartite humanity— thought, feeling, and will— found their sovereign, and language and philosophy, art, poetry, and music, entered the conflict for the recovery of humanity to the fellowship of God, to the dignity of a new allegiance.

The present issue does not involve the success of Jesus Christ. He has succeeded. The only contingency now is whether the church will enter into his victory, and by a holy life and trained faculties aid in extending the victories of the Redeemer's kingdom now, in order that we may share with him in the completeness of his ultimate triumph.

We dishonor Christ and put him again to shame when we refuse to recognize the completeness of his victory. The visionary conjectures concerning what he will do at his second coming are only a plea for the continuance of sin. Such thoughts circumscribe the atoning merit of Jesus, and asperse the Holy Ghost, who is now in the church for the purpose of empowering it for the final conflict.

The only true, unmixed Christian thought is that which discriminates clearly between Christ and his foes, between those forces which proceed from him and those adverse forces that originate in the actions of sinful men. Pure, unmixed Christian thought exalts him to his regal supremacy in every department of his kingdom. It implies the enthronement of him as a living personality in the realm of thought and affection, of ambition, enterprise, and achievement.

It is the recognition of him in that which he is, as certainly and as fully as in that which he does. When the whole church enters into his victory, the whole world will speedily lay its honors and resources at the feet of Jesus.

The power and the authority of Jesus are crystallized in the written word, which is the revealed thought of God, and the true standard of Christian thinking.

As a nation, our thought is not all Christian. We have Christian thinkers and semi-Christian thinkers; but the controlling forces of the state are mixed, and the church is yet in a large degree subordinate to other influences.

At a session of the Utah Conference two of our secretaries spoke on the subject of missions. They pleaded for humanity as only such men can plead. The audience was swayed, like the forest by the storm; heroic hearts were filled with high resolve; but while a group of preachers and laymen discussed the speeches around the breakfast-table the next morning, a dog carried into the dooryard the head of a young woman which had been stricken from her body, as she was sacrificed to a system of pollution, which for more than half a century has been sheltered beneath the American flag.

The saloon and the commercial club and the boards of trade establish the business and political methods of the State. They formulate the code of ethics for the business men of the country. The courts, the theatre, and the secular press create the public sentiment on moral questions, and the religion of Jesus is subordinated to secular thought and local business enterprises. We declare in favor of prohibition in the General Conference; we put it into the dis-

cipline in gilded rhetoric— then go to the polls and vote
for high license, or low license, as advocated by our respective political parties, and send missionaries to foreign
lands on ships freighted with New England rum.

But notwithstanding these alarming facts the church
is continually gaining in aggressive power; and when the
pulpit and the religious press come up to the gospel standard of Christian thought, when the utterances of the
pulpit and the practices of the church shall be truly Christian and flow forth from a holy heart, all opposition in
the world will be speedily overcome. The church is now
daily preparing for this stupendous achievement, and its
accomplishment is now within the range of ordinary spiritual vision, and tinges with celestial beauty the last decade of this golden century.

In the combination of agencies that enter into the
world's progress, the gospel is the pioneer. It is not an
adjunct of other forces, not simply an augmenting force,
it is the creator of forces. The gospel makes commerce.

The prophetic declaration "that every knee shall bow,
and every tongue shall confess that Jesus Christ is Lord,
to the glory of God the Father," is already fulfilled in the
material world. It is a recognized fact in commerce. There
is no standard currency nor coin in the legitimate channels of trade in the whole world but which bears upon its
face the significant *anno domini*. No contract between
persons or states, no bond, or note of any individual,
municipality, or nation, is of any value in any market in
the world, that does not recognize Christ as the Lord;
and in him commerce and the gospel are inseparably
joined for the salvation and progress of man. The gospel
increases values where they already exist, by multiply-
ing man's wants, and stimulating his desires, and improv-
ing his physical condition. The entire bridal outfit of an
African princess consists of a few chalk marks on the
cheek; and the difference between that costume and the

ordinary trousseau in this country, both in cost and style, indicates the change wrought in society by the gospel of the Son of God.

The professional carriers that formerly transported freight from the west coast of Africa to the upper Congo Basin for two cents per day, now receive one dollar and fifty cents for grading on the new railroad now being built over the same route.

The gospel not only multiplies man's wants, and quickens all his faculties, and increases values where they exist, but it creates values where there are none, by stimulating industries and opening new markets.

Less than three hundred years ago Pennsylvania was bought for a few hundred dollars, and paid for in the commonest kind of trade; but now, by the genius of Christian enterprise, its soil and climate and factories, its water and timber and mineral supply, make it one of the most valuable commonwealths in the world.

Less than a hundred years agone the State of Illinois had no commercial value. Wild beasts, Indians, and poisonous reptiles contended for the supremacy, or enjoyed it together. But by the power of Christian enterprise, inspired by the genius of the gospel, that wild, grassy waste, has become worth four billions of dollars, and the enchanting home of three millions of happy and intelligent people.

These facts of history and experience lead to the conviction that there are certain vital forces inherent in the gospel of Jesus that have been operative in society through all the past years of its history, transforming the face of nature, developing values where there were none, increasing those that were in existence, and giving direction to the moral and intellectual forces of society.

The Honorable Hugh Mason, Member of the British Parliament, in a speech before the Board of Trade in Manchester, Eng., said, "Standing in this great commercial city, which sends its productions to every part of the globe, not only to the civilized parts, but to the uncivilized parts, I think I may venture, without bringing any undignified consideration or reflection before you, to stand up for Christian missions even upon subordinate grounds. I look upon the Christian missionary as the promoter and pioneer of commercial enterprises; and many a market in distant lands would have been closed for years against the manufactured articles of Lancashire if it had not been for the devoted missionary who first led the way in an attempt to raise the heathen in the scale of religious and social position."

If the statement of Mr. Mason be true, and there is obligation upon us purely on the basis of commercial advantage, does not the higher motive of Christian love demand of the church that it shall rise to a grander plane of activities, and breathe the spirit and genius of the gospel into the thought and commercial enterprises of this age, and all succeeding ages, and by a more perfect spiritual life and a broader culture direct all subordinate agencies until the whole world shall lay its resources at the feet of Jesus?

To us as a nation God has committed a great trust. We must care for our own land with the great multitude of those continually coming to our shores.

This is the divine order. The great Teacher "came to his own;" and his command to the church was, "Beginning at Jerusalem." This method harmonizes with the divine philosophy: "Make the tree good, and the fruit will cease to be corrupt." "Make the fountain pure, and the water will be sweet." Make this a Christian nation, in fact, and its influence on the world will be Christian.

Throughout the entire period of our national existence, the turbid stream of immigration has emptied its ever-increasing flood upon our shores. These mixed multitudes throng the great cities; they go to the Northwest; they go to Utah, to New Mexico, and Arizona. As a nation we are responsible for the religious culture of these strangers that come to make their homes among our people.

Then we must add to these the neglected and fallen ones of our own families, and the millions of the illiterate and imbruted ex-slaves, and the fetid Indians that still linger in squalor and filth upon our Western borders.

These elements are a perpetual menace to our institutions. There is but one alternative, — we must reach them with the gospel, and recover them to a life of virtue, or perish with them. We must give them a spiritual Christianity of sufficient vitality to transform them into good citizens, or they will corrupt and destroy us.

Statesmen may prepare elaborate disquisitions on finance; they may disport themselves with gilded theories upon the race problem; but the one vital question still demands our consideration: Shall the church be metamorphosed into a semi-religious club? Shall Gethsemane and Calvary be eliminated from the gospel? Shall Christian thought be sensualized, and commerce be debauched? Shall we make merchandise of the bread of life, while the world in a dream of pleasure slides quickly down to hell?

All other questions are diminished in the presence of the one supreme issue: Will the church be true to God in the whole broad realm of Christian thought and Christian activity? Will it measure up to the obligations of the hour and the magnificence of its opportune possibilities?

I believe it will. I am neither an optimist nor a pessimist. I am a Christian, and believe the whole gospel. I have more confidence in the church than ever before. I believe the church is now putting on its strength for the final great conflict. And as I contemplate the near approach of the ultimate victory, my soul thrills with inexpressible pleasure.

The eye that is not spiritually blind can even now see

the beginning of the end. The rays of fulfilled promise now pencil all the east, and make the morning of the future, roseate with the glory of the coming day.

The tremor of invisible forces that now pervades all lands, and thrills and agitates all peoples, is the product of that spirit that is inherent in the gospel. The impulse to a better life is manifest everywhere; it throbs in the heart of all peoples. Everywhere the struggle of humanity is toward the light. The spirit of liberty is in the air; it vibrates in the thunders that reverberate about the summit of Lebanon, and whispers in the hovel of the Siberian exile; it sings about the crests and cornices of the Pyramids, and rustles in the foliage of the Congo jungle. Nation is calling to nation, and tribe is responding to tribe; and the muffled tread of the gathering throng, startles conservatism from its sleep of death. Thrones are crumbling, and crowns are falling like stars in the apocalyptic vision. Empires of spiritual oppression are dissolving into light, to stream their radiance along the highway of human progress.

There is much significance in the fact that six European nations are now projecting railroads to the heart of Africa. Ethiopia is stretching out her hands, and the footsteps of Jehovah are heard everywhere in his omnipotent tramp to his final conquest. The result cannot long be delayed. We misapprehend the facts. Redemption is no longer contingent; Christ has conquered everywhere. He now asks the church to enter into his victory already achieved, that it may share with him in the glory of his ultimate triumph.

When the preparatory work is done, great events transpire at once. Until recently, owing to the rocks in the channel at the entrance of New York Bay, the commerce and the travel of the world were at the caprice of the tides. But an expert engineer went to the heart of the rock at Hell Gate. He tunnelled it in every direction, and packed it with explosives, passing a copper wire carefully through the entire mass. After years of preparatory work by the most skilful workmen and the most scientific methods, the experiment was complete; and on one quiet Sabbath morning, when all nature was in an unsuspecting mood, a little child, miles away from the scene of action in the seclusion of her father's study, pressed the ivory button that loosed the electric spark that converted the potential energy into actual energy, and transformed the stored power into actual force. One single moment of tremulous agony, a groan, a struggle, like the death-agony of a demi-god, and thirteen acres of rock, mingled with dust and smoke and vapor, leaped high into the air, and sank forever out of sight; and the highway of universal commerce was flung open forever.

In this way the captain of the Lord's host is preparing for the ultimate victory of the gospel. God is tunnelling the world, and packing it with his truth. Every text of Scripture is an explosive; every Christian thought, every holy resolution, is a part of the final preparation. Every true minister of the gospel, every Sunday-school teacher, every professor in a Christian school, is a dynamiter. Every toiler of every grade is a helper, preparing for the final victory of Christ.

When the church gets ready, when the world is filled with pure Christian thought, when the ministry shall believe in the Holy Ghost, and accept his fiery baptism, when the supreme moment comes, the Father will let slip one single spark of the pentecostal fire, one single pulsation of his omnipotence, and the whole quivering mass, the hell-gate of opposition, shall be destroyed forever.

The promise of this text shall be fulfilled, the predictions of the prophets shall be performed, the glowing visions of poets and orators shall be realized.

"Jesus shall reign where'er the sun
Does his successive journey run;
His kingdom spread from shore to shore,
Till moon shall wax and wane no more."

His dominion shall be from sea to sea. It is not between two seas, — not from the Mediterranean across the thunder-scathed desert to the Indian Ocean, — but from sea even to sea, until it covers all lands from the "river even to the ends of the earth." Not the Tiber, nor the Nile; but the Jordan, the sacred stream where John preached and baptized, on whose verdant banks Jesus stood while John, with hyssop branch, sprinkled on him the water of separation, and made him a priest of the first order, and where God opened the heavens and poured on him the Holy Ghost, and made him High Priest over the household of humanity, — and gave to him the kingdom. God intended that the pathway of his mediatorial kingdom should be visible in the world, so he, by divine edict, fixed the starting-point.

Jesus began at "The River." The power and authority of the new dispensation, so far as its rites of worship were involved, were conferred upon him at "The River," and all the initial steps for the opening of the kingdom were consummated there. But he bade his disciples begin at Jerusalem, sacred city, the home of David and the prophets. At the holy altar there the infant Jesus was consecrated; and there in his mature years he officiated as priest, and led the daily worship.

This city that had witnessed the scenes of his humiliation, and shared in the glories of his resurrection and ascension, was to be the radiating centre of the new religion. From this hallowed place, where the pentecostal fire fell on the infant church, it was to spread northward where Arctic night rules half the year; and southward to where Antarctic rolls her glaciers up to greet the bending sky;

and eastward and westward until like two prairie fires it should meet by the way, and wrap the earth in auroral brightness from the equator to the poles.

This grand achievement of Christ is now being accomplished by the church. Every day adds some new triumph to his career. The far-off lands are hearing his voice, and responding to his call. The Congo, from the misty shroud of centuries that enwraps her past history, salutes the Nile; and the Nile, from beneath the shadow of her pyramids and obelisks, and out from the drifting sands that for twenty-four centuries have covered her departed glories, proclaims it to the Euphrates and the Tigris; and the Tigris and the Euphrates shout it to the Ganges and the Jumna; and these awake from the sleep of ages and shout it westward to the Danube and the Thames. The Thames rolls it to the ocean, and the ocean wafts it to the islands, and the islands echo it to the shore.

The chorus is still rising; and soon from the Hudson to the Mississippi and Colorado, and from the Columbia and the Rio Grande to the Amazon, one universal paean of praise shall ascend to our God; for the kingdoms of this world will have become the kingdoms of his Son. Then the whole universal church standing on tiptoe shall sing, as it never has sung: —

"All hail the power of Jesus' name.
Let angels prostrate fall;"

and the heavenly choirs, bending low, shall respond: —

"Bring forth the royal diadem,
And crown him Lord of all!"

VI
Peter's Deliverance from Prison

"And when Peter was come to himself, he said, Now I know of a surety, that the Lord hath sent his angel, and hath delivered me out of the hand of Herod, and from all the expectation of the people of the Jews." — Acts xii. 11.

THE INTERPOSITION OF THE FATHER for his saints when in trouble, the mighty deliverances wrought for them in great emergencies, has been to me a source of the keenest enjoyment.

The story of Daniel and the lions, his miraculous preservation from death, was a perpetual fascination to my childish heart, and advancing years and accumulating responsibilities have not broken the charm; and when "the form of the fourth" walked in the midst of the furnace, and the devoted three came forth unscorched from the consuming fire, my youthful soul leaped with inexpressible delight. But the story of Peter's release from prison seems so near and so real that it thrills me with the most intense emotion.

In this brief account, so accurately and minutely

sketched by the historian, there are revealed two centres of influence and of power. One is the prayer- meeting at Mary's house, the other is the scene at the jail.

It was midnight, and Peter was sleeping between two soldiers, chained to each. The time for his execution was appointed for nine o'clock of the coming day; but still he slept. His soul was as calm as a June morning. He was at peace with God and with all the world, and reposed upon the cold stone floor of his cell as serenely as a babe on its mother's bosom.

At the weird and mystic hour of midnight, at exactly low twelve, a light flashed through the dungeon. The darkness fled from its presence, and a voice from some authoritative source spake to Peter, and bade him awake and arise.

In obedience to that mandate, the astonished apostle arose. His chains fell off; he wrapped his garment about him, put on his sandals, and followed the shining messenger as he led the way through guarded portal to the freedom of the street.

When they came to the iron gate that opened to the city, it turned upon its massive hinges at the touch of the angel's hand, and let them pass unquestioned of their foes.

Having gained the open street, the heavenly messenger returned to the presence of God, to report at the throne that the order was executed, and the apostle was free.

After the angel had left Peter, and the fresh, crisp night air had restored him to a normal condition, he knew it was of the Lord; for until then it seemed to him that he had seen a vision, or that some mystic spell had held him in its strange embrace.

The apostle's heart was now filled with praise, and he turned his joyous steps toward the house of Mary. Darkness had spread its mantle over all the earth; nor moon nor star shone out in the vaulted sky. Deep and heavy sleep lay on all the city, but in Mary's house the hour of slumber brought no repose. In that vine-clad cottage on the hillside, at the end of a common street, burdened hearts poured out their strong desire that God would in some manner deliver Peter from the power of Herod.

But what painter, what poet or orator, can picture the surprise with which that tearful company looked upon the apostle when he suddenly stood in their midst? The ear that is never dull had heard the prayer of faith, and he had let slip one single pulsation of his power, and melted off the chains, and freed his servant from the high-handed malice of his foes.

The story of Peter's deliverance appears perfectly natural if we remember God is a person rather than a force. He is the Almighty God. He is the one who hath said, "Ask what ye will, and it shall be done unto you."

There is one more primary fact, — the fulfillment of every promise is predicated upon the petitioner's belief in the Deity whose favor he solicits, and his personal conformity to the divine will.

There is so much said in the pulpit and in the literature of the day about "the power of faith" and "the power of prayer" that the average worshipper is confused; he is lost in the mists of obscure statement; he does not even dream of a personal God. The average worshipper incarnates faith and prayer as agents. He regards these as forces, as impersonal forces. He deifies them in his thought, and calls them "Things," and looks to them for help, and has no conception of a personal Christ whose exclusive mission is to help and to save. But faith and prayer are not agents; they are not forces. They are means to an end; they are the human instrumentalities of approach to God. By these humanity speaks to the Father. But these must reach beyond the clouded atmosphere of doubt, far beyond the darkness and weakness of obscure statement. These conditions that open heaven and secure deliverances must embrace the fact of the *divine person-*

ality, free and unembarrassed by the impersonal forces of the universe.

Suppose we analyze the subject; suppose we formulate one or two simple propositions. Our heavenly Father hears our petitions when we pray. He answers our prayers when we ask aright. The power and authority are all in him. Believing in Jesus as a personal Saviour, and conforming to the divine will, places the petitioner where God can fulfil his promise. It is God who for Jesus' sake pardons the sinner when he repents of his sin. It is God who cleanses the believer, comforts the sorrowing, and strengthens the weak, and refreshes the weary for successful work, and rewards the faithful soul with everlasting life in glory.

The story of Peter's release from prison is one of the most thrilling and exciting incidents in the history of the church. Peter stands before the church in the Book of Acts as Elijah stood before the world in the old dispensation.

Elijah was a man whom not only the people loved and feared, but he was one whom God delighted to honor and trust. When Elijah would, the lightnings leaped from his lips; when he called, the elements obeyed his voice; and when he commanded, the thunders answered from the bending sky. We see him on Carmel, when the issue was fairly joined, when the final test had come, when it was to be determined which was the greater, Jehovah or Baal. Who could be umpire in such a contest?

The appeal was made to fire; to that ancient, chainless, impartial element, fire. "The God that answers by fire, he shall be God." He shall be acknowledged as the Supreme One. Jehovah was an interested party in that issue. So it was at Elijah's command he loosed one single ray from the declining sun which consumed the fuel, the sacrifice, and the altar, and licked up the water from the trenches under the altar.

The same issue is upon us now. It is the issue of every

age, — past, present, and future. But so long as the fire from heaven burns undimmed upon the altars of the church, the world is safe.

This Herodian assault upon Peter was a continuation of the contest between the former Herod and the Nazarene. The regnant prince that instigated the assault upon the infant church was a descendant of the brutal and crafty Herod, who murdered the innocent babes in order that he might thus kill the coming king of the Jews.

This scion of the Herod family, none the less sensual and cruel than his predecessors, saw an opportunity to please the Jews by persecuting the Christians; so he "stretched forth his hand to vex certain of the church." These were days of darkness in the Holy City. When the persecution drove the church out from Jerusalem, and closed every door against it there, God opened every country outside of Judea for his gospel; but the city of David and the adjacent country perished because they put the Son of God to shame, and drove his church from their midst.

But to those hunted and peeled Christians the heavens seemed dark above, and the earth offered no sheltering roof for their aching heads and weary feet. So when depressed and despondent they came back, singly or in small groups, hoping that the storm of opposition at Jerusalem might have passed away. But the persecution had become more violent and extensive. James had been imprisoned; and while in prison, without even a preliminary examination, he was slain by the sword.

In that awful crisis the church looked to Peter as its leader and guide. He was the only earthly hope left it to lean upon. If he should be taken away the church would be left without an authoritative leader. While they were in that state of agitation the news came that Peter had been cast into prison, and that Herod had promised to kill him after the Easter festivities were over.

Matters did look a little dark at that time. A deep, dark, damning crime had been conceived. Herod would not only vex certain of the church, but he would utterly destroy it. He would annihilate the youthful organization. At the supreme moment when the church was celebrating the victory of its founder, he would blot the whole fabric from the face of the earth.

Peter in prison, the doors bolted, an armed guard keeping watch by day and by night at the cell of the royal prisoner, while within the cell were two soldiers chained to the captive.

Under such circumstances escape seemed to be impossible, and death appeared to be certain; for the king had promised, and the day was appointed, and the hour of doom was fixed.

The enemies of the risen Jesus had prepared for a royal banquet. It was to be a high day, a day of universal jubilee, when the intrepid leader of the new movement should be slain.

The enemies of the gospel had calculated very closely. Stephen was dead, James was dead, and all the others had fled for their lives; and with the execution of Peter the last trace of a risen Christ should disappear, and not one vestige of that hated doctrine would remain to disturb the peace of the state.

How the hearts of these persecuted followers of Jesus sunk within them! They were utterly crushed and bewildered, as if all things had suddenly failed them. The church of God that had risen in such beauty and splendor, which had received the baptism of victory on the Day of Pentecost, in one day to become a miscellaneous heap of colossal ruins. Hope prostrated, courage all gone, and no help available in the unequal contest.

At that time evil appeared to be triumphant. God seemed to them to be very far away. Hell was holding high carnival, and rioting in its prospective victory. All through the leaden darkness of its gloomy domain it was the Fourth of July, and every banner was blazoned on the wall, and every streamer flung to the breeze, and every blaring trumpet of the pit poured discordant music on the air. It really did look as if there was nothing the church could do but to sink down in the blackness of despair forever.

That was an awful crisis: Stephen murdered, James slain in prison without a trial, the faint-hearted failing on every side. False brethren were ready to betray them into the hands of the enemy, and angry priests were training their furious mobs for the general fray. The spies were watching every suspected house, and eavesdroppers crouched in the shadows of the night to catch the breath of prayer from some Christian home. But the church did not go to pieces. There was no breaking down in that crisis, there was no conformity to worldly standards then; "but prayer was made without ceasing by the church unto God for him."

Tyrants can do many things. They are potential forces in the world, but they cannot arrest the upward flight of prayer from a believing heart. Conspirators may put the servant of God in prison, or cast him into the lions' den, but they cannot suppress the breath of prayer. Out through the prison bars, over the dusty transom, far beyond the creaking prison gates, prayer flies up to the ear of God.

It may be dark as Egyptian night upon the earth, but the star of Bethlehem still shines in full-orbed beauty and brightness above the mercy-seat. Every heart and every ear may be closed against the child of God; but the ear that hears the young ravens when they cry is pierced by importunate prayer. The eye that sees the falling sparrow notes every want of his obedient children. False teachers may seize every conspicuous place, and fill the world with specious error. The coast lights on the earthly side may all be extinguished, the buoys in the channel may all be destroyed; but the light of divine promise shines on undimmed, and the haven of eternal rest is open to the believing soul.

The church has never seen a darker day than the one recorded in this Scripture. Think of that little group of Christians gathered for prayer, late at night in a cottage chamber, on a side street in the city of David; the doors securely closed, and the gate that led to the city carefully bolted. The occupants talked and prayed in subdued tones, for fear the officers might hale them to prison and to death. Theirs was an awful emergency,— no influential citizen to interest himself for the release of Peter, no one to circulate a petition, and wait on the governor. They were all poor, and there was no money in the treasury. There was no help in sight, for the Pharisees and rulers were all on Herod's side. But when they had reached the end of their effort, then they remembered that Jesus had said, "Verily, verily, I say unto you, that wheresoever two or three of you shall agree on earth as touching one thing, *it shall be done.*" Not some other thing, but "it." The very thing you ask for of a personal God, it shall be yours. God is very definite in his promises, and he requires the petitioner to focalize his faith and his request, to state definitely his desire; and then the Father always answers very definitely. He never gives stone for bread.

This was a critical time, a crucial moment, for those depressed disciples. It was in a special sense a critical time with Peter. It was low twelve, and he was to be put to death in the morning at nine o'clock. It is true they could appeal to Caesar;— but no swift-footed courier could reach the emperor in his home across the sea, and the lightning had not yet been taught to speak for man.

They remembered in their emergency that "help had been laid on one who was mighty to save and strong to deliver." They remembered also that he had said, "Call upon me in the day of thy trouble, and I will deliver thee." He also had said, "Ask what ye will, and it shall be done unto you."

It is a great privilege to carry everything directly to God, conscious that he hears the burden of the feeblest sigh, and that our sympathizing intercessor has indorsed our every request. Think of those persecuted disciples, how their troubles multiplied, how their sorrows pressed upon them; difficulties environed them on every side.

Evil seemed to be enthroned against them; earth and hell appeared to combine for their overthrow. At such a time, how full of comfort, how unutterably sweet, is the fact that Jesus is a helper.

As the church began to pray and to believe, God manifested himself unto them, and they began to understand what the Psalmist meant when he said, "God is my refuge and strength, he is the horn of my salvation." And as they continued to pray, hope sprung up within them; they took on fresh courage; they lost all sense of helplessness and orphanage. "The Almighty God was theirs;" the "Living God was with them." Bolts and bars counted nothing against omnipotence. He was acquainted with all the laws of philosophy, he was familiar with all the combinations of matter. He was their refuge and strength, he was "a very present help in time of trouble."

Once before, Jesus had shown his power over the soldiery. Then there were sixty of them; now there are only sixteen. Once before Jesus had conquered death, and robbed the grave of its prey. Wrapped in his winding-sheet and laid in the tomb, a guard of soldiers stationed about the place, surely it did look as if all was lost.

But Jesus conquered even there. He fearlessly broke the king's seal, pushed back the great stone, and walked away from the place of his incarceration; and the terrified guard fled from the scene of his triumph, and told the story of his victory to those who had put him to death.

So now gates and bars and bolts and soldiers are of no avail. The angel of the Lord descended, the guard was paralyzed at his presence, and he had undisturbed possession of the prison.

Suppose we enter that gloomy abode and look upon the scene within. Stand there a moment beside Peter's cell. A group of soldiers keep guard without; two stalwart veterans are within the cell, to whom the condemned apostle is fastened with two chains. The crucial moment has come. At nine o'clock on the coming day Peter is to be executed. The programme is complete. Everything is so arranged as to make the triumph of the persecutors emphatic. This assault was to be the death-blow to the church; it was to extirpate the last trace of the new movement inaugurated by the Nazarene.

Look upon that scene. Is Peter weeping? Oh, no. Is he dejected? does he moan and clank his chains, and wail out his anguish on the night air? No, no; he is asleep; he sleeps the sleep of the innocent and the pure. Death stands at the door with drawn sword, but what of that? If they behead him in the prison, God will crown him in glory. "The God whom he serves continually," he can deliver his servant, or crown him, at his discretion.

That night, as the apostle lay on the cold stone floor of his cell, God came very near to him; he breathed into his weary soul his own tender good-night, and kissed his troubled spirit into sweet repose; for "So he giveth his beloved sleep."

But while Peter was sleeping, and the soldiers were watching from without, and the keepers of the gate with drawn swords were in their places, God was watching also; and suddenly the angel visitor came. The prison flamed with the brightness of his presence. He touched the prisoner, and the chains fell off; and Peter was free. Instead of the officers of the law coming to lead him forth to the slaughter, it was the angel of the Lord. He had come to take off his fetters and give him the freedom of the outer world. At the touch of the angel's hand, the apostle was liberated. He arose from his bed, and walked away from his cell, away from the soldiers, out through the iron gate into the open street.

When the angel left Peter, and he was recovered from his surprise at what had transpired, he was filled with thankfulness. He thought of that faithful little church up at Mary's house praying for him, and he turned his joyful steps toward that humble place. But the most remarkable part of this story is apparent at this point. The dungeon door opened to Peter, the iron gate swung back of itself; but up at the church, where they were praying for him, every door was bolted. Peter met with no opposition until he came to the house of his friends.

The church had faith, or it would not have prayed. The embarrassment grows out of the fact that they prescribed a method by which the Lord should answer their petitions. Perhaps they thought the spirit might change the heart of Herod, or that the courts would interfere on some technicality, some irregularity, of the legal proceedings; but they had overlooked the fact that God could come in person or by proxy and fling open the prison doors. Because they had made a programme for the Lord, and he had answered without regard to it, they were surprised.

Beloved, learn this one thing: when you pray believe that God will give you "whatsoever ye ask," and not something else, something better. God always gives on the line of your asking; but he always transcends the limit of the petition. He delights to give the very blessing you desire. It is the petitioner's privilege to formulate his request according to any immediate and urgent need, and press his request with importunate faith.

It is a popular delusion that God withholds what we ask, and gives what he will. Such a conception blots out faith, and obliterates intelligent prayer. It emasculates human responsibility and divine alternative, and shuts up the whole scheme of moral government in the iron grasp of fatalism. God holds man responsible for the petitions he makes, but always gives on the line of his asking. "Ask what ye will, and *it* shall be given unto you." — "Therefore I say unto you, whatsoever things ye desire, when ye pray, *believe that ye receive them* and ye shall have *them.*"

The modern heretical interpretation that God will ignore your petition was projected by Satan to neutralize the definite, specific promise of God. When you begin to pray fling the door of your heart wide open; let expectation have the full length of its tether; look for the very thing you have asked for; be as definite in your expectation as you were in your request. Let God have a chance to answer your prayers by whatever method may serve the infinite plan.

On this occasion, Peter had a glorious time with the soldiers and the angel down at the jail, but his first reception at the church was rather cool; but the evidence prevailed and they let him in.

So it is under the delusion of this doctrinal error penitents pray for pardon, but do not believe for it nor expect it until they die. Men pray for a clean heart, but do not think it is possible for God to cleanse them from sinful impurities while they live.

A lack of knowledge concerning the divine character and the divine method of administration, almost entire ignorance of the doctrinal basis of prayer, play strange tricks with man's fears, and hinder him in his efforts to advance in spiritual things.

The soul seeking salvation is afraid of the past. Intelligent persons know that there can be no advancement for any human soul until the past is adjusted. The soul must be square with God, as a prerequisite to the reception of the promised good. Spiritual delinquency is a perpetual bar to Christian progress.

Those timid believers up at Mary's house were not expecting Peter's deliverance at once. They hoped for a change of public sentiment, and an interposition of the courts, a writ of habeas corpus. But God selects his own methods and measures. He took the case in his own hands. The appearance of Peter alarmed the group of worshippers. They supposed that the apostle was already dead, and that his ghost had called to announce the fact to them. But Peter was persistent, he continued to knock, the evidence prevailed, and they let him in.

When Peter had explained it all, he sent a message to James; and after a brief conference with the church, he went forth beyond the jurisdiction of Herod, and left the sensual debauchee to his consuming remorse and devouring vermin. And a few weeks later, while yet the fragrance of cut flowers perfumed his royal palace, and the flattering words of the populace lingered gratefully in his ears, he was "eaten of worms, and gave up the ghost;" for the retributions of Almighty God are as certain and terrible as his mercies are vast and wonderful. This historic fact in the experience of the church teaches some very important lessons: —

(*a*) That Christians are to believe God's promise, and not limit him in his methods of answering. Ask for what you want; believe what he has promised, and receive it by any method he may choose to employ.

(*b*) It teaches us that God was not in the conspiracy. He did not instigate the assault that he might show his power and glory in the deliverance, but he came to the rescue of Peter at the call of the church. God is one. He cannot be divided; he cannot be on both sides in a conflict, by the very nature of his being; he is always on the side of the right.

(*c*) That the power by which the church or an individual Christian gains the victory over its enemies is divine; that it comes forth from a personal God at the time of need; comes in answer to specific, definite prayer. When the conditions of prayer are met by the petitioner, God lets slip a portion of his omnipotence, and his enemies "become as dead men."

The direct highway to all success is by the way of the throne of God. The little band of praying men and women at Mary's house could not go to Peter's aid at the jail nor at the court. They would have shared the same fate. But "they knew their God, and could do exploits." There in that dungeon was Peter upon his bed of stone, shut in behind the bars and bolts, behind the soldiers and the spears. But God's shining messenger of freedom walked in past them all, loosed the apostle, and Peter came out a victor from the very jaws of death. So it would be now if the whole church would really pray, really get hold of God; deal with an intelligent, omnipotent personality rather than with the impersonal forces of nature. Something would transpire, and success would be universal; for the Father has access to all prisons, material and spiritual. He can defeat all conspiracies, and crush the iron hand of the oppressor in all lands.

VII
METHOD OF THE DIVINE GOVERNMENT

"Are not five sparrows sold for two farthings, and not one of them is forgotten before God? But even the very hairs of your head are all numbered. Fear not therefore: ye are of more value than many sparrows." —LUKE xii. 6, 7.

THERE ARE THREE different theories of the divine government. The first and the oldest is known as the necessitarian theory of the divine administration. This theory teaches that everything that transpires in all its minute phenomena was predetermined by the Creator before the first atom of the universe was created, and that consequent upon that antecedent fact there are no alternatives with God or with man.

The second theory is known as the providential or permissive system, which assumes that all evil, both physical and moral, is essential as a factor in the divine government, and is utilized in the gospel system, and made tributary to the glory of God as a working force in the probational life of man, and that God regulates the amount of evil according to his own purpose.

The third theory is based upon the assumption that man is a moral being; that he is a *bona fide* subject of law, accountable to God for his deportment; that he is under the environment of law in the whole domain of his tripartite being, amenable to God, to the state, and to himself ; and, as a creature of law, he volitionates his relation to every other being in the universe.

This theory embraces the fact that there are alternatives with God and with man; that man is a bona fide subject of law, under the operations of grace; and that it is only by the strictest obedience to law that grace becomes available, and is made efficient in the salvation and progress of man. This view of the subject is in harmony with the general principles of divine providence, and with the essential character and attributes of Jehovah.

The text plainly teaches the Father's individual and continuous oversight of the creatures he has made. We regard the fact of divine providence as inseparable from the Christian system; but we regard correct views of providence as essential to correct Christian ethics. The providential oversight is personal, the providential procedure is according to the constitution and laws of the universe, and the providential measures must always harmonize with the principles of eternal right. There can be no caprice on the part of the administrator, nor can there be any coercion of a moral agent; both the subject and the sovereign are under the environment of law.

There are those who regard as providential only such events as are disastrous. When great calamities overtake a nation, when adversity assails a man, or death enters a household, — these events by some persons are regarded as providential. The sickness and death of children are regarded as purely providential; they are spoken of in the pulpit and the press as mysterious providences.

But when we remember that the entire human race is now, and always has been, under the environment of law, and comes into the world under sentence of death, as a direct result of sin; when we consider the whole human family under sentence of death for sin, and add to that fact, the helplessness of children and the ignorance of the nurses, and the thoughtlessness of mothers, — the mystery changes, and it becomes the problem of the ages, that so many children reach maturity as do; and it is inexplicable, except on the hypothesis of God's constant providential care in delivering them from surrounding dangers.

God is sovereign. He governs all, but his government is neither arbitrary nor capricious. God is not a tyrant, and his government cannot be despotic. His administration is according to universal law, both in the natural world and in the spiritual world.

Obedience to divine law, secures both moral and physical health, and gives happiness to soul and body.

Disobedience to any divine law, results in disaster, in suffering, or in death.

God has affixed suffering in its varied forms, as the consequence of violated law. He did this to hedge man into a life of virtue and obedience; and no being, made in the likeness and image of God, ever did or ever could suffer, or sorrow, if sin had not disturbed the healthful relations between that being and God.

There is no lack of harmony in the divine method. God's natural and moral providences both flow forth from himself. God's government is a unit, and his particular or special providences are integral parts of one complete system of government.

The basal fact in this theory, is the existence, and personality of God. If there is no personal Deity, active, intelligent, powerful, and possessing a will, there can be no providence.

1. God, in his essence and person, is one. He cannot be divided.

2. God, in his manifestations, cannot act in such a manner as to contradict his moral character.

Whatever God is essentially in himself, must be the nature of his manifestations. God being essentially holy, can never act contrary to his holy nature. He can never perform an act himself, nor consent to an act by another, that is morally impure, or legally wrong. He cannot do under any circumstances, that which he has made it unlawful for me to do. We err when we think of God only as a given amount of power. We do him an unkindness, when we divest him of his attributes and deify him only as so much force.

The naturalist speaks of God as force operating by law. The materialist says there is no God but force, and under that delusion he continually prates of evolution. The necessitarian says, "God can only act in one way," and is equally incapable of mercy or compassion. But the Bible says, God is our Father; he is a helper; he is a friend.

God is nowhere in the Scripture called force. He is not called power. He is not called omnipotence. But while he possesses all these attributes, the Bible plainly says "God is love." God cannot do wrong to another party while manifesting his love even to his dearest saints. His power and justice, his goodness and mercy, must always be the manifestations of his love. All of God's acts are put forth in harmony with what God is in himself.

We behold in the gorgeous preparation which God made for man in Eden, an illustration of the Father's regard for his children; we get a definite idea of his estimate of manhood; and from the marvellous exhibition of love in the gift of his Son for man's redemption, we can judge of his present affection for his alien and perishing children.

We are at fault in the common conceptions of the divine character. We follow our imagination as it is inspired by fairy tales, or excited by "old wives' fables," rather than the Bible statements of the facts. Thus we have a caricature, rather than a true portrait of the divine character.

The only perfect revelation of God to the world is in the person of the Lord Jesus Christ. The verbal descriptions of the historians and the prophets may be misapprehended, the high-sounding terminology of the theologian may confuse the ordinary mind; but in the man of Galilee we behold "God manifest in the flesh," and in his spirit we see revealed the true heart of the Father. The notion that God in a paroxysm of anger lays waste the fruitful field and flourishing city by the disaster of fire and flood, that he stealthily enters the happy household as a destroyer, the assumption that desolation follows in his pathway wherever he goes forth, — is contrary to every fact in the Bible, and every principle in philosophy.

Our views of the divine character, formed under the instructions of an open Bible, and in the light of the Holy Spirit, ought to be clearer and grander than those conceptions begotten of the mythologies of the ancients, stained with the blood of pagan altars, and entertained by some of the lowest barbarians of the present age.

The wildest Bedouin of the desert will inquire where Allah may be found. When asked what he wants of Allah, he replies, "If I could catch him, I would spear him through, for he lays waste our fields, destroys our cattle, and kills our wives and children."

Christians living in the light of an open Bible should entertain more exalted ideas of the divine character than those unlettered children of the desert. The true conception of deity is, "That God is a self-existing, self-determining, intelligent personality," that he is governed by the laws that inhere in himself, that his divine nature directs all his movements.

The divine sovereign moves the planetary system as he desires. There is no friction, because no inanimate atom resists his will, that is, the divine method in the realm of his natural providence.

But man is a moral being; he is a creature whose happiness depends upon his obedience to law, God moves the natural universe by his own invisible power; but man, as a volitional being, determines his own personal relations to God and his laws. The fact of sovereignty is not dependent upon power alone. Sovereignty is a fact of relationships.

It is a fatal mistake to assume that there are no determining forces outside the will of God. If we assume that God plans and executes every event that transpires, then there is no being in the universe that can suffer pain or be unhappy, except by an exhibition of the grossest tyranny and the most intense cruelty on the part of the administrator, but by this concession to error the conception that God is love, is logically eliminated from the thought of the world.

As a subject of moral government, man has real volitional power. He possesses a *bona fide* power of himself, originating with him, neither instigated nor delegated, but belonging to him as man, — the ability and responsibility to determine his relation to law. The uncoerced power to accept or reject any proposition is an elementary constituent quality of every accountable being. God's moral government is a government of many alternatives. If there are no contingencies in the divine government, there is no logical possibility of a special providence. If there is but one determining force in the universe, and that is the will of God, man is not a moral agent, but a conspicuous part of a minute, systematic, and intense despotism.

We stated in the opening paragraph of this discourse that there were three recognized theories of moral government. We now formulate a universal proposition. One of these theories must be the true one, and only one of them can be the correct one, as it is logically impossible to combine them.

(*a*) The first theory assumes that God does everything that is done; that he sets in motion all influences; that everything, including that which we call sin, and all the sequences that flow from it in the form of moral and physical evil, flows forth of the divine will, and all these together work out in concert the secret purpose of Almighty God.

We object to this theory because it makes God the author and abetter of sin. It declares that moral evil is essential to the accomplishment of the divine purpose with man. This view of the divine government constitutes sin, a necessary factor in the government of God, the principal training force in the process of human culture and advancement. If we accept this theory, we impeach the moral purity of Jehovah, and abolish the moral agency of man, and eliminate all idea of rewards and punishments, by blotting out all distinctions between virtue and vice, thus transforming the moral universe into one vast crushing despotism.

(*b*) The other view, known as the permissive system of divine government, varies but little in statement or sequence from the first.

It was conceived and brought into existence as an apology for the first. It is a covering of gilded tapestry, woven by the artistic hand of genius to conceal the atrocious deformities of the former theory. In conception and logical results they are the same. This theory assumes that all moral and physical evil, are blessings in disguise, that those things that seem to be evil are the gracious scaffolding on which the favored few climb up to God, while the great surging mass perish without help.

That system assumes that all disastrous events by

land or sea are permitted of God for some good though invisible purpose. It is assumed that God permits evil-minded men to do things that in themselves are wrong, in order that he may bring good out of it to some individual or community.

The class of events usually denominated permissive providences embraces the most gigantic crimes, the most malignant and diabolical schemes, in the history of iniquity.

The assassination of President Garfield, that act of infamy that hung a pall over the nation, and plunged the Christian world into the depths of sorrow. The burning of the steamboat Sultana, when seventeen hundred men perished in a moment, and ten thousand hearts were made sad with an unutterable anguish, and a shadow black as night flung over ten thousand happy homes by one fiendish deed that could only have been born in hell.

The Ashtabula horror, the great fires at Chicago and Boston, the giving way of the dam in the Mill River, the Johnstown flood, and all kindred events, though clearly the result of negligence or crime, are all classed as permissive providences; and although a thousand helpless mortals perish without time to lisp a prayer for pardon, and many other thousands are suddenly left in hopeless orphanage and poverty, we are called upon to accept of it as the achievement of a compassionate God. Verily, the theology that can associate a loving Father's hand with deeds of that character, and make him a party to them, is worthy to have been conceived in the most obscure period of the Dark Ages, and to have been evolved from the upas mists, of pagan philosophy, that hung like the raven wing of night, over the whole earth when the light on the altar of truth had been quenched in blood.

God permits moral agents to do as they will during the period of their probation, subject always to the environment of law, by which they are finally judged. A moral agent acts in a given way because he chooses to do so. If he is a moral agent, God can neither grant him immunity from the law, nor withdraw from the party his legal restraint, because always the power that determines the act is located in the agent.

It must be evident to every thoughtful mind that if God permits any event to occur for some good purpose, and in order that it may occur he withdraws his divine prohibition, he must first will the event to be, for God cannot act without "willing to act;" and however revolting it may appear to man, and however malignant in the eyes of human law, all parties connected with those disasters are not only absolved from blame, but they are honored of God according to the Scripture that says, "Whosoever doeth the will of God abideth forever."

Therefore, if the doctrine of permission be true, the perpetrators of all these dark deeds go right up to glory, while their hands are yet dripping with the blood of their innocent victims; and, furthermore, under such conditions, no civil government has a legal right to hang Guiteau or Booth for doing the will of God.

God permits moral agents to act in a given way, because they are moral agents. If the determining power were not in them, they would not be agents at all; but God never licenses, nor permits, any being in heaven or earth or hell, to do wrong for any purpose whatever. Sinai thunders against all evil doing, and is as terrible to wicked men as when canopied with the cloudy pavilion of Jehovah, and it puts its fiery prohibition between man and all uncleanness; and never in any emergency of man, nor in the unfoldings of the divine plan, does it become necessary that evil should be done by angel or man. And a permissive providence of the nature above described is morally impossible, the impossibility being grounded in the constitution and nature of God.

(*c*) The other theory of the divine government, and the

one which we believe to be correct, and the only one that can be consistently held in harmony with the fact of the atonement and priesthood, and intercessory office of Jesus Christ, is based on the revealed fact that the government of God is alternative, and under the environment of law. This method enables the divine Father to continually adapt himself to the necessities of each individual member of the human family; and, while each individual man constantly changes his relations, and daily determines existing possibilities into facts, God never leaves him, but continually through the priestly merit of Jesus seeks to save every child of man from evil of every kind. God aims to secure the greatest possible good for each individual, and thus reach the highest state of good for all in this age and in all coming ages, in this life and in eternity.

The text says, "Five sparrows are sold for two farthings," and not one of them is forgotten. Not one of them falls to the ground without the notice of the Father; and God says to his people, "Fear not, ye are of more value than many sparrows."

These words of the Master teach us that, as man rises above the sparrow in the significance of his relationship to God, even so the Father's care for him increases as his value is greater than the sparrow.

Thus we perceive that, as God does not strike down the almost worthless sparrow, nor burn their carefully prepared nests, but that he judges the cruel boy by whose ruthless hand the sparrow falls; and as the Father's care for man, increases in breadth and intensity in proportion to man's advancement above the sparrow in the scale of being— the compassionate Father cannot conspire against his child, but sympathizes with man in all his sufferings and sorrows to which the apostasy of Adam has exposed the race. In all of these, "We have an high Priest, touched with the feeling of our infirmities."

"He, in the days of feeble flesh,
   Poured out strange cries and tears;
And in his measure feels afresh
   What every member bears."

A perfect criterion on this subject is embraced in the fact "that God cannot act contrary to his holy nature," and that he cannot deal coercively with a moral agent, amenable to the *regime* of law under which he was created.

Government by law, implies the fact that the first office of the law is the protection of the subject, and the second is the punishment of the transgressor, the violator of the authority of the law. It is because of this fact that the violation of law results in disaster to the offender.

There is but one way of escape from violated law; that is, by vicarious redemption. So far as this principle applies to man as a sinner, the penalty of the law which he violated in Eden was arrested and held in suspension by the "redemption that is in Jesus Christ." But the sequences of sinful action cannot be arrested; they flow forth from the act, and are not penal; they belong to the act, and are not affected by the law; they continue forever.

Therefore, as we are mutually related to each other by the ties of social life, by politics and commerce and consanguinity, and as we are now in a probational state with sinful surroundings which flow forth of Adam's transgression, as sequences of his act, it is impossible but that society should become involved in the disasters of our mistakes and crimes.

This view of the subject enables the thoughtful mind to see clearly that the world is not now as God made it. It enables man to harmonize the justice, the mercy, and goodness of God with man's present condition of suffering and sorrow during his earthly life.

We have seen that in redemption the law was not suspended. The penalty of the law was arrested so far as it related to man, but it was executed upon the Redeemer. The law is not suspended; the law has not abated one jot of its claim on man. The penalty of the law was met by man's vicar, in order that grace and mercy might bound unto all. But law is still regnant in every department of the universe.

The suicide knows that poison kills, and in his despondency seeks its aid; but when he has swallowed the fatal drug, no remorse, no degree of penitence, no vehemence in prayer, can change the result. The deed was his own deliberate act; and that which proceeds from an act as a legitimate sequence cannot be changed, even by the special act of Almighty God. He may pardon and save the offender; but the sequence of the action flows on forever.

Logic, experience, history, and the Word of God agree in their testimony that moral and physical evil come upon humanity as the sequences of the transgression in Eden. "And the Lord God said unto Adam, because thou hast harkened unto the voice of thy wife, and hast eaten of the tree, of which I commanded thee, saying. Thou shalt not eat of it: cursed is the ground for thy sake [for the sake of thy sin]; in sorrow shalt thou eat of it all the days of thy life."

Thus we perceive that it does not require any additional legislative or executive act of the Almighty to send a curse. The earth is already cursed because of sin. The earth has passed through many changes since the curse fell upon it. The structure of the earth, the soil, the climate, and the seasons, all share in the original sentence.

Under the influence of this curse, the very elements that should be tributary to man's highest enjoyment are full of peril. The life element of man becomes a dangerous foe; the atmosphere becomes pestilential with contagion. Every vesicle of air becomes the habitation of countless microbes; and that which should vitalize the blood and give vigor to the whole man, now fills the organism with cholera and typhoid germs. Occasionally the lightning leaps out from the rifted cloud and smites to the death in a moment, or the cyclone and tornado slip out from their hiding-place and fall upon the defenceless community, and the hail and flood complete the physical ruin.

These conspiracies of the elements are the perpetual reminders of the catastrophe in Eden. Not one of them is a normal manifestation. They perpetuate the story of the apostasy, and rehearse the fact of the curse that still rests upon the earth as a sequence of Adam's transgression.

In the light of these facts we discover that the moral and physical evil that come upon the human family in their homes and in their personal relations with each other are the sequences either of sinful actions or ignorant and thoughtless mistakes. The ravages of disease, arising from man's changed relations to God, are augmented by the violation of the sanitary laws, and the neglect of suitable hygienic measures. We look out upon this beautiful earth clothed in splendor and fragrant with flora and fruitage; but consumption, like an angel of death, hovers over it all. We see cholera, and the yellow plague, that bronzed reaper of the sunny southland, sweeping their untold millions into the grave. Again we look, and behold intemperance, the legalized crime of municipalities, holding in its right hand the certificate of authority from Christian communities, and on its brow the seal of protection from the state, marshalling all its forces to consume both soul and body on its bloody altar. Epidemics of fever, of smallpox, join in the carnival to reap the great harvest of death.

The superstitious notion that for so many centuries connected seasons of unusual sickness with the anger of God, and regarded these odious and loathsome forms of disease as the chastening agencies of heaven, is slowly fading out before the light of advancing science and the unfolding glories of a pure gospel.

There never was disease in any country or age but what originated from violated natural or sanitary laws, and was propagated by specific germs or by infectious touch; and no form of disease was possible in Eden.

That mysterious and inscrutable providence, about whose inexplicable deeds we have heard so much from the pulpit and the press, upon closer examination proves to be the product of defective drainage, damp walls, unwholesome food, no ventilation, poisoned wells, and great malarial deposits.

Suppose you were to visit some of those plague-scourged cities of the past or the present, see the festering graveyards pour their deadly contents into every well and cistern, take notice of the loathsome cesspools forcing their distilled death through all the porous earth, producing contagions that sweep like a tornado over the land; and the soul grows sick under the stupid and ignorant wail concerning the mysterious dispensations of an incomprehensible providence.

Is it not time we would dispense with that impious and profane insolence which in the name of religion flaunts its filth in the face of Jehovah, saying these came from his benevolent hand as his holy messengers of some unseen good?

God speaks to the world now, as he spake to his servant in the past: "Wash you, and be clean." Be clean in your person; be clean in the food you eat, and in the water you drink, and in the air you breathe. If you expect the favor of God in this world or in the world to come, be clean in thought and in word, and be clean in your deeds and in your life.

VIII
God's Love for Humanity

"For God, so loved the world, that he gave his only begotten Son, that whosoever believeth in him should not perish, but [should] have everlasting life." —John iii. 16.

THE LOVE OF GOD to man as manifested in Christ Jesus is the profoundest mystery of heaven and earth. The divine affection, as exhibited in the redemption of a sinful race, no man or angel can fathom.

Jesus said to the astonished rabbi who sought an interview by night, "God so loved the world." He appears to have purposely chosen that phrase, "so loved," that he might excite the wonder, and then inspire the confidence, of humanity.

Not one of the inspired writers attempts to analyze love. John says, "Behold what manner of love the Father hath bestowed upon us, that we should be called the sons of God." He does not attempt to define it, nor describe it. He appears to stand a little apart from the world, and gaze in wonder upon the manifestation of this love. Its magnitude, its nature, its incomprehensibility, awed him into silence, or overwhelmed and oppressed him.

"God is love;" and his essential nature is the fountain of all life, and the inspiration to all action. Love being the essential quality of the divine personality, it is of necessity a primary force in the construction of the universe. That love is a primary force in the government of God, is a fact not generally apprehended. It is a fact that lies outside the immediate realm of the consciousness, and has been shrouded in the mists of error for ages.

That love should be a primary force in moral government, is as natural as that life should be a primary condition of animals and men.

God is love, and God is life, are equivalent facts. Love wherever manifested is of God, and God is the essential fountain of light and life.

Love and life and light represent God in the domain of animated nature, and in the realm of thought and affection.

Sin causes moral darkness, sin obscures the truth. The love of sinful things perverts the judgment, debases the moral nature, and subordinates the will to the passions. In the natural world, the dense, dark, portentous cloud shuts out the light of the sun, and shrouds the earth in gloom. In like manner, sin throws its sable shadow athwart the moral sky, and shuts out the light and life and love of God from the human soul.

As the fleecy mists of a November storm shut out the stars, so in the absence of love, star after star declines, till the deepening gloom of sinful night shuts out the light of heaven from the human soul, and shrouds its present and its future in the darkness of impenetrable night.

To disperse the night of sin, and roll back the clouds, and bring in the glad morning of endless day, God sent his Son into the world.

There was a time far back beyond the rolling centuries

of the past when all the world appeared to be in waiting for the coming of the Prince of Peace. Costly gems, precious jewels, and lustrous pearls, gathered from all lands and stored with great care, were ready to be brought forth by loving hands on his coronation day. All the nations of the earth shared in this feeling of expectation. The desire for a deliverer appeared to spring up in the human heart from the universal consciousness of need.

Even China in her isolation shared in this feeling of expectation. Shut in behind her massive walls, her gates of adamant bolted by day and night from the darkness of her self-imposed exile, she looked with longing eyes and anxious hearts for the coming of him who had strength to break the power of sin and roll back the darkness of moral night, to lift the burden from the stricken soul and fill the crushed and sorrowing heart with conscious life and peace.

In the land of David the light of divine promise had kindled this hope to a white heat. Every birth was looked upon as a possible epoch, and as the probable advent of the promised seed. But the Jews fondly thought that the coming king would build again the throne of David and reconstruct the fallen nation; and that the glory of the new empire would as far exceed the glory of Solomon as Solomon's splendor excelled the sceptred sheik of the desert. The Jews supposed that Christ would come to them only, and that his glory would add new lustre to the names of Moses and Abraham.

The growth of selfishness in the Jewish heart was beyond computation. Prejudice and ungodly ambition culminated in spiritual ruin. Formalism and materialism dominated the religious thought of the nation, and ruled with despotic power in church and state.

But the fortuitous moment came; the glad hour of the world's release was accomplished; the Saviour was born. The star led the men from the East, filled with wonder and admiration, to where the King of kings and Prince of Peace was cradled in a manger.

When Jesus was grown to manhood and had entered upon his public career, the Jewish rabbies [*sic*] saw beams of hope tinge all the sky. When the elements obeyed his voice, when disease yielded to his touch and evil spirits fled from his approach, visions of the coming victory over all their foes filled all their broad horizon. But as he began to speak of some of the features of his kingdom, declaring that it was not of this world, that it was a spiritual dominion, they deliberately rejected him. The Jews traced their ancestry through an unbroken lineage back to him who had received the promises. They could not abandon Abraham and Moses to receive new leaders, and they would not accept deliverance from one whose origin they knew not, from one who was without parentage and without credentials, except so far as his works attested his mission to be divine. They thought it incredible that one who was himself a man could give salvation to others, and bring in everlasting righteousness. But in the face of all opposition Jesus continued to assert that he came to give life, abundant life; a life of beauty and spirituality; a life born of pure, perfect, unsullied love; a life which would secure to its possessor a crown of glory in the heavenly world.

Man's need of a Saviour was so intense, was of such a nature, and involved such interests, that "God gave his only begotten Son;" delivered him up for all; gave him freely, in order that he might also give eternal life to as many as would receive him.

I think we fail to get the true significance of the word perish. It is from *apollumi*, "to destroy." No ray of light ever entered the lens of a destroyed eye. The organism of the body perishes at death. Without the salvation of Christ, soul, body, and spirit must perish forever. That word perish includes the curse and consequences of sin in this life, and the final penalty of the law in the world which is to come. The curse of sin sweeps the broad area of human activities in this life, and reaches downward to the lowest depths of fathomless perdition.

If God had not so loved humanity, Adam would have perished at the first offence. Then the law would have taken its course without interruption, and the penalty, with all it implies, would have been executed upon the first offenders. No stream would have issued from that corrupted fountain to flow on forever and poison with its putrid waters all the coming ages. If God had not so loved the world, death's fatal dart would have quenched all the life of Eden at one fell stroke.

But God so loved the world that "he gave his only begotten Son." Wondrous power of love! Love of the Father to send; love of the Son unto death; and through the matchless power of this infinite love, humanity has life, and hope, and heaven; for the cross of Jesus stands between the world in ruins and the yawning chasm of a pitiless and eternal hell.

In the current thought of this age, there is a fatal error in regard to redemption; there is a persistent unwillingness to accept the divine statement that because of sin the world is lost. There is a covert or open rejection of the fact of universal guilt. There is a fixed purpose to deny the fact of man's moral corruption as a sequent of the fall, and emasculate it from the theology of this period.

These self-appointed leaders of Christian thought, by rejecting these doctrines, also reject the divinity of Christ and his vicarious atonement. In the pulpit and on the platform, Jesus the Christ is put in contrast with Socrates; and these reformers of Christian doctrine attempt to bridge the chasm of man's apostasy with the dangerous expediency of an imperfect morality.

But the sacred writings do not speak of Jesus as a moralist, nor as a reformer. He is not an adventurer among the sons of men. He is the Holy One, come forth on his mission of redemption.

There is an unlimited difference between virtue and holiness, between morality and spiritual life. The Bible states as the fundamental fact of its doctrinal teaching, "That the whole world is lost because of the sin of Adam;" and we must accept as its logical correlate the other fact, that unless a substitute should be accepted by which the original culprit is released, he must perish at the hands of the law. If the law had taken its course when Adam sinned, the human family would have begun and ended with the first pair. These are facts which are inseparable from a redemptive system. It is because of these fundamental truths that the work of Christ cannot be exemplary. It must *be*, therefore *it is*, priestly and sacrificial.

As a logical deduction from these basal truths, we have the irresistible conclusion that virtue alone is not sufficient to save the soul; that pardon and regeneration do not embrace all of man's needs. These must be supplemented by moral purity. We also perceive that these different religious states are neither the product of churchly culture nor of disciplinary processes. They are the purchase of the "Redeemer's blood," and come to each separate individual as a divine gift.

Man in his unconverted state is a condemned criminal at the bar of sovereign justice; but, through the mercy of God, pardon and life are freely offered to him if he will return to his allegiance to God.

By virtue of the sacrificial merit of Christ, man comes upon the stage of life in a state of initial salvation, and is lost only because he rejects the offered pardon, because he will not surrender himself to God.

Suppose we go to that prison where the condemned criminal expiates his guilt. He looks through the iron grating that shuts him out from the world; he pines for the freedom of his native hills; he longs to look upon the purple-clouded sky that canopied his boyhood home; he sighs for the melody of the woods; he pants for the freedom of his youth. These are his continuous desires; but his real wants lie very far back of his desires. His real needs lie outside of the realm of his thoughts. The possession of all he covets would not make him happy. His needs lie very far beyond the freedom of the outer world. It is not the warm hand of an earthly friend pressing his own outstretched palm that will satisfy his soul. He may secure all of these, and yet perish.

What his guilty soul needs, and what he must have, or die eternally, is peace with God. He must have pardon and life, his soul must be liberated from the bondage of sin. He must feel the thrill of conscious purity. The Son must make him free, which is liberty in the broadest and grandest sense. "He that hath the Son hath life." "And ye shall know the truth, and the truth shall make you free."

In any system of redemption, the redeemer is everything. If the gospel system is redemptive, Jesus is everything. "He is the well of water in the soul, springing up into everlasting life." He is the vine pulsating with life. Christians are the living branches. When the life of Christ flows unobstructed through the soul, clusters of sublimest joy hang golden and purple upon the pendent bough. "This is life eternal, that they might know thee, the only true God, and Jesus Christ whom thou hast sent."

It is not enough that a man be thoroughly orthodox in his belief, nor is the healing power in the act of believing. The atonement of Jesus Christ is the enabling act, it is the meritorious cause of reconciliation; but Christ in his divine personality is the fountain of salvation. The virtue that heals and saves a sin-polluted soul goes out of the Christ.

The faith that brings salvation is not a gift from God,

but the act of the penitent seeker. He rests all on the atoning merit of Christ, and looks to him alone. He returns to a true allegiance to Christ, and accepts and receives everything in him.

The divine order of salvation is pardon, life, and purity. Then to the saved only come power, comfort, consolation, victory, and everlasting life in heaven.

Salvation is not a sequence of churchly culture; no ecclesiastical rites can bring the soul into fellowship with God. The entire period of man's probation may be filled with all the ecstatic bliss of earthly loves, the beatitudes of this world may crown all his circling years, and lay their varied treasures at his feet, and yet leave him to perish outside the fold of salvation.

Deliverance from the dominion and impurity of sin cannot be found in any system of man's devising. Though these systems should contain the garnered thoughts of all the centuries, carefully attempered to the highest wisdom of the age, they cannot give salvation from sin. The soul athirst for the waters of life can find rest and satisfaction in Christ alone.

When a sinner is pardoned, or a believer is wholly sanctified, when consolation reaches a sorrowing heart, whatever want of humanity is satisfied, virtue goes out of him. There must be the personal touch, — the expectant seeker and the personal Christ must meet.

All who really believe in Jesus and receive him in his fulness, find that which science cannot give them; find what no human theory or formulated creed can give; find what no ritualistic machinery and no ecclesiastical juggling can impart. They find peace, they obtain hope and joy, they enter upon everlasting life.

Men love that which to them appears lovable; "but God commendeth his love to us in that, while we were yet sinners, Christ died for us." By the apostasy, man was not only in danger of being lost when he died, but he was absolutely and helplessly ruined. He was corrupted in his essential nature, stained by sin in his spiritual being, alienated from his Father's house, and in revolt against the King of heaven. And under those conditions God gave his Son to die for him. "Herein is love," not that man loved God, and saw in Christ the priceless remedy for sin, but God in Christ Jesus loved humanity.

While man thus stood before the law, condemned, polluted, and helpless, God saw and pitied him, and gave his Son a ransom for the lost.

No man ever measured the extent of human depravity, for no one ever saw human nature unredeemed. Nor can any one comprehend the odious nature of sin, or sound the unfathomed depths of its impurity. So deep is its stain, so dark and vile its nature, that nothing but the blood of the Son of God could wash it from the soul. God looked upon man, ruined by sin and writhing under the fearful penalty of the law. He saw what agony the soul of Adam must endure throughout eternal ages unless redeemed and saved; and because he loved him, he sent his Son to rescue him, to heal his wounds, and take away his pollution, and save him with the power of an endless life. God saw that the alienated race could be reclaimed; he saw that the broken column of fallen manhood could be rebuilt; that the ruined fabric of a sinful soul could be readjusted by the Holy Ghost. God saw that the whole fallen structure might be re-erected and cemented by the blood of Jesus; that it might be beautified and embellished with its lost holiness, and stand forever a monument of praise to its Redeemer's name.

The power of true love lies in the fact that it always seeks to bless others. It always finds suitable expression. While intense admiration may be silent, love must have utterance. It must exert itself. Hand and voice proclaim the existence of genuine love.

"With pitying eye the Prince of Peace
Beheld our helpless grief.
He saw, and O amazing love,
He ran to our relief.
Down from the shining courts of bliss,
With joyful haste he fled;
Entered the tomb in mortal flesh.
And dwelt among the dead."

Such was the love of Jesus for humanity. A monument of love; love crystallized into action; love shining and moving through all the ages.

The cross of Jesus was visible to him through all the period of his earthly career. Its shadow fell across his cradle, and made the gloom of the manger ominous of coming sorrow. The objective point of his life was the agony and shame of the cross. These confronted him at the beginning of his life, and were continually within the horizon of his vision.

"It was meet that a deep darkness expressive of the anger of God, the evil of sin, and the anguish of the Saviour, should cover the earth; that nature, unable to look upon the scene of suffering, upon the features of her expiring Lord, should throw a veil over the transaction, and conceal the sufferer from her astonished gaze. It was altogether proper that this darkness should cover the universe; that all the bright lights of heaven should grow dim above the cross of Christ; that not one orb should venture to shine while the bright and morning star was under eclipse. It was exceedingly proper that from the dying brow of Jesus the shadow should sweep outward over suns and systems, over constellations and firmaments, until, save only the throne of God, all the universe should be shrouded in darkness and gloom."

The darkness came; nature spread a pall upon the universe; and when the shadow had passed away, there hung Jesus on the cross— dead.

Redemption's work was done; mercy had prevailed; justice was satisfied; love was triumphant; the embargo was removed, and full salvation was free for all mankind.

Although the work of redemption is complete, and Christ has power to save instantly, and save to the uttermost, many perish because they will not come to him and receive eternal life as a gift.

One of the saddest facts in the history of the world is that many loved ones reared in Christian homes have been misled by the gilded baits of error, and wandered very far from God. Forgetful of a mother's prayers, forgetful of the anguish of a father's heart over an erring child, forgetful of the garnered wealth of a Saviour's love, they turn away from him, and, like the child lost on the prairie, perish in sight of home.

The focal point of human destiny is the human will. God's love cannot compel the obedience of a moral being. It provides unlimited help, but leaves manhood uncoerced. No child was ever lost until by its own choice it went away from God, and no adult can be saved until there is a complete submission to the will of God.

All the abundance of the divine mercy, the infinite wealth of love, the wonderful exhibition of the divine willingness, is contingent. The experience of full salvation is predicated upon man's return to a true allegiance to God. All that the Father has done in the way of preparation, the unlimited outflow of prevenient grace, is done that the Father may freely bestow eternal life upon all who will believe on his Son.

True belief implies submission to God. Genuine faith produces obedience to the authority of Christ and conformity to his will. To all who thus return to God he gives everlasting life. Wonderful gift; mysterious, incomprehensible, elusive, indefinable principle, which God calls life, with the qualifying adjective eternal added.

Who can tell us what life is? We know much of its phenomena, but what is life? What is eternal life? The world is full of life, but death is always present.

"Death rides on every passing breeze
  And lurks in every flower.
Each season has its own disease,
  Its peril every hour."

The air is variegated with birds of beautiful plumage and melodious voices. The summer atmosphere swarms with living creatures. The falling snowflake brings down from its aerial home a world of animalculine life. The waters of the earth are peopled with innumerable forms of life. The earth itself is instinct with life. Its countless tribes creep or run or climb, or remain quiescent. Everywhere life is manifesting its presence; but it is of brief continuance. The momentary life of the inhabitant of the snowflake, or the twenty-four hours of the coral, or the threescore years allotted to man, mark the duration of earthly existence. But the flowing stream rolls on; it issues from a continuous fountain, and swells and enlarges as it sweeps onward. The same stars rise and set upon this generation that shone above the tent of Abraham, or shed their radiance on the glory of Rameses. For six thousand years this stream of life has emptied its ceaseless flow into eternity with no perceptible increase of that unknown quantity.

Does any one measure the significance of that term in the text, "everlasting life"? Who can put that divine phrase in the alembic of thought, separate it into its original parts, and give a complete analysis of its essence? Is there one scientist on the earth who will arrest a single ray of solar light, analyze it, and give its primary elements? Is there one expert physiologist that can tell the origin and constituent qualities of that mysterious force which we call life?

But the text speaks of "everlasting life," endless life, eternal life. It is more than a period of unlimited happiness, more than existence with unlimited duration. God is its origin and source of perpetuation. It is fellowship with him. It is his own life animating the tripartite child of God as in the morning of his first creation.

No new qualities will be added in heaven; the accumulating eons make no contributions to it. Time is not a factor in its existence or engagements. Its significance is in its origin and continuance.

Everlasting life! Language staggers under the weight of its meaning. The imagination sits silent and bewildered, and contemplates its import with folded wing. Life with its unlimited possibilities unfolding through endless years! The surroundings may change continually, but no new element or quality is added to the life. New delights, new joys, new sources of enjoyment, may surprise the soul at every beat of the heart, but it is the same life marching to the music of endless years. Time may grind down the mountains till those granite heaps are reduced to a level with the plain; the pitiless waves may corrode the shore till the rocky barriers disappear and the mad waters are set at liberty; these disintegrating forces may continue operative until the entire globe is reduced to its original elements — but there will be no diminution of the eternal years. New stars may begin their courses, grow old, and pass away; but the tide of everlasting life sweeps on with ceaseless flow. New constellations may be reared in space, measure their course, and disappear; but it will yet be morning in heaven, and the swelling tide of endless life pours on afresh, and feels the bounding pulse of everlasting youth.

IX
REDEMPTION VS. EVOLUTION

[This is a Full Text of the Sermon as Preached at the National Camp-meeting at Sewickley.]

"He that committeth sin is of the devil; for the devil sinneth from the beginning. For this purpose the Son of God was manifested, that he might destroy the works of the devil."—I JOHN iii. 8.

THE SCRIPTURE CLEARLY and distinctly sets forth the fact that there is an eternal and uncompromising hostility between sin and holiness; between Jesus Christ and his adversary. The fact is very definitely stated that the entire process of the recovery from sin, so far as it relates to salvation, is by divine power. We must discriminate between that which is involved in the act of salvation and the growth of Christian manhood after the work of salvation begins.

The salvation of the human soul is not by evolution, but by redemptive agencies. In the process of salvation, evil is not subjugated and made tributary to the spiritual advancement of the individual, but the odious thing is to be utterly destroyed.

Sin is not a necessary factor in the government of God, embraced in his original plan. Sin is the uncoerced act of a moral agent, — an act which, when executed by our federal head, instantly changed the relations of all the spiritual forces in the universe, and inaugurated a curse whose destructive waters have overflowed all lands and swept the shores of all ages.

For the arrest of this curse, and for the destruction of its cause, the Son of God was manifested. Whatever is under the dominion of the devil, or emanates from him, is uncompromisingly opposed to the kingdom of Jesus Christ. And the highest good of man and the glory of God require that the offending thing be utterly destroyed.

A certain class of public teachers affirm that sin is a necessity; that it is an essential factor in the government of God; and that its ultimate tendency is toward a healthy condition of society; and that a state of sinfulness is the normal condition of the soul. They assume that evil is like an abscess on the body, which carries off effete and poisonous matter, and is the result of a recuperative process which is imperceptibly carried forward, and will necessarily end in perfect health. They declare that sinning is a necessary process, that no one can abstain from it, and that holiness will eventually be evolved from this mass of corruption.

These teachers affirm that all instrumentalities and all agencies are alike with God. That everything indiscriminately aids in the accomplishment of his purposes. That wicked men and devils as effectually do his will as the burning seraphs that circle the throne. They affirm that "so soon as a purpose leaves the sacred precinct of the volitions, God seizes it, and makes it subserve his ends, even though it should have been evil in the worst sense in its conception."

It is impossible to harmonize this theory with the facts

in the case. It is a strange philosophy that thus unites God and his sworn enemy in special effort to accomplish that which is impossible without the union of good and evil. This theory concedes that there is an arena of action where neither Christ nor the Holy Ghost can operate; a department of salvation which they cannot jointly accomplish; an outlying region given over to evil that good may be evolved therefrom.

These semi-scientific philosophers continually affirm that there are shades of Christian character that can only be brought to view by the force of evil influences; that affliction and trial polish the soul, just as the diamond receives its lustre while in contact with the lapidary, — the severe and long continued friction imparting a brilliancy not otherwise attainable.

They assert that God subjects his children who trust him to that degree of affliction by loss of property or friends, or by loss of health or position, that will insure to them the degree of purity and development that is well pleasing in his sight. According to this theory of salvation, the devil must either turn the lapidary, or hold the unwilling subject hard against the revolving wheel.

When Jesus proclaimed his gospel, he stated as a fundamental fact in the philosophy of truth, "that no fountain could send forth both bitter and sweet water," that "a house divided against itself cannot stand." "And if Satan cast out Satan, he is divided against himself; how shall then his kingdom stand?"

The church has through all its history denied that God was the author of evil. Therefore, if moral or physical evil, or both, are necessary for the salvation or culture of man, we must concede that there is a part of his salvation that God alone cannot accomplish. But the text affirms that Christ was "manifested, that he might destroy the works of the devil."

The Bible is explicit in the statement that Jesus Christ

and the devil are sworn eternal foes; that there can be no collusion, no agreement, no contract between those persons; that when the few are saved by the joint effort of Jesus and his adversary, the great mass of unfortunates who are lost shall be turned over to Satan as his well-earned share of the spoil.

The first prophetic vision of these renowned contestants reveals Jesus to us as the conqueror.

The first promise given to humanity is one of victory, and presents to the injured race a Saviour bruising Satan's head, while yet his heel is wet with the poisoned slime of the serpent's venomed fang. And from that time to the present period there has been no armistice, no cessation of hostilities. The Christian peace is not one of negotiation, but of conquest.

Satan in his craftiness has attempted negotiations, but without success. When he had failed in his efforts with the Master, he was content to surprise and capture some subordinate. If he cannot utterly overthrow, he will embarrass and hinder to the extent of his power. He will come to you with flattering pretensions, he may kindly offer you aid, he may suggest to you methods of success as he did to Jesus in the wilderness, he may promise to shield and protect you from danger; but he is a liar from the beginning, and will deceive you if you trust him.

He is no more worthy of confidence now, than when within the sacred enclosure of Eden he won the heart of Eve, and with lying words plunged the race into fearful ruin. He is no more the friend of God now, than when in the wilderness of Judea he assailed with all malice the suffering Saviour with the vile insinuation, "If thou be the Son of God, command that these stones be made bread." Why suffer here in this wilderness? If you are the Son of God, all power belongs to you. You only have to speak the word, and those unshapely and worthless stones that cover the mountainside shall be transmuted into nutritious and satisfying bread. But Jesus replied, "It is written that man shall not live by bread alone, but by every word that proceedeth out of the mouth of God."

You cannot bow the devil out of society. You can't compromise him out. He will negotiate and remain. He prefers rather to affiliate with swine than to leave the coast, for all he gets by compromise is clear gain.

One fundamental fact of orthodoxy, a fact which is supported by the most advanced science, is "that life is the gift of God." The divine Creator fashioned man after his own ideal from earth-dust, that is from original elements from which he made the earth, and then "breathed into his nostrils the breath of life." And in man's recovery from sin, the Redeemer pursues the same method. "Except a man be born of the Spirit, he can in no case enter into the kingdom of God."

The spiritual life is the gift, received and perpetuated by the obedience of faith; while all affiliation with evil, all distrust and disobedience, produce disaster and death, the same as in the beginning.

It will be necessary for us to discriminate between that which Jesus does, and that which his adversary does; between the works of Jesus, and the works of the devil.

What may be truly denominated the works of the devil? What are his achievements, and what are the sequences of his victory?

The whole may be grouped into two classes,— sin and its results, or actions and the sequences that flow from them. Sin is the action of man under the delusions of the enemy. Suffering and death are the sequences of that act. The term sin is generic, and includes all evil agencies by which it propagates itself and becomes universal in its diffusion. Sin is the prolific source of all evil. Suffering and death are its legitimate fruits. They are to be destroyed. No sequent of sin can become a factor in the process of salvation from sin. "God shall wipe away all tears from their eyes; and there shall be no more death, neither sorrow, nor crying, neither shall there be any more pain: for the former things have passed away."

The forms of evil in the world are almost innumerable; but standard authors on philosophy have reduced them to two general classes, — natural and moral evil.

Natural evil is the pain or suffering which arises from outward condition and events, or from causes which are independent of the immediate action of the human will.

Moral evil of every sort flows from sin; but in the present state of society, where all are estranged from God by original sin, and where all are in a probational life with sinful surroundings, so far as we can see the relation of sequent and action, some evils are induced by our own conduct, some by the misconduct of other parties; and some evils, such as sickness and death, arise generally from causes far outside of and antecedent to the will of any living being. Sin and its ultimate results are first and last the work of the devil; and for their extirpation Jesus came into the world.

Sin is an offence against God; it is a violation of his law. It is, therefore, an insult to him. Sin introduced anarchy and discord into the moral universe, and invaded the moral rights of deity. It is a gross wrong against God, an impudent effort to subvert him.

But sin is a great damage to the sinner. It debases his moral nature; it effaces the image of God from his soul; transforms him into the likeness of Satan; and is a source of perpetual grief to God.

Every act of sin, whether by fallen angels or wicked men, is a direct contribution to the sum total of evil in the universe, and directly at war with God. Sin is not only a wrong done to God and the sinner, but it involves the moral condition of all men.

The effects of a sinful act run on to the end of time. They involve other parties remote from the scene of action in time or in space. The evil influences of a man's sin are more lasting than the memory of his crimes. By his disobedience he inaugurates a curse which he can never stop, but which will sweep onward to the end of time.

Sin is a destroyer. It is a desolating force which injures society in its most vital parts. It spreads wretchedness and woe throughout all the world. It brings untold anguish and misery into the daily lot of earth's toiling millions.

To sin, and sin alone, we attribute all the suffering that ever was in this world, or ever will be in the world to come. All the suffering resulting from disease, from the multitude of social evils, from war, famine, and pestilence, from crime of every conceivable character, is directly attributed to sin. These have filled the earth with desolation and woe, with sorrow, anguish, and death.

To dry earth's tears, to assuage earth's sorrows, to arrest the onward rush of disaster and death, is the distinctive mission of the Son of God. He was manifested that "the wilderness and the solitary place might be glad; and that the desert should rejoice and blossom like the rose;" and the waste places of the earth be as fruitful as Carmel.

The process by which Jesus shall accomplish this work, and the agencies which he will employ, are not always clearly perceived. There is a great deal of confusion in the religious teaching of the period. We are assured by one class of teachers that salvation is a gradual process accomplished by the attrition of events; that "the price of perfection in grace is pain." We are taught that sin and virtue act and react on each other, and evolve holiness; that all things, including sin and its sequences, tend to the same end.

To read the current literature of the age, or listen to the common utterances of the pulpit, one would be persuaded that nothing ever went amiss; that no purpose of God was ever disturbed by the actions of men. Necessitarianism dominates the religious thought of the world.

It is not only assumed that God overrules sin and makes it tributary to his glory, but that the most wonderful exhibitions of his grace are necessarily preceded by the most overwhelming visitations of physical ill, or the most violent dispensations of moral disaster; that the highest type of Christian character is evolved from the deepest abysses of spiritual ruin. But the Bible does not contain one word or intimation of salvation by evolution or by law.

Redemption and evolution are not synonymous terms. They are not similar in their methods.

Evolution is that process by which the power inherent in vegetable, animal, or spiritual existence yields to the potent influence of law from without, and constantly presses toward some more mature state, or bursting through all known limits assumes new forms of life with still greater possibilities yet unfulfilled.

Redemption is that process by which one person does for another, or for a group of the same species, something which it is impossible for them to do for themselves.

In the relation of these two theories to the salvation of man, one class of teachers adopt the nomenclature of the scientists, who find the origin of man in the lower departments of the animal kingdom, from which he has been gradually pushed up and rounded out to his present dimensions by the power of inherent forces acting on inherent possibilities.

These religious evolutionists are necessarily gradualists. Instantaneous salvation in any stage is not possible by their methods. They mould their creed according to the popular thought. Following their leaders, they look for man's salvation by a process similar to that of his creation. Hence they deny that there is any such thing as a conscious religious experience in a state of completeness. They affirm that religious advancement goes forward slowly during the whole period of human life, and culminates in heart purity only in the act of death. But the

Bible says the salvation of the soul is by the redemption that is in Christ Jesus the Lord; and if your salvation is to be accomplished by him, he can complete it to-day as well as a thousand ages from this time.

The doctrine of redemption is based upon the antecedent fact that God created man holy, and that by sin, which is always a voluntary act, man forfeited this holy state. If this be true, if man be alienated from God by sin, if there ever was a lapse of his fidelity, then it is impossible for him ever to recover his lost estate, except by the means of redemption.

As the forfeiture of man's holy state subordinated him to evil and the consequent corruption of his moral nature, and subjected him to physical death, his disinthralment from the ultimate and farthest reaching consequences of sin cannot be accomplished by the action of natural law, but is secured by the mediation of a third party, — by the priestly merit of a Redeemer.

The Redeemer of man is nowhere spoken of as a divine evolver. There is no such thought in the economy of grace. Redemption implies the loss of something. There must be forfeiture first, or redemption is not conceivable.

If the salvation is accomplished by growth or by culture, if any part of it is evolved, man is neither guilty nor defiled. He needs neither pardon nor cleansing. He requires only strength and guidance. But if man is a sinner, his salvation can only be accomplished by another.

The name of Jesus is indicative of his mission, "His name shall be called Jesus, for he shall save his people from their sins." Jesus did not come to teach man how to save himself. He nowhere says that by a tortuous pathway leading through deep defiles of moral darkness, infested with fierce temptations, extending over weary years of wasting toil, over mountain-paths of imminent peril, he will direct man to a place of safety.

The Bible tells the glad story of redeeming love; it tells

the sorrowing penitent the joyful news of a present conscious salvation, through the help of One who "bore our griefs and carried our sorrows," and by "whose stripes" humanity is healed.

Jesus Christ satisfied the claims of violated law; redeemed, and now holds in trust for all, the alienated estate, the forfeited birthright of moral purity. Not only so, but the means by which this salvation became an experimental fact in each human soul are redemptive agencies. They proceed from the same source with the salvation. "Christ gave himself that he might redeem us from all iniquity, and purify unto himself a peculiar people zealous of good works."

The Pharisees charged Jesus with casting out devils by satanic power. They said he was in collusion with the adversary. But Jesus called attention to the fundamental fact in philosophy: "Every kingdom divided against itself is brought to desolation; and every house divided against itself cannot stand." "Now if the adversary expel the adversary, he is at variance with himself; how then shall his kingdom stand? Besides, if I through Beelzebub expel demons, through whom do your sons expel them? therefore they will be your judges. But if it is by the divine co-operation that I cast out demons, then God's royal majesty has unexpectedly appeared among you."

It is evident from these statements of the Master, that whatsoever originates in sin, or remotely proceeds therefrom, can never become a gospel agent, but is something that is to be destroyed. As sin includes in itself all evil agencies by which it propagates itself, and becomes universal in its diffusion, so the atonement of Christ is the fountain of all the gospel agencies; and whatsoever does not proceed from that source is no part of the gospel machinery.

The agencies of the gospel by which the benefits of the atonement become the facts of conscious salvation may be grouped into three classes: (1) The written word; (2) the Holy Ghost; (3) human instrumentalities.

Heubner says: "The chief purpose of the manifestation of Christ was the cancelling of sin and the sanctification of man by means of reconciliation. Hence to continue in sin frustrates the purpose of Christ, and contradicts his holiness." Rhinehard says upon this text, "He takes away the deception of sin by his doctrine."

There is nothing ambiguous in the written word. The Holy Ghost tears off the mask, and exposes sin in all its hideousness. He floods the soul with light, and "makes wise unto salvation."

The written word contains all the commands and all the proscriptions, reveals the nature and consequences of sin; and with equal clearness points out the conditions of salvation and the ethics of Christian practice.

"Jesus takes away the punishment of sin by his death," so that sin is not punished in this life at all. By his death Jesus removes all liability to punishment, and opens wide the fountain of salvation to every child of man. "The Holy Ghost is a revealer;" he takes freely the things that are God's, and gives them to all who ask. He takes away the dominion and corruption of sin by his Spirit and example. "By grace are ye saved."

It is God's prerogative to cast out the man of sin and cleanse the soul from inbred corruption, God only can forgive sin; and as he pardons the guilty and remits the punishment due to sin, so also by an act of divine power the Saviour purifies the soul from the heredi-tary defilements of sin. Whoever, therefore, retains a sinful nature by keeping possession of his depravity resists God, and hinders Jesus Christ from destroying the works of the devil.

Inasmuch, then, as all the agencies of salvation are under the control of the divine will and the will of man, by the union of these forces Jesus becomes an uttermost Saviour, and man the possessor of an uttermost salvation.

Holiness of heart as a personal experience is therefore not only possible for the few, but is obligatory upon all. But there is another field in which the redemptive power of Jesus is to be exerted. There is one work yet to be accomplished that is exclusively Christ's work, and we cannot give the full scope and meaning of this text without reference to it. It is in a department of Satan's empire where no other instrumentality can go; it is in the grave.

The theory of salvation by development has no place for the resurrection, therefore it must get rid of it. The redemptive system is impossible without it. Death is the culmination of sin. "As through one man sin entered into the world [and in him all sinned], and through sin death came, so also death passed upon all men." "Then inordinate desire having conceived, produces sin; and sin, being perfected, brings forth death."

If every human being upon the face of the earth was wholly sanctified to God, and the earth was covered with the pristine beauty and made fragrant with the odors of ancient Eden, if Satan still held the seal of the tomb, he would be the victor. The Son of man must not only capture and hold some of the outposts of Satan's kingdom, but he must of necessity go into the heart of his empire. Death's old throne must be demolished and destroyed; his quiver broken; his arrows gone and lost forever in the deepest shades of oblivion.

There is no reason why we should understand or explain the method of the resurrection in order to know the fact. "Christ is the resurrection." It is his work to accomplish this ultimate victory of the gospel. The resurrection of the dead by the power of Jesus Christ is the crowning fact of the gospel. This is the culmination of the Saviour's warfare, the climax of his victorious effort, without which all the rest is marred and broken, bearing the impress of inglorious defeat.

The resurrection of the dead is the crowning fact of the New Testament. It gives emphasis to all the other doctrines of the gospel. "However obscure may be the references to the resurrection in the Old Testament; with whatever apparent lack of enthusiasm the triumph of life over death may be anticipated there; no sooner do we reach the threshold of the New Testament than we hear voices from within proclaiming the resurrection of the dead. The sign of the Son of man is advanced above; the graves around are seen with their head-stones loosened, the turf broken, and 'I shall arise' written in golden characters over each narrow house. The central figure bruises death under his feet, and points with his cross to his empty grave where life and immortality are seen cleaving the clouds, and coming forth with beauty and healing in their wings."

Jesus gave this doctrine prominence in all his utterances, and the whole system stands or falls with this: "Marvel not at this: for the hour is coming, when all that are in their graves shall hear his voice and come forth."

We do not stop to answer questions in philosophy. If we accept the redemptive system we must accept that which is inseparable from it. If man is redeemed by the precious blood of Jesus, this grand climax must come in its proper order. So certainly as death is the culmination of sin, the resurrection of the body is the culmination of the redemptive effort.

As the entrance of sin brought suffering and death, so also is the resurrection of the body and its restoration to a state of immortality as legitimately the fruitage of the atonement as pardon and purity.

So important is this fact in the gospel system, that Jesus proclaims himself the "Resurrection and the Life;" and from his empty grave floods of meaning and hope flow forth over the New Testament page to bless the world, forming a connecting link between the resurrection of

Christ and the rising of his people, giving abundant proofs of the first-fruits and of the full harvest that shall follow. "For this purpose was the Son of God manifested, that he might destroy the works of the devil;" and as a soldier of Jesus we place ourselves with him in the work of destroying the devil's kingdom, that we may share with him the triumphs of his cause when the victory is complete.

X
THE NECESSITY OF HOLINESS

"Follow peace with all men, and holiness, without which no man shall see the Lord:

"Follow peace and obtain the sanctification, without which no man shall see the Lord." — HEBREWS xii. 14.

THE SIMPLEST INTERPRETATION of this text embraces the fact that heaven is a holy place; and if you ever enter heaven, or enjoy heaven, you must, as a prerequisite to that fact, obtain holiness.

Holiness signifies the state or quality of being essentially pure. Holiness is not predicated of action, but of being. It implies purity, integrity of moral character, freedom from the pollution or uncleanness which arises from the act of sin. Purity in essence is primarily different from innocence. Every child in the human family is perfectly innocent at the time of its birth. Guilt is the result of an overt act of violation of law. Therefore, while all children are innocent, not one is by nature essentially pure. Holiness is that part of full salvation by which the hereditary uncleanness of sin is removed from the spiritual nature of man.

The term holiness when applied to the Supreme Being signifies perfect moral purity. God's holiness is absolute, independent, and underived. Holiness in man is relative, dependent, and derived; but it is essential holiness.

The doctrine of holiness is not obscurely hidden away among the more important truths of the gospel. It is prominent and conspicuous and emphatic everywhere in the Word of God. It is the climax of the redemptive effort so far as it relates to salvation, and appears luminous with divine beauty on every page of Revelation.

Holiness of heart, being a part of man's salvation, must of necessity be accomplished by God alone. No other being can save. Salvation cannot be a product of ecclesiastical rites, nor churchly culture, nor of growth. And if God commands us to be holy, and provides the means to accomplish that end, no man can refuse to comply with the command without incurring great peril to his religious state.

If God commands us to be holy now, it is not only possible, but it is obligatory upon all men; for obligation is always equal to the possibilities of every case. Therefore, as the text commands us to follow peace with all men and "the sanctification without which no man shall see the Lord," we must assume that it is as much a Christian's duty to be pure in heart as it is to be at peace with God and with his neighbor.

But we know man is not pure by nature, we know he cannot make himself pure. But God commands him to obtain purity, and tells him where and how this precious quality may be secured.

Correct views of the method of salvation greatly enhance man's progress in the divine life; and erroneous doctrines not only hinder, but may utterly paralyze, every effort of the seeker after purity.

Heart purity is not a product of growth, therefore no individual ever obtained it in that manner. It is not obtained by growth entirely, nor in part, if holiness is any part of man's salvation; or, if it is essential to complete salvation, then no jot or tittle of it can be grown.

The assumption that holiness is the product of growth misleads and utterly ruins the religious life of many anxious Christians. Those who teach this doctrine are unscientific and illogical. They entirely fail to discriminate between purity and size. They fail to perceive that growth has regard to increase in proportions, without any regard to constituent elements.

The apostle affirms that holiness is essential in order to enter heaven, but neither size nor age sustains any such relation to the glory land. God can save a child one day old as easily as he could save Methuselah with the coronet of a thousand years upon his brow. God can save the smallest soul that thrills with immortality as easily as he could save Daniel or Paul. Neither size nor age count anything with God, who himself filleth all things, and is eternal.

But the text says holiness is an essential element of salvation. The apostle affirms that "no man," great or small, learned or ignorant, cultured or uncouth, sage or sensualist, king or peasant, priest or prophet, shall enter heaven, except he shall first have been made holy. Therefore, if it should appear that the vital part of man's salvation, the essential element of it, is by growth, may it not all be by growth? The relation of holiness to pardon and regeneration is such that, if it is a possible product of growth, pardon and regeneration are both possible products of growth.

There is but one salvation, notwithstanding its various crises and stages of progress. Salvation is a unit; it is one salvation; it is wrought by one agency. In a logical process, the greater must always contain the lesser. If we apply this rule to the process of salvation, we must accept the fact that holiness, being a part of the one salvation, and being the lesser part, it is embraced in the original process, and wrought by the one supreme agency.

There is danger at this point of a fatal error; for, if heart purity is possible as a product of growth, pardon and life are both possible attainments by growth; and if we accept the position that salvation is a possible product of growth, we sweep away at one fell stroke the priesthood of Jesus Christ, and supersede the divine method of salvation by a process purely natural or entirely human, and eliminate the personality and agency of the Holy Ghost from our system of theology, and exclude Jesus Christ and the Holy Spirit as factors in the salvation of man, and make salvation the product of the impersonal forces of nature.

The embarrassments on this subject grow out of a misapprehension of facts. The seeker after the truth confounds growth with salvation; he fails to distinguish between development and redemption. These are not at all alike; they do not belong to the same family. The seeker after the truth having once become confused, further fails to discriminate between the two states of purity and maturity; between the fact and the process of being made clean, and the fact and process of being made large and old.

In all cases where the Scripture speaks of growth in grace, in all its allusions to Christian character and manhood, to the maturity of experience, there is a clear distinction made between those states and the simple and instantaneous experience of heart purity. The one refers to the advancement of the Christian in the divine life, and the other indicates that act of sovereign grace whereby God saves a sinner from the pollution of sin.

The Christian grows into a state of maturity. He goes on to a state of ripeness by a gradual process; but when it is a question of salvation, no being in the universe can impart salvation except the eternal God. No man ever grew one jot or tittle of his salvation. The very conception of such a thing is an idolatrous movement of the soul.

Entire sanctification is the removal of whatever lingering elements of depravity remain in the soul after conversion. If there is no residuum of impurity in the soul after regeneration which needs to be removed, then there is no need of, and no possibility of, a second work of grace; but if there remains something in the form of impurity, it can only be removed by cleansing. It never was, and never can be, grown out of the soul. No vagary of the imagination was ever more unscientific and impossible.

The converted man may and ought to get a constant victory over all outward and all inward sin. He may vanquish temptation at all times, but the latent impurity that remains in the human soul after conversion yields only to the cleansing blood of Jesus.

Entire sanctification is a process that makes clean. It signifies a purification. The word sanctify, in its original root, and in all its derivatives and synonyms, means "to make clean," or "to purify." It never expresses the idea of age or size, it never indicates life or more life. It refers alone to moral quality or condition. The original word, αγιαζω, or αγασμος, signifies "to purify," "to cleanse that which is set apart for holy uses," or it implies the state of being holy.

That the purification from sin is in a large degree accomplished at regeneration, we know. That fact has never been called in question by persons of common intelligence. All standard authors in Methodism have always affirmed this. But without one exception every Methodist writer that has been recognized as authority up to the present time, has also affirmed with equal force and clearness that entire sanctification was subsequent to regeneration, and was wrought by the Holy Ghost through faith.

Richard Watson says, "That a distinction exists between

a regenerate state and a state of entire sanctification, or perfect holiness, will generally be allowed. Regeneration is concomitant with justification; but the apostles set before the church, both in the prayers they offer and in the exhortations they administer, a still higher degree of deliverance from sin, as well as a higher growth of Christian virtues."

This higher degree of deliverance from sin is not obtained by good works. It is a spiritual state, distinct from, but never separate from, the primary stages of salvation.

By this act of purification, God restores the soul to a state of healthfulness. Every function of the spiritual nature is invigorated, and adjusted to its proper sphere of activities. We are thus compelled to admit that if the primary stages of salvation are wrought by the Holy Ghost, surely every finishing touch must be by the same divine agent. If it requires the agency of the Holy Ghost to bring a sinful soul into a state of initial salvation, surely nothing but almighty power can complete the work. "Faithful is he that calleth you, who also will do it." But it requires care at this point to distinguish between that which the candidate does when he submits to God, and that which God does for him, and in him, when he sanctifies him wholly.

In seeking the blessing of a clean heart there must be a deep and abiding conviction of the need of purification, a consciousness that it is needed now.

If persons advanced in Christian life can recall their experiences, they will discover that when they sought God in the pardon of sin, it was after the Holy Ghost had convicted them of sin; and they fled from guilt and the condemnation of a violated law because there was no other way of escape, for they knew that without reconciliation they were lost beyond recovery. And in the same manner the soul under the light of the Holy Ghost becomes conscious of remaining depravity, becomes conscious of the remaining elements of the carnal nature. As the spirit leads, and the seeker obediently follows on, he comes to loathe the inherent corruption of his nature, and cries mightily to God for deliverance from its power; and in answer to this earnest pleading, God heals the soul of its native impurities.

As to the time at which this experience should be obtained, no man may enforce an ironclad law. The best time, because it is God's time, God's promised time, is, doubtless, very soon after conversion; but there is such a diversity of teaching on this subject, such confusion of theories, and such a barrier of prejudice against the whole subject, that earnest and intelligent Christians do not all progress with equal rapidity.

When a soul is converted, when a penitent sinner is first brought "from darkness to light," from a state of natural wickedness into fellowship with God, and becomes a member of the divine family, when the burden of guilt is removed and the new life permeates the spiritual nature, the soul is filled with joy, and the peace is so profound that he does not at once discover the foe that lurks within. The well-informed individual at that particular period of his experience can understand Charles Wesley's hymn, where he says: —

"And I could not believe
That I ever should grieve,
That I ever should suffer again."

The regenerating energy of the Holy Ghost, the transfiguring power of omnipotent love, have overthrown the old order of things, and transported the soul into a new realm. But the carnal nature is not exterminated. There is a residuary element of impurity that under favorable circumstances will manifest its presence and its life, not always in expressions of anger, or in exhibitions of pride. Very many unconverted persons are ethically cool under the aggravating circumstances, while very many Christians fail to control themselves under a very slight temptation. There are other and more inviting outlets for the carnal nature than those afforded by anger or pride.

Carnality more frequently manifests its presence in a believer's heart in some secret way, — some covetous desire, some unholy amusement, some fondness for a former uncleanness, some secret affiliation of the heart with some forbidden sensual pleasure. It is generally at the solicitation of some secret sin which had a controlling influence over the soul in its unregenerate state that the young convert is lured from the path of duty, and betrayed into a temporary apostasy.

The favorite method of sinful indulgence gets the strongest control over the passions and appetites, and puts its peculiar impurity deepest into the soul; and after conversion the nature is weakest in that department, and most susceptible to those influences that formerly dominated its actions. It was the recollection of the leeks and the garlic, the cucumbers and the melons, that caused Israel to say, "We loathe this light food;" and the secret recollection, some cherished memory of some former uncleanness, has caused many a believing soul to fall.

When a converted person holds a parley with some special temptation, and some slumbering appetite is awakened, he is in danger of being swallowed up.

When the believer gets such a view of himself as enables him to perceive that there remains a taint of impurity interwoven with every fibre of his being, when the Holy Ghost opens to him the substratum of his moral nature, and reveals to him his impurity, and impresses him with his utter helplessness, he extorts from him the reluctant confession: "O wretched man that I am! who shall deliver me from this body of death?" And it is not until then that God answers by fire, and makes him every whit whole.

But in order to reach this experience there must be an intelligent consecration of the believer to God. It is not a pledge to do more work, and better work for God; it is not a consecration to any department of work; it is a complete submission of soul, body, spirit, mind, position, and estate to God.

Consecration and sanctification sustain the same relation to each other that repentance and conversion do. They are essential to each other. Consecration is the act of setting apart any person or thing for holy uses. A believer's consecration implies the devotement to God of the entire man. It embraces every power and faculty, every capability, every impulse and energy. Everything the man is, everything the man has, all he hopes to be and to have, for time and for eternity, goes over to God without equivocation or mental reservation in this covenant of full salvation.

This may be and often is done at once; but it is a work that is so comprehensive, and brings the soul into such intimate relations with God, that we instinctively approach it with the profoundest reverence. We stand in its awe-inspiring presence as Moses stood before the burning bush. We enter here with holy caution, as the high priest went into the Holy of Holies.

There can be nothing more repulsive to a refined nature, nothing more out of harmony with good taste, than the irreverent and flippant manner in which some persons talk about consecration and the "blood of the Son of God." We are often pained at the coarse and abrupt manner in which professedly good people appear to rush into the presence of God.

Then occasionally we meet those who go through the process of consecrating their sins to God, — their unholy appetites and objects of unclean indulgence. You cannot consecrate these. You may keep your appetite for some sinful thing, and fight it all your lifetime, and God will let you. But if you will surrender your uncleanness, God will destroy it at once.

Every sinner gave up his sins in order that God might convert his soul. Consecration is the act of surrendering your regenerated powers to God, that he may cleanse them and sanctify them to his own service.

We assume that the candidate for the experience of holiness is a converted man. If he is, he is not an habitual sinner. He gave up all his sinful practices in order that he might become a child of God. God now commands him to lay aside all filthiness of the flesh and of the spirit, and perfect the holiness that was largely accomplished at his conversion.

When all sinfulness is abandoned, and every unholy purpose and every filthy practice of soul and body put away, the candidate for a clean heart comes where it is possible for him to make a believer's consecration, where he can "present his body a living sacrifice, holy, acceptable to God, — a reasonable service." Then the language of the heart will be, —

"Take my life, and let it be
Consecrated, Lord, to thee.
Take my feet, and let them move
At the impulse of thy love.
Lord, I give to thee my life and all, to be
Thine henceforth eternally."

No candidate can pass this portal into the Beulah land of unfolding mysteries, who is not duly and truly prepared, worthy and well qualified. No chance here for the Ananiases to keep back part of the price. Head and heart, hands and feet, intellect, affections, and will, wealth and social position, — everything, without reserve, goes onto the altar of obedience. This is the strait gate and narrow way that leads to the full-orbed life of fellowship with God. There is no smuggling here;

and no surplus baggage ever enters this sacred gateway.

This stage of religious progress necessarily involves a second crisis, an essential preparation, in order to a distinct second work of grace in the heart.

Men may evade the issue, they may rear a wall of prejudice; but the fact lies back of all this, and is in the constitution of nature and grace; the founders of Methodism put it into our hymns, and we have sung the doctrine and experience for more than a century. It is in the Discipline signed by every member of the Episcopal Board from Wesley to the present date. The purest utterances of the pulpit, and the most eloquent statements of the official press, have voiced this doctrine to the world for more than one hundred years. The lyric bard of Methodism set it to music, and our hearts caught the inspiration, and we have sung it around the world; and still the chorus rises, and the church echoes the glad song:—

> "Breathe, oh, breathe thy loving spirit
> Into every troubled breast;
> Let us all in thee inherit,
> Let us find that *second* rest.
> Take away my bent to sinning,
> Alpha and Omega be,
> End of faith as its beginning,
> Set our hearts at liberty."

The objector to a second crisis insists upon it that he made a perfect consecration when he sought the Lord in the pardon of his sins. He further insists that he has not backslidden, that the offering he then made is still wholly on the altar; and he further affirms that it is neither necessary nor possible for him to make a new or a better consecration.

But the very nature of consecration implies a careful daily examination of relationships, and a daily devotement of all to God. The continued increase of knowledge, the breadth of wisdom arising from new experiences, make a renewal of consecration a necessity; and we repeat in the language of that grand old hymn,—

> "High heaven that heard that solemn vow,
> That vow renewed shall *daily* hear,
> Till in life's latest hour I bow
> And bless in death a bond so dear."

A very little attention to the force of language will obviate all difficulty and remove all embarrassment from the subject.

To the honest objector we propound the question: What is implied in what you call a penitent sinner's consecration? and what does God require of him? What are the rights and privileges of a penitent sinner? What is his relation to God?

The honest objector replies, stating that he absolutely and unconditionally surrendered to God; he submitted to his law; he gave himself— gave all. The language of his heart was,—

> "Here, Lord, I give myself to thee;
> 'Tis all that I can do."

There was nothing else possible to him, and there was nothing else required. His relation to God at the time was that of a condemned criminal flying from the terrors of a violated law. Mercy was his only plea. He was a sinner, dead in trespasses and in sin. All that he could do was to lay down the arms of his warfare and plead the merit of the world's Redeemer.

A condemned criminal has no rights. He has forfeited everything. He cannot mortgage nor deed property; he cannot make a will. The State makes provision for all his effects.

The sinner is an outlaw, perfectly helpless of himself; but God for Christ's sake receives him, pardons all the past, adopts him into the heavenly family, and in Christ Jesus his Redeemer, the Father invests him with all his forfeited rights.

Every step of his return is through the boundless mercy of God. It is only through the merit of Jesus that his return is possible, that his sins are pardoned, and his spirit made alive from the dead. Previous to that time a consecration is impossible in the nature of things. The penitent had no rights, privileges, or possessions, that he could consecrate.

The first step of a penitent sinner is to seek reconciliation with God; to secure an adjustment of relations with him. When this is accomplished, God calls upon him as an obedient child to consecrate, to set apart to him, these regenerated powers, this redeemed and renewed manhood. As a sinner, God commands him to repent and be converted. As a son, he beseeches him to "present his body a living sacrifice, holy, acceptable to God, which is his reasonable service."

Nothing less than this constitutes a believer's consecration; and no unconverted man can conceive of such a relationship to God as the one implied in this covenant.

This kind of consecration necessarily brings the believer into a new relationship with God; brings him to where the cleansing is possible; brings him to that point where the covenant of full salvation may be fulfilled, and by the agency of the Holy Ghost become a fact in his personal experience. When the seeker of this form of religious experience has surrendered his prejudices, and has passed out of the realm of speculation and abandoned the habit of theorizing, there is but one thing more which is necessary for him to do, — he must accept and receive the Lord Jesus for this specific work of cleansing now.

Salvation is always in the present tense. Personal faith in Jesus Christ is always in the present tense. It cannot be prospective when it relates to salvation. It is not more faith, but a focalization of faith, — faith in a present Saviour for a present help. Do not misapprehend. Faith does not begin here. Faith has brought the seeker every step of the way. Now, at the altar of full salvation, faith must focalize. Fully conscious of his impurity the seeker must now receive Christ as his sanctification. "Receive him;" do not be deceived and seek a great blessing. If you do, you will fail. Seek Jesus; honor your personal Saviour by receiving him as your purifier.

There is no danger in the reception of the truth. It is specious error that produces fanaticism. Come to Jesus as a perfect, present Saviour. You can have no refuge but in him.

"When wounded sore, the stricken soul
Lies bleeding and unbound,
One only hand, a pierced hand,
Can salve the sinner's wound.

When sorrow swells the laden breast,
And tears of anguish flow.
Only one heart, a broken heart,
Can feel the sinner's woe.

When penitence has wept in vain
Over some foul, dark spot.
One only stream, a stream of blood,
Can wash away the blot.

'Tis Jesus' blood that washes white;
His hand that brings relief;
His heart that's touched with all our joys.
And feeleth all our grief.

Lift up thy bleeding hands, O Christ;
Unseal that cleansing tide;
We have no shelter from our sin,
But in thy wounded side."

XI

THE TWO CHIEF FACTORS OF THE GOSPEL,— THE BLOOD OF ATONEMENT AND THE HOLY GHOST

[Preached at the Round Lake National Camp-Meeting]

"But now, in Christ Jesus, ye who sometime were far off are made nigh by the blood of Christ. For he is our peace, who hath made both one, and hath broken down the middle wall of partition between us. Having abolished in his flesh the enmity, even the law of commandments contained in ordinances; for to make in himself of twain one new man, so making peace. And that he might reconcile both unto God in one body by the cross, having slain the enmity thereby. And came and preached peace to you which were afar off, and to them that were nigh. For through him we both have access by one Spirit unto the Father." —EPHESIANS ii. 13-18.

WE HAVE READ the entire paragraph which contains the one compound proposition to which we invite your prayerful thought.

The alienated race is re-established in the favor and fellowship of God through the atoning merit of Jesus as the procuring cause, and the Holy Ghost is the essential agency of approach to the Father, and at the same time the active, efficient instrumentality by which the transformation into God-likeness is wrought, and the purification of the moral nature effected.

In everything that pertains to the theory and practice of the Christian religion there are two indispensable factors, — the atonement of Jesus Christ, and the personality and office of the Holy Ghost; and the faith that does not embrace both of these is spurious.

Infidelity has signified its willingness to accept Jesus as the model man, and assert his martyrdom to the cause of truth, provided the church will abandon the idea of his vicarious merit, and give up the hope of salvation through his blood. They are willing to unite if they are allowed to construct the platform.

The scientific world has indicated its willingness to accept the morals of Christianity and unite with the church in extending its beneficial influence on society, if the church will renounce the idea that there is any supernatural power in the gospel.

But while liberal Christians and fierce assailing sceptics unite for the overthrow of the church, and while weak and corrupt men are willing to compromise for the sake of peace or for personal gain, the church, the real vital portion of Christ's mystic body, is ready to go to the stake rather than surrender the two fundamental principles of the gospel indicated in the text; viz., satisfaction through the blood of atonement, and the divinity and supernaturalness of the Holy Ghost.

The more closely we adhere to these, and the more earnestly we insist upon them, and the more firmly our faith grasps them, the more vigorous and uniform will be the spiritual life of the church. We must not forget, however, that these fundamental truths do not stand alone; they necessarily involve others that are very important.

The sacrificial death of Jesus Christ as the basal truth of the gospel system implies that the beings for whom he died are sinners, condemned sinners, helpless sinners, powerless for self-recovery.

It implies further that God is a righteous governor, whose violated law demands satisfaction for sin, and that the Saviour who shed his blood for this purpose is a divine Saviour, being so near the throne that God does, through his merit, send the Holy Ghost into the world to accomplish man's salvation.

It is impossible to construct a platform of truth of sufficient breadth to accommodate the world, and of sufficient strength to save the multitude anxious for salvation, and leave out these primary truths. But the two principal ones involved in this discussion are fundamental. These are the Jachin and Boaz that support the majestic temple of gospel truth.

A penitent at the altar seeking salvation, who feeling himself a sinner helpless before God, and pleading the merit of Jesus' blood as his only hope, and relying upon the renewing power of the Holy Ghost, cannot fail of success, if he do not doubt the efficacy of that blood and the power of that Spirit.

But it is equally true that there is no ground of hope, not one word of encouragement, for any who turn away from the cleansing fountain of sacrificial blood and reject the office of the divine Spirit, who was sent into the world to purify and comfort the hearts of believers.

In the heroic days of Methodism, when whole congregations were prostrated by the power of the Holy Ghost, these specific doctrines were believed and preached and accepted; and it was not until the philosophy of Unitarianism, and the blighting influence of Fatalism in one form or another had crept into the pulpit and diffused themselves abroad, that the power of Christian life began to wane in the Methodist Church.

But a new era has dawned upon us. The emasculated gospel of sensationalism, with its periodical harvests of disappointment, is being swept away by the rising tide of Gospel truth which is now rolling over the entire world. We are learning more and more that a sinner smarting under the stings of an awakened conscience cannot be satisfied with anything less than the atoning blood of Jesus. When the "pains of hell" get hold of the sinner they extort from him the reluctant confession: —

"Nor bleeding bird, nor bleeding beast.
Nor hyssop branch, nor sprinkling priest,
Nor running brook, nor flood, nor sea,
Can take the dismal stain away.
Jesus, Thy blood, Thy blood alone.
Hath power sufficient to atone.
Thy blood can make me white as snow,
No Jewish type can cleanse me so."

The whole church in all its branches is rising again to the grandeur of the thought that all men everywhere may come directly to Jesus and be instantly saved. We are just opening our eyes to the fact that no amount of burden-bearing, no process of human suffering, no tornado of sorrow and affliction, can purge one stain of sin from the soul. We are waking from the deathlike slumber of formality and legalism; just beginning to apprehend the significance of the fact that Jesus Christ was crucified in man's stead; that "by his stripes we are healed;" and that we rise to newness of life through faith in his blood, rather than by the tortuous process of penance. We are learning to discard self and trust Jesus alone for salvation, and as the gathering throng presses onward to the crimson stream, they join the full chorus of the church: —

"To the best fountain of Thy blood,
Incarnate God I fly.
Here I can wash my guilty soul,
From stains of deepest dye."

And when the conscience is thoroughly roused, the soul does not linger long on doubtful preliminaries, but in the language of genuine penitence cries, —

"Just as I am, without one plea,
But that Thy blood was shed for me —
And that Thou bid'st me come to Thee,
Lamb of God, I come! I come!"

But notwithstanding the fact that thousands are rejoicing in the consciousness of a Saviour's love, it is equally true that there are many excellent people, upright in all their actions, prayerful in their habits, conscientious and obedient to the divine law, earnest in their sympathy with every good work, firm in their reliance on God, orthodox in their belief in Christ and in the Holy Ghost, whose faith in these great truths is so vague and indefinite *as to time*, that it brings them neither present comfort nor power. There are many pulpits that make frequent allusions to the sacrificial blood that cleanseth from all sin. They speak of the Holy Ghost as the sanctifier of believers, but their reference to these truths is incidental, their argument evasive and obscure, tending rather to the subordination of those great truths than to give them prominence. It will avail nothing to give these doctrines a nominal place in the creeds, or even a conspicuous place, if we so cover them up with philosophical speculations and illogical reasoning, that they neither animate the speaker, nor warm and move his hearers. These two principles in the gospel system are set forth in the Scriptures as burning truths, and when accompanied by the Holy Ghost they set on fire all the rest, and pervade the whole church with vital energy, thrilling it with the power of divine life from apex to periphery. When the faithful pastor beholds sinners panting for life and salvation, when burdened souls are crying out for the living God, he leads them directly to the blood, and prays earnestly for the descent of the Holy Ghost. The bugle call of the church to-day is, "Come to Jesus." It has taken us a great while to learn the important lesson.

For ages the types and shadows flitted before the mind of God's ancient people, occasionally alternating with the dark and deceitful rites of paganism. But in due time Christ came. He shed his blood upon the cross, went up to the mediatorial throne and sent the Spirit into the world, and now the "Spirit and the bride say. Come." Although for many centuries of the Christian era these truths were obscured by false teachers or seemed under eclipse, the Sun of righteousness has dispersed the clouds of error, and the light of his beams has enabled us to read the Apocalypse aright, and we discover that in the conflict of ages the overcoming forces are the "Blood of the Lamb," and the testimony of the saints that the blood "cleanseth from all sin."

The business of the church is to save men from sin and build them up in holiness. God never designed it for any other purpose, and the work of salvation, like every other business, is to be done in a straightforward manner; it is to be done intelligently.

God is the perfection of wisdom and intelligence, and he will not have his methods superseded by the austere rites and monkish superstitions of fanatics. He is displeased with the stupendous frauds of those who "teach for doctrines the traditions of men."

Notwithstanding God made the way of salvation so plain that a wayfaring man of moderate ability could pursue it with safety, men have woven about it the gauze of mysteriousness, and obscured it with the effete notions of paganism, until scores become discouraged and turn away from the path of life and drift downward to everlasting night. The experience of the church in all the periods of her history confirms the fact that the largest degree of success in all spiritual work is connected with the steadfast presentation of Christ as the only way of salvation, not by virtue of his martyrdom, but through the merit of his atoning blood. From the time the apostle preached to the church at Corinth a crucified Christ as the "power of God" and the "wisdom of God," to the present period, that minister has done most for the world, most for God, most for himself and for humanity, who has preached most clearly and forcibly "redemption in the blood of Jesus, even the forgiveness of sin."

All preaching that does not offer full salvation and invite to Jesus now as the only promised time is comparatively a failure. Whatever else may be presented, however eloquently spoken and earnestly enforced, without these it is in a great measure fruitless.

The successful evangelist after he has aroused the conscience and awakened penitence, directs the mourner to Jesus, assuring him that—

"There is a fountain filled with blood.
   Drawn from Immanuel's veins;
And sinners sprinkled with that blood,
   Lose all their guilty stains."

When Jesus spake to Nicodemus of the necessity of the new birth, he taught him that the Holy Ghost was the regenerating agent; and the hosts of successful workers now in the field are winning glorious victories by the simple story of the cross. The experience of every perfectly saved soul is "that the blood cleanseth," and the pathway of recovery from all backsliding leads straight to Calvary, and the returning wanderer receives the Father's welcome beneath the shadow of the Saviour's cross; and the enduement of power that prepares the minister, the class-leader, the superintendent, and Sabbath-school teacher for successful work in their respective fields, is given in answer to pleadings as direct and fervent, and a faith as specific, definite, and unyielding, as that which characterized the disciples while they tarried in the upper chamber for the Master's blessing.

We know from experience that monastic rites are fruitless of good results. "Bodily exercise profiteth nothing." Prayers, watchings, fastings, of themselves never bring peace and joy to the heart.

> "Not all our groans nor tears,
>   Nor works which we have done,
> Nor vows, nor promises, or prayers,
>   Can e'er for sin atone.
>
> Relief alone is found
>   In Jesus' precious blood;
> 'Tis this that heals the mortal wound,
>   And reconciles to God.
>
> High lifted on the cross,
>   The spotless victim dies;
> This is salvation's only source,
>   Hence all our hopes arise."

Prayer and fasting have their respective places in the Christian system, but are useless except when they are the language of living faith, at whose omnipotent bidding the Spirit applies the blood to the stricken soul, and fills it with love and peace.

As these two primal truths become more clearly understood, they will come to have greater prominence in our experiences, and become the controlling forces in the life-work of God's people.

It has been clearly demonstrated in the past that a

Christless gospel cannot arrest the attention and save the world from sin. The preaching that warms and energizes the speaker and startles and surprises his hearers, the hymns that thrill the soul and melt the heart, are full of Christ; and the experiences that edify the saints and alarm backsliders, the exhortations that interest and move the godless, and the faith that brings and keeps the consciousness of a present salvation, always have direct reference to the Spirit and the blood.

We know these doctrines have been abused and are still liable to abuse. We confess that fanaticism has characterized the action of men on the subject of religion in all ages; nevertheless there is but one safe way for the church, — we must give to these fundamental doctrines the same prominence in our faith and lives that God has given them in his word.

Let the pulpit be true to its mission; let the trumpet give forth no uncertain sound; let the instruction of those who are appointed spiritual guides be such as becometh sound doctrine; let the whole church, by an earnest study of the Scripture and the handbooks of our theology, fortify themselves against the assaults of error from whatever source it may come; let the pulpit call after erring men and offer them present salvation through the blood of atonement, and stop not at the initial point in the Christian pathway, but "have boldness to enter the holiest by the blood of Jesus, by a new and living way, consecrated for them." Against the doctrine of instantaneous full salvation through the blood of atonement there remain operative at this time two prominent and dangerous heresies: —

The first is that "death is a factor in the salvation of man." The logical sequence of this error gives rise to the widespread delusion, that regardless of his habits of life, when his days are accomplished, man has only to die and go to heaven. It is assumed that death is a purgatorial rite joined to the blood and Spirit to cleanse the heart and kill the inbred man of sin.

This is one of the inseparable sequents of gradualism antagonized by the text; for the Scripture teaches that the blood cleanses "from all sin," without the least assistance, "from the pangs, agonies, arrows, or sweats of death."

The other popular error is that physical and mental suffering have a purifying influence on the heart, and are gospel factors in the salvation of the soul. This is paganistic or demoniacal in its origin and influence, and is out of harmony with every attribute of Deity. This is not a new form of error; it is as old as the Christian religion, and has stamped its vile impress on every page of the world's history; and we are unconsciously and thoughtlessly receiving these specious delusions from an accommodating pulpit and a patronizing press.

It must appear to every thoughtful mind that if the apostle gives us the true idea in the text, — if we are saved by the operation of the Holy Ghost, "through faith in his blood," — then the notion that suffering purifies or is essential for discipline, or that the world is benefited in any sense by the introduction of sin into it, or that there will come to the individual Christian greater good by the blasting of his hopes; *or that any sequent of sin can contribute to its removal*, is a fierce delusion and a dangerous heresy.

But if the text is true and our reasoning is true, these theories are not true, and those who thank God for evil, and ascribe their salvation to their afflictions, attribute to evil that which the text affirms is done by the Spirit of God.

This subject is beautifully and amply illustrated in the Scriptures: we go in our imagination and stand beside the prophets of Baal on the summit of Carmel; they are cutting their flesh and mutilating their bodies, but their

God answers not. They become frantic with rage, and thrust in their lances and hold up their lacerated and bleeding arms, and entreat in vain.

But the prophet of God prepares his altar and arranges his sacrifice, and while his white locks tremble in the mountain air, he lifts his placid brow toward heaven, stretches forth his arm like a sceptre of power, and, obedient to the command of his unwavering faith, the fire descends and consumes the offering. I go back over the highway of history for two thousand years to the days of Christ's personal ministry; I journey with him to the land of Gadara; I see the demoniac coming out of the tombs, cutting himself with sticks and stones, and bleeding and haggard he stands before the Saviour of men. Jesus says to the evil one, Come out of him, and straightway the devils leave the man and enter into the swine; and true to their devilish instincts to destroy, they hurry the whole herd to the depths of the sea. And in no case did Jesus impose any afflictive rite on any one who sought relief at his hands.

But all those austere ceremonies which have disgraced the lives of professors of religion and embarrassed the church in all ages proceed from the weakness and corruption of human nature; they are excrescences developed and moulded into form by Oriental philosophy, and incorporated into the Christian system in the early part of the second century.

This fondness of human nature for that which *is useless* and afflictive is the product of pagan philosophy and the fruitful source of all fanaticism, and under its potent influence arose the pillar saints of the fifth century. Among them was Barodatus, a monk of Syria, who lived in a box, and James, one of the same fraternity, who was loaded down with chains about his neck and waist, and who continued for three days and nights in prayer prostrate upon the ground, his body nearly covered with snow, and his hands extended pleadingly toward heaven. Others sat on posts with uncovered heads until they died of sunstroke or exhaustion; while others bruised their bodies with rods, or distorted their features with self-inflicted pain, that they might thus propitiate the favor of God. It seems strange that after two thousand years of the Spirit's teaching, with an open Bible before us, men should yet be found who proclaim these "old wives' fables" from the pulpit; who still insist that moral and physical evil are essential factors in the government of God; who still assert that what we call sin is a necessity; that sickness and sorrow and suffering are indispensable to the progress of the race; who still aver that the tornado is the messenger of God's justice, the plaything of the Almighty, and works out his unalterable purpose, whether it sweep away churches or breweries, whether it overthrow wicked men or destroy innocent women and children.

When the Spirit begets the new life all of man's relations to law are changed, but his outward surroundings remain the same; he is still on probation in a world where sin has inaugurated a curse, and in which he cannot have peace except while he submits to the authority of law. And after he is cleansed from all sin, the pathway to heaven is one of obedience and loyalty to God; and although evil assail him at every step of his advancement, it cannot harm him if he remain true to God; grace is given every moment. Faith in the blood as a continuous state of the heart gives perpetual victory to the soul, the benefits of the atonement are received without interruption, he is supported in trial, conquers every foe, and is enabled to make the most of himself, for himself, for God, and humanity; and is enabled daily to say, "Now thanks be unto God, who always causeth us to triumph in Christ, and maketh manifest the savour of his knowledge by us in every place."

God never sees anything the individual does or suffers, either as the procuring cause, or as the condition of his salvation. God sees us always in the attitude we are in toward the atonement. "The Father hath put all things into the hands of his Son," hence he can see no one except in his relation to the blood of Calvary. The only place of meeting for God and the sinner is the cross of Jesus Christ. The only place where God can receive an offering that can be acceptable in his sight is where the sinner recognizes the atonement and relies on that alone. It is because of that atonement that you and I have any hope about us. It is because of that atonement that the saints in all ages have been enabled to rejoice in Christ Jesus, and have no confidence in the flesh. "God always sees the blood, and because he does, it is impossible for a penitent to be rejected from the altar of salvation. He sees the blood, and the tears of the Magdalene are dried by the Spirit's touch. He sees the blood, and Simon is triumphant in Satan's sifting-time, and walks the yielding sea with unfailing faith. He sees the blood, and Paul bears the thorn of flesh without a murmur, and records his triumph in a Roman cell. He sees the blood, and John, wrapped about with an asbestos garment, comes out of the boiling oil unhurt and full of rejoicing. God sees the blood, and Stephen, the martyr, breaks away from his murderers to pillow his bleeding head on his Redeemer's bosom. He sees the blood, and the dying thief, from the jaws of infolding damnation, leaps up to receive a harp and a crown. God sees the blood, and the sigh of the thoughtful and contrite is registered, the painstaking endeavor is recorded; faith is accepted for righteousness; the struggle after purity is ended; the believer is triumphant in affliction; there is light at eventide; death, the last enemy, is destroyed; the trumpet sounds; the graves open; the angels shout the welcome, and eternity unfolds through all its everlasting years the grandeur of its beatific vision— and all this because at this moment, and every moment, God sees the blood by which all things in heaven and in earth are reconciled unto himself. It is because of that blood, and the sight of that blood in heaven, that we are this moment out of hell. Again and again, from the scenes of impurity and oppression, from the place where the demon of war sits and howls, from the deck of the slave-ship or from the slave-pen, from the defiled and sultry streets of the slave metropolis, from the places of demoniacal oppression and wrong, from the place where theft and lust and murder prowl and prey, a cry has gone up many a time; a cry loud and strong for vengeance against the oppressor; ay, and the Judge, it may be, with his eye bright and piercing and quick, has had the sword in his hand, and the sword has been brandished for destruction; and then he has looked at the man at his right hand, and the bared and brandished weapon has gone back again to its scabbard, and the oppressor has been granted a respite." And to-day as we gather about this altar and look unto Jesus for salvation, God sees the blood, and the penitent soul is forgiven, and the seeker after purity made whiter than snow. God sees the blood, and the sanctified soul, with all its infirmities, passes unhurt through the trials of life, triumphs in a dying hour, and goes home to join the blood-washed company on the other shore.

When I was very small I was strangely impressed at times with my father's singing. He often sang of the blood. He would sing in a low, soft voice of peculiar sweetness, as if rehearsing to some one near him, and as if the listener were as much interested in the song as himself. This was his favorite hymn:—

"Forever here my rest shall be,
    Close to Thy bleeding side:

This all my hope and all my plea,
> For me the Saviour died.

My dying Saviour and my God,
> Fountain for guilt and sin;
Sprinkle me ever with Thy blood,
> And cleanse and keep me clean.

"Wash me, and make me thus Thine own,
> Wash me, and mine Thou art;
Wash me, but not my feet alone,
> My hands, my head, my heart.

The atonement of Thy blood apply.
> Till faith to sight improve;
Till hope in full fruition die,
> And all my soul be love."

I did not then understand its significance; but years afterward it was made plain. When we stood by his bed-side and sang hymns of praise while his launched bark lingered a moment on the crystal wave, we sang the same hymn that had given him so much strength and comfort in the battle of life. The two worlds seemed to mingle into one; the radiance of the God-man's countenance made the valley of death luminous with the divine glory, and the heavenly choirs bending low seemed to swell the triumphant song, and in that hushed moment we could almost catch the glad refrain, — Made white in the blood of the Lamb!

XII

ENTIRE SANCTIFICATION, AN INSTANTANEOUS WORK WROUGHT BY THE HOLY GHOST SUBSEQUENT TO CONVERSION

"And immediately his leprosy was cleansed." — MATTHEW viii. 3.

ENTIRE SANCTIFICATION, OR full salvation, as embraced in Methodist terminology, is the removal from the moral nature of a believer of the elements of depravity that remain in the soul after conversion. It is not the canceling of guilt, nor the act of overcoming the inertia of spiritual death; it is not more pardon nor more life; it is the purification of the moral being from the remaining defilements of a sinful nature.

Leprosy does not symbolize guilt, and it does not represent death. It represents the uncleanness of sin. It demonstrates the fact that life may exist in its full vigor in the physical organism while it is diseased, permeated with the virus of impurity. And Jesus uses this fact to illustrate how it is that the moral impurity remains in the heart after the Christ-life has been imparted to the soul.

In healing the leper, Jesus represented to the church the divine method of purification. When Jesus bade him "be clean," immediately his leprosy was cleansed."

The leaden mists that lie about the subject of holiness would all disappear if teachers would be more accurate in their statements, and give the true significance to the terms they use. The word used to express an idea should be properly defined, and should be a perfect exponent of the idea expressed.

The Bible speaks of a state of grace, variously denominated "holiness," "heart purity," "perfect love," and "entire sanctification." These terms are never used interchangeably with the words regeneration and justification.

Entire is a qualifying term, used to express the completing of a fact or a process; and when so used indicates that some part of the achievement more or less had been previously accomplished. Hence we have the fact that entire sanctification is a part of man's salvation which is not accomplished by the act of regeneration. The process of entire sanctification is that of cleansing. It is not at all like pardoning. It is entirely different from regeneration, and it reaches an entirely different result.

The condition of the soul after it is sanctified is that of purity, not only guiltless, and alive from the dead, and adopted into the family of God, but clean, consciously pure within.

The experience of full salvation embraces the consciousness of the individual that he has been purified from inherent corruption, and that as a result of that process through which he has passed he is consciously pure.

Webster defines sanctification as "the act of God's grace by which the affections of men are purified from sin and exalted to a supreme love to God." The word "entire" is a qualifying term, and indicates the degree of purity secured, or the extent of the sanctifying power experienced.

According to the lexicon, "entire" is a term signifying "completeness in all its parts," "full," "perfect," "comprising all requisites in itself," "without defect."

According to this definition, entire sanctification is a state of unalloyed purity of heart; a condition in which the moral nature is perfectly renovated; a condition in which the grace of God has removed all sin from the heart.

This work of the complete restoration of moral purity to the human soul is a part of man's salvation. It is that without which he cannot enter heaven. It is God's work, and is wrought by the Holy Ghost, and is done at once; or it is a gradual work which God has left to be accomplished in some other way.

Adam Clarke, the great exegete of the period, says, "In no part of the Scripture are we directed to seek remission of sins *seriatim*, one now, and another then, and so on. Neither in any part of the Bible are we directed to seek holiness by gradation. Neither a gradation pardon nor a gradation purification exists in the Bible."

Anything is instantaneous that is done at once. "Occurring without perceptible succession," "as the passage of electricity through a given space."

If the experience of heart purity is reached by a gradual process after conversion, it must be either by growth or by elimination of impurity by penance. For those who believe it to be accomplished by death recognize it as an instantaneous work; for death always does its work at once.

If entire sanctification is a gradual process by development, it is a contribution to the work of salvation by the addition of some element or quality that God intentionally omitted at conversion, or was unable to supply. If this work is accomplished by penance, it is a contribution to the work of salvation by the gradual removal from the soul of some unholy essence or quality which God intentionally left in the soul at conversion, or which he was unable to remove at the time.

Both of these theories have their advocates whose honesty and Christian integrity are not called into question. But a clear view of what constitutes entire sanctification, and only a limited knowledge of the laws of growth, will demonstrate the absolute impossibility of obtaining this experience by growth.

A fundamental law of growth is "everything after its kind," and six thousand years of recorded observation have produced no exception to this law.

Growth has no element of construction in it. Growth is the gradual accumulation of such particles as constitute the animal or plant when first formed. Growth has regard to increase in proportions, but cannot change the quality of any substance.

But the doctrine of holiness by growth is embarrassed by another difficulty, — growth never changes the relations of persons nor things. Law gives precedent to the first occupant. Wheat is never sown in the forest for the purpose of removing the underbrush and uprooting the giant oaks. These occupy the soil by right of inheritance. Not one instance of displacement by growth is "recorded in the history of the world.

For years after the forests have been felled, the stumps of massive trees remain in the best cultivated fields, scarred and blackened by the laborer's hand, demonstrating the fact that the growth of the most valuable crops by the most vigorous and improved methods of culture can never eradicate these pristine monarchs of the soil. They yield only to the stump- lifter, or to fire.

Sin is indigenous in the human soul. Although it is a usurper, it has the primary possession of the soul by hereditary descent; and we could as easily displace the Norwegian forests by the introduction of the fragrant magnolia from the banks of the Mississippi, or extirpate the primeval forests of North America by transplanting to its midst the stately palm from the Syrian desert, as we could grow sin out of its native soil by the most refined and elegant processes of culture.

However vigorous the growth of spiritual life may be, if sin in the form of depravity or native uncleanness remains in the soul after conversion, even if it be held in a state of suppression, it cannot be grown out; but as salvation is by priestly rite it yields at once to the power of God. As we perceive that depravity cannot be removed from the soul by culture, is it any more reasonable to suppose that we can wear it out by ascetic rites and austere ceremonies, by purgatorial flames, or by physical and mental suffering in this life?

The idea of purgatory, as taught by Rome, is more reasonable than the Protestant notion of salvation by the attrition of pain; for Rome has regard to the penalty of the law. But if purgatorial purification is a myth, and is an offence, as taught in the Catholic Church, why should the Protestantism of this century change the locality of purgatory, and parade it through all their forms of worship.

The doctrine of salvation by the attrition of sorrow has its advocates in all lands and among all peoples. It appears to be a necessary part of every system of theology or philosophy that limits the priestly merit of the Lord Jesus Christ. It is the *dernier ressort* of naturalism in the campaign against the sacrifice of Calvary.

"How shall I get rid of my sin?" asks the devotee of his priest at the shrine of paganism, "Drive your sandals full of spikes, and walk five hundred miles over the burning sands of the desert," replies his priest. "How may I be sanctified wholly, and fitted for heaven?" inquires the earnest Christian of his pastor. "Don't sin any more than is necessary to keep you humble, and bear patiently all

the afflictions your heavenly Father sends upon you,"
replies the average spiritual adviser of the period. A single
quotation from one of the most popular preachers of the
century will be sufficient to show the extent to which this
doctrine has been ingrained into the popular belief.

"Before the wrought iron can become steel, it must be
heated by means of charcoal, and made to pass through
a process of cementation until it is blistered by fire and
freed from a portion of its carbon; and then the merciless
hammer must do the rest, and complete the work. Before
the coal gas which at night illumines the city and beautifies its temples and parks is fit for use, it must be freed
from carbonic acid, tar, resinous compounds, and other
impurities which dim its brilliancy; and this is accomplished by first subjecting it to an intense heat, and then
passing it through water, cooling it in condensers, and
transmitting it through tubes and purifiers.

"And just so it is with the growth and spiritual progress
of the soul. The friction and attrition, the purging and
the purifying, the heating and the cooling, the *sinning
and repenting to which we are subjected,* the very difficulties and painful experiences we have to encounter, and of
which we are so apt to complain, are the necessary conditions of our spiritual progress."

But that entire theory is wrong; the very philosophy
upon which it is based is false. Sinning and repenting are
not the necessary conditions of spiritual advancement.
Man is not saved by the operations of natural law. Man
is not saved by the proscriptions of the moral law. Man is
not saved by disciplinary processes under the law. Salvation is by another process. Salvation is by the redemption that is in Jesus Christ. It is by sacrificial blood that
man is saved. It is because of the blood the Holy Ghost
transforms and renews and cleanses the moral nature.
Salvation is all accomplished through the priestly merit
of Jesus; and if it is, as the Scriptures teach, that salvation

is by redemptive agencies, it is wrought for us by another, and is all accomplished by divine power.

Sinning and suffering are inseparable. No sin was ever committed that did not produce suffering. These are what Jesus came to save us from, and it is absurd to talk of them as conditions or agencies of salvation. But as sin has in itself all the elements by which it diffuses itself abroad and becomes universal, so also does the atonement of Jesus Christ possess in itself all the elements and all the agencies by which sin is to be destroyed.

Pain is a product of sin; it is something that is to be destroyed. As it is a sequence of sin, it must cease in the ultimate victory over evil, when "God shall wipe away all tears from their eyes... and there shall be no more crying, nor pain, for the former things are passed away."

The conception of gaining salvation by suffering is one of the oldest forms of paganism; it is the emphatic and controlling principle in every system of idolatry known to man. It was incorporated into the Latin church from pagan Rome, and has propagated itself with a greater or less degree of distinctiveness among all creeds and classes. It has dragged its slimy trail across four thousand years of the world's history; and to-day it stands beside Christian altars, and with insulting mien challenges the blood of the Son of God.

Theodore Parker, that prince of sophists, said, "In the next life, I hope to suffer until I learn the mastery of myself, and learn to keep the conditions of my higher life. Through the Red Sea of pain I will march to the promised land, the divine ideal guiding before, the Egyptian actual urging from behind." There is no Christ in his theory; no virtue, no purity, except that which is ideal and evasive; while evil as personified by the Egyptian taskmaster is the only actual and impelling force that can stimulate man in this life.

These doctrines both dishonor Christ and leave Calvary without an offering, and humanity without a Saviour. Both of these theories make the instantaneous salvation of a soul impossible by any method whatever. They virtually disrobe the Christian system of every divine element, and enthrone the impersonal forces of nature instead.

Every standard writer in Methodism, from John Wesley until this moment, has taught that the completing act of salvation, or the experience of heart purity, is wrought instantaneously by the Holy Ghost; that salvation is conditioned upon the faith of the seeker; that salvation is by successive stages; and the remaining impurity that lingers in the moral nature after conversion is not removed at that time, solely because the candidate neither perceived his own needs, nor apprehended the remedy which God had provided.

However tedious the preparation may be, however tortuous the pathway of approach, when it comes to the work of cleansing, that is the work of God; and no other being can do it, and it is accomplished at once.

But there is another line of approach to this subject. If sin is an instantaneous act, salvation must be an instantaneous process.

All men concede sin to be an act in which there is no perceptible succession; hence the results of sin upon the moral qualities of the soul must be instantaneous. However slowly Adam and Eve approached the fatal act, however insidious the process of temptation may have been, the culmination was sudden; guilt ensued at once. "When lust hath conceived, it bringeth forth sin; and when sin is executed, it bringeth forth death."

During the six thousand years of the world's rebellion, no act of man has exceeded the audacity with which Adam confronted his Maker when dragged from his place of concealment. Turning like a base coward against her whom God had given him, and whose honor was intrusted to his care, he hurled into the face of Jehovah the charge of complicity: "The woman thou gavest me has conspired against me; she beguiled me; she is the guilty cause of my fall; she accomplished my ruin."

The defilement of man's moral nature was not a gradual process. When Satan entered into man he seized every organ, and diffused himself through every fibre and tissue of soul, body, and spirit. This temple of the living God so suddenly defiled became the habitation of every unholy and vile thing.

Salvation is the divine process by which sin is destroyed from the soul. It is the complete recovery of man from the catastrophe of the garden.

Heart purity, which is a part of man's salvation, implies the complete renovation of the moral and spiritual nature of man. It implies the restoration of the individual to a state of harmony with God, the establishment of correct legal relations with him, and the cleansing and adjustment of those moral qualities that constituted him the Son of God at his creation, and which were interrupted by the apostasy.

The process by which this is accomplished must be a reversal of that by which this moral ruin was wrought. There must first of all be given the full consent of the party that God shall come in and occupy the heart. The candidate for heart purity must render a complete, willing, cheerful obedience to all the commands and requirements of the gospel.

When the penitent sinner fulfils the conditions of pardon, God, in the exercise of the divine prerogative, immediately pardons all the past; then the Holy Ghost quickens the soul into a new spiritual life. This is in harmony with universal experience. And when the regenerate soul entirely devotes himself to the Father, when he gives God permission to wholly possess his heart, as suddenly as Satan defiled it God enters and restores perfect moral order and purity to the soul so recently polluted by sin.

When the believer comes as perfectly into sympathy with Christ as the unregenerate soul is with the spirit of the world, something will transpire at once. Let any true seeker after purity surrender as completely to the Holy Ghost as the ungodly man does to the spirit of the world, and as suddenly as the unrestrained air will fill a vacuum, God will come into the soul, and the seeker will have a vivid and an instantaneous experience of heart purity, — an experience in which there is no perceptible succession.

The phraseology of the Bible supports this view of the subject. The direct statement of the word is: "That his name is called Jesus because he saves his people from their sins;" "that Christ Jesus came into the world to save sinners;" "that he is able to save to the uttermost all that come unto God by him." The Bible not only states "that he forgives sins," but that "he cleanseth from all unrighteousness;" "that if we walk in the light, as he is in the light, we have fellowship one with the other, and the blood of Jesus Christ his Son cleanseth us from all sin."

There is not one place in the Bible where it speaks of any part of salvation being accomplished by growth. No intimation is given in the Bible of any kind or degree of salvation as a result of pain or sorrow. It never once speaks of any form of gradual salvation. The Bible continuously announces to the world of perishing sinners that "now is the day of salvation." The accepted time of the Lord is the present.

But we may put this argument in another form. Entire sanctification is a part of man's salvation. Jesus Christ is the only Saviour, and the salvation of each individual is his own personal work. Whatever Jesus does as his own personal work, he does at once. When Lazarus had lain in the embrace of death four days, Jesus came to Bethany, and standing by the grave where his dead friend lay, in the presence of the weeping multitude, he bade him come forth; and the dead man heard and obeyed his voice. He stood by the gate of the city travel-stained and weary. He bade the *cortege* stand still when he touched the bier and gave the weeping mother her child in perfect health. He said to the blind man who cried for mercy, "Receive thy sight;" and filled both soul and body with perfect radiance. In the text he said to the leper, "I will; be thou clean. And immediately his leprosy was cleansed."

This omnipotent Jesus, whose voice the winds and sea obey, at whose touch disease retires, and at whose command death restores the prey, "is of God, made unto us wisdom, righteousness, sanctification, and redemption." He is a competent Saviour. He is no novice. He is no adventurer. He is the mighty to save; the world's Redeemer. The preliminary steps are all taken; the preparatory work is all done; the atonement is made; the blood is sprinkled; the Father has accepted the sacrifice, and now only waits for the church to accept and receive him.

That the divine method of salvation is an instantaneous process, we have the statement of the Christian world. It is in evidence that cannot be impeached that pardon and regeneration are experiences without perceptible succession; and we have the recorded testimony of multitudes who have died in the triumphs of full salvation, and the thousands of living witnesses who now enjoy the blessing of heart purity and testify to that fact. And these all with one accord affirm that they are cleansed from their inherited impurity by the blood of atonement, and that by the agency of the Holy Ghost it was an instantaneous experience.

And the evangelist by divine authority records the testimony of the entire church above, and you cannot impeach them without rejecting all revelation. John beheld a great multitude that no man could number, composed of the saved ones of all the ages and all climes and classes,

embracing all tribes and all nationalities, and compre-
hending all the periods of time; and they all with united
voice testified that Jesus Christ, the great High Priest of
humanity, had "washed them from their sins in his own
blood."

But we formulate again with the same result. Salvation is a free gift conferred upon the trusting soul through
the merit of the Lord Jesus Christ, The act of giving,
whether conditional or arbitrary, is an act without perceptible succession; hence we conclude that experimental holiness is an event, an epoch in religious progress
that occurs at once.

Shall we not then honor the Lord Jesus with a present,
continuous faith that ascribes to him all saving power,
and secures to us a present victory over all impurity? Let
this be the language of every heart: —

"Jesus, a word, a look, from thee
Can turn my heart, and make it clean.
Purge out the inbred leprosy.
And save me from my bosom sin.

My heart which now to thee I raise,
I know thou canst this moment cleanse;
The deepest stains of sin efface,
And drive the evil spirit hence.

Be it according to thy word;
Accomplish *now* thy work in me;
And let my soul, to health restored,
Devote its deathless powers to thee."

XIII
FULNESS OF THE DIVINE PROVISION

[Full Text of the Sermon Preached at the National Camp-meeting at New Castle, Pa., Sabbath, a.m., 1885]

"For all things are yours." —I CORINTHIANS iii. 21.

THE FACT THAT ALL TRUE Christians belong to Christ is the primary fact that entitles them to the possession and use of all things. All things are yours, only because you belong to Christ. If you in reality belong to him *now*, all things that belong to him are yours now.

It is your right as an individual to appropriate and use your own goods. God keeps nothing exclusively for himself. He has given up all; emptied heaven, emptied himself, surrendered the crown jewels of his spiritual kingdom, for the salvation of man.

God having given his Son for man's redemption, freely gives himself in all his divine fulness to every one who will receive him.

When God created man, he gave him, as his own divine heritage, every attribute and every constituent quality of his own divine nature. These exalted qualities are not endowments. They are the elementary constituents of manhood. And the Father manifested his appreciation of his child by appointing him to the lordship and super-intendency of his estate.

This original supremacy in every department of his being and activities is the sum total of what man lost by becoming an apostate from God. By his disobedience in Eden, man became the slave of the circumstances he was appointed to rule.

In the work of redemption, the honor of individual su-premacy is restored to man in Jesus Christ, who is him-self exalted to universal power and authority at the right hand of God. This is the sum total of redemption, and embraces all the subordinate and co-ordinate doctrines and experiences of the Christian religion.

It is by virtue of the sacrificial and vicarious merit of the offering on Calvary that the whole creation is now placed at the disposal of each individual Christian. "All things are yours." In Christ everything the Father has is made to subserve the purpose of his love, and promote the present and eternal happiness of his children.

The popular delusion that the Christian system is nar-row, and that it is the promoter of ignorance and the es-sential element of bigotry, is not only refuted by the text, but universal history proves it to be false. As the emanci-pator of humanity and the inspiration of progress, Chris-tianity stands alone. Every other system of religion cir-cumscribes the intellect and enslaves the passions.

To strike the manacles from mind and limb, to liberate the conscience and enlighten the understanding, is the distinctive mission of the gospel. The Author and Founder of the Christian system came to this world for the express purpose of undoing heavy burdens. He came to fling open wide earth's gloomy prisons of soul and body, that the oppressed millions of humanity might be free. By no force of arbitrary interpretation can this bondage be applied to the body alone. The charge Jesus made against the Pharisees is a sufficient illustration of this fact: "Ye bind heavy burdens and grievous to be borne, and lay them on men's shoulders."

There is no tyranny so cruel, no bondage so relentless, as that which enslaves the mind. There is no slavery so brutalizing, so debasing, as the slavery of passion. The despotism of prejudice, and the enthralment of ignorance and passion, are more to be abhorred than the fetters and scourge of the oppressor who makes merchandise of the souls and bodies of men.

Christianity is the only system of thought that ever gave to man the idea of claiming for himself, and of granting unto others, liberty as large as the compass of his own mind. It is no argument against this fact to admit that in all ages some professors of Christianity have been exceedingly narrow in their range of thought, and fierce and cruel in their persecutions.

The fault is not with the religion of the gospel; the difficulty is concealed in the weakness and corruption of human nature. It is because men do not advance to the higher and broader experiences of the Christian religion that they neither feel its power nor appreciate its privileges. Reared with the Bible in their hands, living beneath the noontide glories of a full-orbed Christian day, the great body of the church is yet in the thraldom of prejudice, and in the Egyptian night of spiritual gloom.

There is no book that so pointedly and so severely rebukes narrowness and bigotry as the Bible. There is no creed so comprehensive in its range of thought as the Bible; nothing in the literature of the world equal to it in the grandeur and poetic beauty of its sentiment.

Not only does Christianity seek to wrench the chains of bondage from man's encumbered soul by entreaty, by command, by the display of the danger-signal, but it adds the golden promise of exalted inspiration; it holds up before him the glorious incentive of untold riches and honors, upon the reasonable condition that he will give up his selfishness, and by divine fellowship and assimilation become broad-hearted and benevolent, holy and godlike in character.

From the inception of the Christian religion to the present time, it has had to contend with adverse forces. All the native tendencies of the soul are against it. There is in humanity a spirit of hostility to goodness. There is inherent in humanity a disposition to shrinkage, — a tendency toward contraction and waste. Outside the life that is in Christ Jesus there is a perpetual ebb-tide toward absolute degeneracy. It was for the arrest of these tendencies, and for their removal from the human heart, and for the destruction of the causes that produce them, that Christianity was established.

The idea of salvation by evolution is contrary to all philosophy, and finds no support in universal history. Evolution is a new name for the old doctrine of "eternal procession;" but when there is once a break in the endless chain of procession, evolution is forever lost. And if there has been no break, no salvation is needed, and none is possible; for there has been no catastrophe, and there is nothing to be saved from. The survival of the fittest would never have been heard of but for the fostering care of Him whose life is the light of men.

As stated above, the natural trend of humanity is toward a state of absolute degeneration; and it is the supreme mission of Jesus to arrest this downward tendency. For this purpose he poured his life-blood into the veins of an expiring world. He turned disaster into victory; he gave the world a new lease of life, and gave humanity an upward impulse in progress which to the soul that keeps fellowship with him shall never end.

No man was ever more conscious of the blighting effects of sin than the author of this text. He could speak from the depths of his own personal experience. By nature Paul was an egotist; by training he was a bigot; by practice he was a bold persecutor pursuing unto death for opinions' sake. But by the grace of God he was liberated from all these, and became a cosmopolite of all the ages. As a Christian Paul was a star of the first magnitude, whose orbit swept round the farthest outlying planet of truth, and across the richest and most diversified fields of religious experience.

In outlining his own personal creed the apostle presented a constellation of principles embracing the essential elements for the highest standard of Christian attainment; and truth is the foundation on which he rears his massive superstructure. "Whatsoever things are true, whatsoever things are honest, whatsoever things are just, whatsoever things are pure, whatsoever things are lovely, whatsoever things are of good report; if there be any virtue, and if there be any praise, think on these things."

This comprehensive creed embraces everything that is valuable. It is as if the apostle had said, "Search for the truth as for concealed treasure; appropriate to your own needs all that is good, whether it come from Athens or Rome, whether it be perfumed with the breath of Arabia or scorched by the Ethiopian suns."

> "Seize upon truth wherever found,
> Among your friends, among your foes,
> On Christian or on heathen ground,
> The gem divine where'er it grows."

Glean carefully the fruitful fields of philosophy and history; appropriate the uncounted treasures of science; explore the untrodden heights of religious experience; give to your soul the freedom of the universe in its pursuit of knowledge.

Having enjoyed this exalted privilege for himself, the apostle was anxious that the whole church through all the ages should share it with him. Some of the Corinthian church had turned aside to glory in men, and factions were formed as a result of it. Some had selected a favorite,— Paul or Apollos, Peter or John. Having administered a kindly rebuke to the spirit of clannishness which had such early development in the church at Corinth, he said, "Therefore let no man glory in men;" your ecclesiastical organizations, though valuable and important, are always subordinate to the divine personality; "for all things are yours."

This text is the key to the situation. It indicates the royal highway to a state of perpetual victory, to the complete recovery of the forfeited supremacy. "All things are yours" in the covenant of redemption. All there is in the department of personal salvation is subject to draft now. The present tense of that verb is the golden wand of the divine magician whose single touch transforms defeat into success and turns disaster into eternal triumph. It is as if the apostle had said, "Why do you reject so much, and why do you accept so little? Why do you boast of your poverty? You are not poor. Why then remain in a state of perpetual pauperism? Take freely of your Father's munificence. All those boundless provisions of mercy and love were made for you. God calls them yours. You need more. The church at large confesses that it needs more."

In order to prepare the church for its mission, it absolutely requires all the great Provider has in store for it. That the church has taken a part of the great inheritance is evidence against it. By refusing to take more you shut out others to perish. By that act you declare to the world that you prefer a narrow sphere of action. You select from your father's estate a small portion; you call it by name; you throw around it a wall of prejudice and call it the universe, and in your isolation imagine that all that lies beyond the confines of your enclosure is a waste, howling wilderness.

God created man a king; made him to be a dweller in all lands; made him to be a traveller who should be familiar throughout all his domain. He created him with power to pass over seas, to scale the highest mountains, to visit the distant stars. And it is only as man takes in this broadening prospect that he is fitted for life in its highest and noblest conceptions and activities.

In the work of redemption the whole broad realm of religious experience was opened to every human being equally by the sacrifice of Calvary; and a worldly, sensual, thoughtless, ignorant, or indolent ministry cannot, without guilt, enclose from humanity any portion of the Saviour's freehold of salvation. Half systems in religion, like half truths in philosophy, are dangerous in their tendency. To reject any portion of God's precious gift of salvation mars the symmetry, and prevents the development of the whole.

The crowning glory of the gospel, the ultimate climax of the divine effort, is the experimental holiness of each individual member of the human family; and if the church rejects this, it obscures and subordinates the chief end of the Saviour's passion. "Christ loved the church, and gave himself for it; that he might sanctify it with the washing of water by the word, that he might present it to himself a glorious church, not having spot, or wrinkle, or any such thing; but that it should be holy and without blemish."

By rejecting full salvation by faith, and substituting any other method, the party so doing eliminates the divine element from the gospel. He makes a religion of his own; makes it of divine material it is true, but entirely of human construction in every essential part, and all human just at the point where human nature most of all needs the divine help.

Man can do much for himself in the department of culture. He is entirely responsible for the development of his character. He must conform his life to the standard of divine ethics. But the leopard can change his spots, and the Ethiopian can bleach his skin, easier than man can by any process of culture, or by conformity to any ethical code, remove the hereditary elements of impurity from his own soul.

Holiness is nothing more nor less than full salvation. It is the climax of the divine procedure in the recovery of man from the thraldom of sin. As advocates of a complete atonement, we must accept this as a possible experience; and if so, then it is obligatory upon all men. If we cannot do this, to be consistent we must erase the doctrine of atonement from our creed entirely.

It will be apparent to all persons that holiness as an experience is not to be sought separate from the primary stages of salvation. Salvation is a unit, and without the essential preceding stages holiness would be as an inverted column; it would be a pyramid with its base in the air.

Holiness is the ultimate climax of the "redemptive system." It is the crowning glory of the Master's work; and to obscure it, or to emasculate it, from the Christian system, is a crime against Christianity, and an assault upon its author.

Christianity is not merely an accumulation of facts, any one of which may be rejected without loss, and all of which are at the discretion of the receiver; the Christian system is complete, and it is because of this fact that it is authoritative and obligatory; and being thus perfect it covers the entire need of humanity in this life and in the life to come. As a sinner, man needs all the gospel to save him perfectly from his sins. As a Christian, man cannot be dissevered from the gospel; he needs it all, and needs it all the time, to keep him pure, and to round out his character and give him strength equal to the emergencies of this life. These no partial system can supply; but the perfect gospel makes provision for a complete salvation, and for almost unlimited growth afterwards.

But there is one other aspect of this subject. As a converted man may remain unsanctified and in a very limited sense be unholy because through ignorance or prejudice he does not receive Christ as his purifier, even so many holy people remain narrow and circumscribed and uncouth and full of prejudice, because they are encompassed with the infirmities of the flesh, and receive only a fraction of their inheritance.

It is at this point in her experience that the church discovers the vastness of her needs and the infinite abundance of her resources. The church at large needs the teaching of the text made clear to its apprehension, and pressed affectionately upon its understanding, and thundered by day and by night upon its burdened ears. Conscious that this text is true, whenever we find persons claiming a limited portion of their inheritance, we will cheerfully let them have that; but we must also press upon them the obligation to receive infinitely more.

Among the qualities invoiced to the Christian, we find pardon, purity, power; we find sonship, sustenance, comfort in sorrow, consolation, victory, and glory. These are the purchased inheritance of the church; and they are embraced in all things which belong to each individual child of God.

There is a mistaken and dangerous humility that sings,—

"Let me be little and unknown,
Loved and prized by God alone."

This sentiment may be correct in a limited sense; but there is a broad distinction between humility and indolence. God wants stalwart men in the field. The cause demands trained men, who can endure hardness as good soldiers of Jesus Christ; and he has made ample provision for growth, for training, and for achievement.

Contemplating the vastness of the divine supply, Charles Wesley sang, —

> "Let me no more in deep complaint
> My leanness! oh my leanness! cry.
> Alone consumed of pining want,
> Of all my Father's children, I.
>
> The painful thirst, the fond desire,
> Thy joyous presence shall remove;
> But my full soul shall still require
> A whole eternity of love."

"All things are yours." The provisions of the text are perfected. The resources of God belong to the Christian now; they belong to him on the basis of his personal relations to Christ. Every department of God's dominion is laid under tribute for the sustenance, culture, happiness, and progress of man, — the physical, the ethical, the intellectual, and the spiritual; yea, —

> "All the joys which mortals know,
> From God's exhaustless fountains flow."

The whole broad kingdom of nature belongs to you. Full of sustenance for your bodies, ample in its opportunities for your advancement, full of the grandest lessons of him who formed it, God speaks in the ten thousand melodious voices of nature, proclaiming his Fatherly regard.

Behold the scenes of beauty and abundance, of grandeur and sublimity, that adorn the face of nature. What displays of the divine goodness and power, what exhibitions of infinite love! The sun that mounts in golden splendor by day, and the moon that shimmers in silver radiance by night, and the stars that hold their midnight revel around the burning throne, were all made for man. Yours are the grain-scented fields, the verdant prairies, the moaning forests, the broad rivers, the foaming oceans, the thundering cataracts, the gray old hills. For you the Himalayas lift their crests of snow to greet the rising sun; and for you the Rockies stand in all their rugged grandeur, and fling back their darkening shadows from his declining ray.

To the Christian also belongs the entire realm of art. The productions of the pencil, brush, and chisel, the frescoes and carved work of ancient temple and modern gallery, are all yours, — the silent, effective auxiliaries of your aesthetic culture.

The whole unbroken domain of literature is the rightful heritage of the church. Homer and Virgil and Shakespeare and Milton, penned their glowing periods for you; and Demosthenes and Burke poured forth their fervid numbers for your advantage; and philosophers and orators of all lands, and of all the centuries, have brought their offerings to this shrine and kindled the fires of their genius for your illumination.

The entire realm of science is yours. There is no controversy between science and the gospel. Whenever there is an apparent antagonism, the truth of science is not clearly perceived, or the expositors have not correctly rendered the text. The voice of God in revelation can never contradict what he has spoken in nature. The demonstrated truths of science must be accepted, whether they harmonize with established creeds, or antagonize them. Newton and Herschel, walking among the stars, are your friends; and Agassiz and Miller, searching among the ancient formation of rocks, or in the depths of the sea, bring forth their facts for you.

All theology belongs to you. Augustine and Arminius are both dead; but the two great systems of doctrine formulated by them still survive, not as the ultimatum of theological statement, but as the scaffolding on which the student of to-day carries up his work to completeness.

All religious thought is by divine right the heritage of God's people. The fathers, before the Reformation, gave their generous contributions to this department; and Luther and Melanchthon, and Calvin and Wesley, and the vicar of Madley thought for all the ages.

The Bible unsealed, and without priestly embargo, is embraced in the "all things" that constitute the spiritual wealth of the children of God. In this sacred volume the prophets, apostles, and evangelists have recorded their glowing visions of the kingdom of God for the benefit of his subjects. For you Sinai pealed forth its prescriptive utterances, and Calvary and Olivet sang their anthems of victory. Here we behold the massive majesty of Moses; and listen to the startling descriptive periods of Job; and are amazed at the rapid, vehement utterances of Ezekiel "rushing like a fiery torrent from the hills of the Lord." We stand trembling in the fitful glare of poetic enthusiasm of David, flashing for a single moment in the glory of a triumph, and then dying away into a pitiful wail of penitential sorrow. Here we see Daniel's awful figures standing up in their stateliness, "waiting for the fulness of time;" and we behold Isaiah rushing from amid all these confused splendors, "into the Holy of Holies, to snatch a single live coal from the altar of God." Then we are thrilled and overwhelmed with the bold and incisive declarations of Peter, the grand double climaxes of Paul; and we are charmed and enraptured, and stand with uncovered brow, in the presence of the mingled rainbow glories with which the beloved disciple finally envelops the head of the man of Galilee.

To every individual Christian belongs the unexplored realm of religious experience. The Beulah land opens its portals to the adventurous feet of every child of God. Every one on the same terms may freely enter this wonderful region of mountain and valley, of field, vineyard, and landscape, adorned with odorous shrubs and trees of fragrant foliage and flora, whose pendent boughs are laden with golden and purple fruitage; beautiful land, where the saints of all the ages break their golden vials, and pour their incense like the mingled perfume of ten thousand odors on the burdened air; that mysterious land, where "the eye hath not seen nor the ear heard, neither have entered into the heart of man the things that God hath in reservation for them that love him." That illimitable region, that like an unrimmed sea stretches onward forever, which the Father hath filled with good things, and which the Spirit alone revealeth to man.

The past is yours. Its history and biography, its disasters and defeats, its victories, its scientific discoveries, its illustrious achievements, — all are yours. You cannot afford, with the reckless spirit of a free religionist, to sweep away the record of the past. You may not enter this temple, hoary and honorable with years, and with iconoclastic hand despoil its wealth of treasured good. Let us rather stand to-day, with uncovered brow, in its dim and dingy aisles, and gaze upon those sacred faces that adorn its grimy old walls, and reverently listen to the resounding footsteps and the echoing hymns of praise which proceed from the generations of worshippers that crowd its ancient altars.

But the present is yours also. Momentous period! Six thousand years of human history compress their gathered weight of responsibility into this single moment. This is the focal point of all the ages. We are standing on the advance line of opportunity. Ever- broadening fields of usefulness are now open before us; along their valleys mighty engines of progress bear their precious freight, while on every side rivers of knowledge, rising on the mountain heights of the past ages, and drawing their supply from the accumulated experience of sixty centuries, deepen and widen as they roll on, ever pouring their golden treasures at our feet.

"We are living, we are dwelling
    In a grand and awful time;
In an age on ages telling,
    When to be living is sublime.

Worlds are charging, heaven beholding
    Thou hast but one hour to fight;
Love's pure banner now unfolding,
    On, right onward to the fight.

From the crimes that men are crushing,
    War's dire curse and whiskey's wrong;
To deliver him, now rushing,
    Arm thee well; be strong, be strong."

The future is yours. Whether of storm or flood, of persecution or poverty, of success or defeat, of gray hairs, unsteady hand, faltering steps, of lingering years or premature decay, the future in its infinite series of cycles belongs to you.

You may not sit like a group of mourners about the grave of the dear dead past, nor linger aimlessly in the cosey nooks and shady arbors of the luxuriant present. The present is for preparation; the future is for achievement. If you are really worthy of the age in which you live, if you are equal to the opportunities that crowd your pathway, if the blood of a chivalrous ancestry courses untainted through your veins, you will advance to give battle to the leagued legions of evil.

If you really are consecrated to God, if you have clasped hands with the infinite One for the right, the hardest circumstance that lifts its bronzed form and flashes its lurid crest in your pathway shall crumble to dust at one stroke of your resistless power; and like as when the setting sun is overcast with the dark thunderclouds he struggles through the sulphurous gloom, and with ten thousand streams of liquid fire he melts the black destructive mass into a rosy light which from the glowing heavens smiles its triumph to the verdant earth, even so, through the sullen gloom of defeat and disaster gleams the radiant promise of the text, telling humanity amid all its sorrows and its embarrassments, of an incorrupted future which is yet all its own.

Jesus is yours— the Alpha and the Omega. The living, personal Christ *is* yours. The unmeasured depths of his love lie open to you; the infinite riches of his divine affection are subject to your command. With the living, personal Christ enthroned in your heart, you join the rapturous song:—

"Fade, fade each earthly joy;
   Jesus is mine.
Break every tender tie;
   Jesus is mine.
Dark is the wilderness,
Earth has no resting-place,
Jesus alone can bless;
   Jesus is mine.

Farewell mortality;
   Jesus is mine.
Welcome eternity;
   Jesus is mine.
Welcome, O loved and blest,
Welcome, sweet scenes of rest.
Welcome, my Saviour's breast;
   Jesus is mine."

Heaven is yours. What magic is in that word! How indescribably thrilling the train of emotions that respond to its magnetic power! How like an unfolding reality it stands as the synonym of eternal glory— stands as the only reality when the transient shall have forever faded away. When the shaded pilgrim land shall vanish before the closing eye; when the unwitnessed splendors of the celestial world shall lie around you on every side; when the veil of flesh that now darkens all the future and conceals all its glory shall fall away; when the aching heart shall be forever still; when the hands shall be gently folded above the pulseless breast; when the lashes shall be drooped for the last long slumber, and the freed spirit shall soar away to enter the unimagined joys of the heavenly home— then, and not till then, will you find remuneration for toil, and reimbursement for earthly losses. In heaven every one will find appreciation and honor for the faithful. In heaven there will be glory and dominion; there will be a throne and a sceptre for the victors of all the ages; there is the better and the enduring substance. "All things are yours; and ye are Christ's and Christ is God's;" and with this bond of omnipotence, man, redeemed and saved, is forever bound to the eternal throne.

XIV
THE SYMBOLISM OF THE TEMPLE

"And the house, when it was in building, was built of stone made ready before it was brought thither; so that there was neither hammer nor ax nor any tool of iron heard in the house, while it was in building."—I KINGS vi. 7.

THE TEMPLE AT JERUSALEM which was built by Solomon was a visible "symbol of the church of Christ." It was a complex type, representing the glory, strength, splendor, and magnificence of the church on the earth, and symbolizing the variety and beauty and perfection of the church above,— "that house not made with hands, whose maker and builder is God."

Solomon, King of Israel, was the architect and builder of the beautiful structure that stood on Mount Zion; and Jesus Christ, the Lord of glory, is the supreme architect and builder, the living head and "royal sovereign," of the spiritual habitation of the children of God.

The visible temple was situated on Mount Moriah. The significance of this name is "to see"; "the place of instruction." The name Moriah, or Moreh, embraces the root elements of the name of Jehovah. It is equivalent to "the place where God is seen and known;" the mountains of myrrh; the place of divine communion and fellowship.

The best traditions and the strongest evidences unite in support of the opinion that the temple stood near where Abraham had made preparation to sacrifice his son a thousand years before this date, and where David met and appeased the destroying angel who was visible above the threshing-floor of Oman the Jebusite.

The work of the temple was commenced in the fourth year of Solomon's reign, three years after the death of David, and four hundred and eighty years after Israel passed through the Red Sea to a life of independence and personal freedom. It was on the second day of the month of Zif, which was the second month of the sacred year, which date answers to the twenty-first day of April in the year of the world 2992. By the wisdom of Solomon and the divine direction, this stupendous edifice was erected without the sound of an axe or hammer, or any tool of iron being heard therein during the period of its construction. The stones were all hewed and squared and numbered in the quarries where they were raised by derricks prepared for that purpose. The timbers were cut and prepared in the forests of Lebanon, and conveyed by sea in floats to Joppa, and thence by land to Jerusalem. The whole superstructure was then erected by the use of wooden instruments prepared for that purpose.

When the building was finished, the whole fabric fitted so nicely and was so exact in all its parts that it appeared as if it might have been the product of some celestial genius rather than the workmanship of man.

It will be profitable to trace the analogy between the visible temple which once stood on Zion's hill, and that spiritual building, that celestial structure, being reared in the heavens, the ultimate home of the saved of all ages. (*a*) The temple at Jerusalem was composed of a great variety of material, — stones of great diversity, all of the metals known and used by man, and all the different species of valuable wood. These were brought from all the different countries of the globe. This symbolizes the heavenly temple. When it is completed it will consist of the different grades of spiritual being, — archangel and seraph, and the souls of men made perfect. But in a very particular sense it represents the different grades of the saved. The men of high degree and those of lowly birth; the men of wealth and those weary toilers from among the poor; the philosopher, with his scales weighing the atom or the mountain, and the peasant with ever increasing wonder at the productions of genius; the children of God from every nation and tribe, from every city and hamlet, — all are alike precious to Christ, and all are equally pure who enter that holy place.

But the text teaches us that the same differences of intellectual power and attainment, the same distinguishing qualities of moral power, the same diversity of taste and culture that characterize the people of God in this life, will continue to manifest their presence and power in the heavenly state. All will be alike in moral quality, all will be equally holy; for no impure thing can enter heaven.

But happiness is not dependent upon knowledge, but always arises from the moral condition of the party. Every person in heaven will be perfectly happy because they will be perfectly holy. Each one in heaven will fill some niche where he will contribute by his presence and his fitness to the general harmony and happiness of all. "There is one glory of the sun, and another glory of the moon, and another glory of the stars, and one star differeth from another star in glory," but not in starship. Thus it will be in the heavenly state, — places for all, happiness for all, employment for all, growth, progress, and improvement for all.

In this life we give and receive. We exchange thought; we bestow and receive affection; we teach and receive instruction; and all of us realize that there is a higher bliss in giving than in receiving. It will be so in heaven, because this is the primary law of our being. It has been the myth of the church throughout its history that all intellectual distinctions will be obliterated in the heavenly state. This is but an irridescent dream; such a consummation is forever made impossible by the constitution of the human mind. We concede that such might be the case if the mind perished in death and we all began anew on the other side; but if we accept the fact of man's natural immortality, we must also accept its collateral fact, — the individuality of man, — and the other fact that death is the culmination of a disaster; it is not and cannot be an agent. It cannot change anything. In view of these facts, we discover that there is no provision made anywhere for that which is lacking in natural capacity, nor for that which is forfeited by neglect or abuse. Death can have no more effect on the intellectual faculties or on the moral qualities of man, than the crossing of the equator in mid-ocean could produce upon the passengers and crew of an ocean steamer. It is a single event in the endless journey.

Suppose that to-night at exactly six o'clock some poor degraded inebriate should be converted. Fifty years of criminal dissipation have shrouded all his faculties and blunted all his sensibilities; they have incrusted his moral nature with the accumulated depravity of unbridled sensuality, and left the intellect blighted, and the spiritual nature shrivelled to a cinder. But Jesus saves, as he saved the thief on the cross; saves all there is of him; saves him perfectly. Then suppose that at the expiration of twenty-four hours this man should die. He has scarcely recovered from the surprises of his conversion until his blood-washed spirit is ushered into the presence of God, and overwhelmed with the brightness of the excellent glory. He has not had time to adjust himself to his new environments in his probational state till it suddenly closes forever, and this converted and sanctified debauchee enters upon an unchangeable state of existence in the presence of God.

Suppose, further, that at the hour that this converted criminal died, and in the same city, it should have transpired that Bishop Matthew Simpson died also; and suppose that the souls of those two parties should have arrived in heaven at the same moment. Would the simple fact that both were saved constitute them alike, intellectually and morally? Would they stand before God equal in the attainments of manhood? Would death rob the one of his wealth of religious culture, the product of his native genius and sixty years of incessant toil and achievement? Would death despoil that lofty soul of its stupendous growth, the fruitage of half a century's effort? Would the destroyer enter the very presence of God and conquer there by blotting out of existence at one fell stroke the fruitage of a lifetime devoted to God? Could God be just and rob the one that he might imburse the other for losses sustained as the prolific sequences of a life of sensuality and crime?

(*b*) The temple was composed of separate blocks of marble and individual pieces of wood, sheets of gold and loops of silver, with furniture and decorations too elaborate to name in this discourse, each made for a definite purpose, and all answering a specific end.

This celestial temple will be composed of individual Christians. Humanity is not saved by households, nor by churches. It will avail nothing to be a Methodist or a Baptist, if you are not more than a Methodist or Baptist. If you are not saved, the outward trappings of ecclesiasticism will add fierceness to your condemnation, and if you are saved it must be by the personal touch of a living Christ. No being in this universe will ever lose its individuality. This law is regnant from archangel to animalcule.

Each saved person has his work to do in the church; and if it is done and accepted of the Lord, it will fill its particular niche in the temple, and the worker will receive his reward. The gold and silver, the marble and the wood, the brass and the productions of the loom, each had its proper place. These could not change. They were utilized according to the general law of adaptation.

God designs each Christian to do his own work, first in the development of his own character, then in helping to save others. God designs every one to do his work well, and fill up perfectly the measure of his usefulness in this life that he may also shine in the brightness of his Father's glory in the upper temple.

We have a conviction that many who are obscure in this life will prove to be the finest gold there, and doubtless occupy conspicuous positions there. Lazarus went from the dog-house of the rich man to the bosom of Abraham. The gold often lies unseen in the surrounding earth, and the finest marble may be buried in the *dibris* of the quarry; but God sees the obscure ones, and he will gather them from the remotest corners of the earth, and assign them to their proper place in his temple.

(*c*) The text says these blocks of marble and beams of cedar were all prepared in the mountains and in the quarries. All the material that was used in building the temple was dressed and polished and numbered and made ready for use before it was brought to the building, and if it was not perfect it was thrown aside with the waste. There was no fitting done there. There was no omission nor delinquency corrected at the temple. There was neither hammer nor axe nor any tool of iron heard in the house while it was in building. No finishing touch was put upon any-thing that became a part of the temple or its furniture after it was brought to the building.

God teaches us by these symbols, which are far more impressive than argument, and as impregnable as logic, that all preparation for heaven is made before death. All who enter heaven are prepared for that event in this world. They are fitted for me place in that spiritual temple. There are no purgatorial fires there for the removal of lingering stains. There is no pool of Bethesda where the impotent are made strong. No mistakes will be corrected in heaven; no apologies will be made; no wrongs will be piled up within the gate waiting for redress. There will be no ad-justment of difficulties between alienated persons in the heavenly state.

The church is the workshop. The world is the forest and quarry; it is the place where the workmen of all classes and all kinds succeed or fail. The competition is open and unlimited, except by the strictest rules of the craft. "No man is crowned except he strive law-fully." It is here in the church that the rough ashlars from the quarry are all squared, polished, and num-bered; here in the mountains the beams are hewed and framed and finished, and the various metals are re-fined and shaped. It is true that in the church there is confusion and strife, there is discord and contention, there is the sharp conflict of opposing dogma, and fre-quently there is the clamor of ungodly ambition and the greed for position and for power; but the work of God goes steadily forward to its final victory.

When the temple was in process of erection there was jealousy and dissension among the workmen; there was ambition and fraud and conspiracy and murder. But when all these prepared materials were brought together, the grand superstructure rose into being without the least friction.

"Then towered the palace;
Then in awful state
The temple reared its everlasting gate.
No workman's steel,
No ponderous axes rung,
Like some tall palm, the noiseless fabric sprung.

Majestic silence! then the harp awoke,
The cymbal clanged, the deep-voiced trumpet spoke;
And Salem spread her suppliant arms abroad.
Viewed the descending flame, and blessed a present God."

Thus it is in the spiritual temple. Silently the great superstructure is being pushed up to its completeness. This is the period of preparation. The workmen have been called from refreshment to labor; the material is being prepared in all lands. When your work is finished, the carriers will remove it to its place. If it is perfect, it will pass the grand overseer; but if it is defective, it will be heaved over among the rubbish to be trodden down in the mire.

The temple at Jerusalem was typical and transient; it utterly perished; not one stone was left upon another that was not overthrown. The despoilers took up the foundations in their vain search for concealed treasure; but this spiritual temple whose glory it foreshadowed shall endure forever.

"David, the man of war,
The alien host o'erthrows;
Type of that mighty conqueror
Who trod down all his foes.
Who in his mortal days,
By having all subdued,
Heaped exhaustless stores of grace
To build the house of God,
David's immortal Son,

Magnificent in power,
Sublime on his celestial throne
He reigns for evermore.
The real Prince of Peace,
The Solomon from on high,
He rears his house of holiness,
And bids it reach the sky."

(d) This subject suggests a very personal inquiry. Will we be polished stones in this heavenly temple? Will we occupy some place in the wall, or be utilized as furniture in this celestial edifice? Will we shine with supernal brightness in some conspicuous niche, or fill some delightful alcove? Or shall we be cast off with the rejected material to perish under the feet of the workmen.

Without doubt some who are now present need the removal of some remaining prejudice; some of us need the lingering elements of selfishness eliminated from the soul, and a brighter lustre imparted to the spiritual man. The whole church needs a new baptism with the Holy Ghost, by whose silent but potential force every human being that accepts Christ is made new and fitted for use.

Beloved, "be fit for the wall; square thyself for it; polish thy spirit for it; do not be satisfied with thy present attainment. Be not content with such knowledge as is necessary to maintain thy present position; put thyself on the stretch for more; cherish the aptitudes thou findest in thyself, and it is certain thy time will come. Thou wilt not be left in the way; the builders will be glad of thee. The wall will want thee to fill a place in it as much as thou shalt need to occupy a place in the wall."

In the light of these facts we perceive that "we are laborers together with God" in the erection of this spiritual temple.

Every Christian is a laborer employed by the supreme Architect to prepare material for this stupendous edifice.

One by one the stones are being finished in the quarries. One by one the beams are being hewed and polished on the mountains. The smiths are refining and shaping the metals, and the carvers are "engraving the mystic cherubim," the stately palm, and the fair flowers, on the olive wood. The weavers and the dyers are fashioning the blue and the purple and the crimson. Every ship from the distant ports is freighted with precious material or exquisite furniture. God is building every day. Our friends are falling about us on every side, and passing to their respective places in the heavenly temple.

The stones of which the temple was built were quarried from the heart of the mountain on which the building stood. We go back in our thoughts across the gulf of three thousand years; we take our place beside the stone-cutter in the gloomy vaults a thousand feet beneath the ancient city. There, in the dimly lighted cavern, the workman wrought for years on a single stone. He did not know where it was to go, neither did he know the place it would occupy in the building. Before him was the marble, rough and irregular from the quarry, an unpolished and shapeless mass. On the trestle-board the architect had drawn the pattern into which he was to transform the irregular block.

Time sped on apace; his work was done. He put his own private mark upon it, and the carriers removed it to its place. Worn and weary, he laid down his implements of labor, and started for the light. He straightened up his bowed form; he brushed the dust and labor stain from his faded garments; he wiped the grime and sweat from his face; he went up the narrow pathway of ascent and soon stood on Mount Zion. The temple had just been completed, and its untarnished beauty gleamed and flashed in the brightness of an Oriental sun.

When the day of dedication came, he followed the

multitude into the house; and when the glory of the Lord filled the temple, he beheld in the archway just over the mercy-seat the stone on which he had wrought so many years. It was there, a lasting memorial of his fidelity, giving its silent but emphatic testimony to his skill, publishing his fame to the generations of zealous worshippers that should seek that altar through all the coming years.

It was enough for him. The labor and the darkness of the quarries were all forgotten in the triumphs of that glad hour. The weariness was all gone. The thrill of rapture, and the pulsation of power, and energy of returning youth, filled all his being; and when the organ pealed forth its sacred melody he joined with the multitude in the chorus. Then—

"Each pillar of the temple rang;
   The trumpets sounded loud and keen;
And every minstrel blithely sang,
   With harps and cymbals oft between.

And while those minstrels sang and prayed,
   The mystic cloud of glory fell;
That shadowy light, that splendid shade,
   In which Jehovah deigns to dwell.

And thrice resplendent from above
   The cloud of glory beamed;
And with unmingled awe and love
   Each beating bosom teemed.

They bowed them on the spacious floor
   With heaven-averted eye;
And blessed his name, who deigned to pour
   His presence from on high."

Beloved, we are now in the quarries. We are beneath that city whose foundation is Christ, and whose duration is eternal. We are at work on the material for that spiritual building which the supremer Architect of the universe is rearing in the skies. Jesus is the true model. He is not simply an example to humanity; he is the true model of manhood. We are not commanded to act like him, but we are to be like him.

The word of God is our guide; it is our light; "sole torch in the darkness of this world." By the light of this sacred volume, and by the agency of the Holy Ghost, the toilers in the church are to transform the shapeless blocks of a sinful and sensual humanity that lie bruised and broken all about them into symmetrical and polished Christians, into perfect stones for the celestial temple.

In the divine plan, the method is from the inception to the finish by successive stages. God works upward from the atom to the planet, to the system and the universe; from the material to the spiritual; from the ordinary or coarser to the refined and sublimated; from the sinner to the victorious saint— by successive stages.

"The temple once which brightly shone
    On proud Moriah's rocky brow,
Not there doth God erect his throne,
    And build his place of beauty now.

The sunbeam of the orient day
    Saw naught on earth so bright and fair;
But desolation swept away,
    And left no trace of glory there.

But God who raised that chiselled stone
    Now builds upon a higher plan;
And rears the columns of his throne,
    His temple, in the heart of man.

O man! O woman! know it well.
    Nor seek elsewhere his place to find,

That God doth in his temple dwell, —
The temple of a holy mind."

"Ye are laborers together with God." "Ye are God's husbandry. Ye are God's building." The time is near when the workmen will be called from labor to refreshment and reward. Each piece on which you have wrought, bearing the impress of your own private signature, will soon be carried to its place. Then the skilled workman will brush the dust from his garments, and wipe the sweat from his brow, and lay down forever the implements of his toil; and, standing erect, run up with joy the shining way, and join the multitude on the sea of glass.

I pray that when you are there you may see the spiritual substance on which you have wrought for the whole period of your lives, radiant and lustrous with beauty, conspicuous in some select niche of the great temple. Then when the great organ of eternity shall peal forth its notes of praise, and the garnered saints of all the ages shall unite in the "song of Moses and the Lamb," we may join in that paean that shall roll through the vaulted heavens and fill perfectly the measure of his glory who "redeemed us with his own precious blood," and saved you by the agencies of the Holy Ghost.

XV
THE FACT OF POWER, OR FORCE AND PHENOMENA

"And suddenly there came a sound from heaven as of a rushing mighty wind, and it filled all the house where they were sitting. And there appeared unto them cloven tongues like as of fire, and it sat on each of them. And they were all filled with the Holy Ghost, and began to speak with other tongues, as the Spirit gave them utterance." — ACTS ii. 2, 4.

THERE WERE TWO EXTERNAL manifestations intimately connected with the opening of the gospel dispensation. There was a sound, and a light. The one saluted the ears of the disciples, the other was visible to their eyes.

The sound was like the rushing of a mighty wind. It was not a wind, it was like the rushing of a mighty wind. It was the noise that was like the wind; and it was the noise that filled the house.

But neither the noise nor the light was the Holy Ghost. In the history of the inauguration of the gospel there is the constant recognition of two aspects of propagandism, — force and phenomena.

As Jesus came "eating and drinking," conforming always to the legal environments of his humanity, so the gospel conforms to the philosophical order of the universe, — that force and phenomena are relative and inseparable parts of all achievement, and that in the gospel, as in the physical world, the force is antecedent to all of that which is seen or heard or felt. Force is the active cause of all phenomena; force produces all that is seen or heard or felt.

In the Pentecostal inauguration there was the "rushing sound" and the "flashing light." In connection with these manifestations there are two facts stated: (1) "They were all filled with the Holy Ghost." (2) "They began to speak and testify," There are two aspects of nature, — force and phenomena; and there are two aspects of the Christian religion, force and phenomena.

We state a primary fact in all philosophy, that there was never any phenomena in any department of the universe except as the product of antecedent force.

Force is power in motion or in exercise. It may be an army. It may be an agent, such as water-power, steam, or electricity. It may be intellectual or psychological force, such as an argument or an appeal to the conscience or to the passions. Force may be purely physical, as indicated in the change that takes place between two inert bodies, putting them in motion, and bringing them to a position of rest after changing their relation to each other.

Power and force are not the same. Power expresses the idea of capability, or the measurement of capability. But force is power in operation; it is the measure of exerted power. This is illustrated by the pressure of the air at the earth's surface, which is equal to a force of fourteen pounds to the square inch. The capability of the air is much greater than that. That represents the measure of its normal manifestation. Any departure above or below that point is a departure from the standard manifestation, and is subject to the will and laws of the sovereign Ruler of the universe. The gospel is under the same authority, and accomplishes its mission subject to the same law.

On the day of Pentecost there was the audible and visible manifestation. There was also the filling with the Holy Ghost; and after that the testifying. But back of all that was seen and heard and achieved, there was an adequate force.

While these external manifestations were producing their impressions upon the senses, something transpired in those disciples. A mighty revolution was wrought in the substance and fabric of each soul. After that event not one of that company was like his former self. Their whole being was sublimated, and their lives became suddenly exalted. They were possessed of a new energy; new conceptions of the nature and character of God were given them; new purposes and plans rose into being, and this life seemed at once invested with a new significance.

These disciples became witnesses to the ultimate power of the gospel. These disciples had witnessed the miracles of Jesus Christ; they had heard his promise of the Holy Ghost, and had received and believed the promise. But now he was come, the promise was fulfilled in them, and now they were divinely qualified to open the campaign for the subjugation of the world.

The force that wrought all these changes was the Holy Ghost. It was not wrought by the Word alone, the gospel was not yet written; it was not simply the influx of new ideas, nor the impulse of a new love. It was the achievement of the Holy Ghost, who in his divine personality is the spiritual force of the gospel; and the evangelism of all ages and all places is helpless in proportion to the extent that the other gospel factors are emphasized to the exclusion of the Holy Ghost.

Philosophy demonstrates the fact, and universal experience confirms it, that there never was in nature nor in grace any phenomena, except there was antecedent to it a sufficient force. The sunbeam is a force, a secondary force; moisture and grass in the soil are forces. The growth of grasses and grains and trees and animals is phenomena.

Life is a primary force. Twenty-five years ago it was taught in the schools that life was the product of force. By investigation we perceived the error, and the thought of to-day has changed to correspond with the facts.

Favorable conditions augment force and make it efficient. The leverage of the overshot wheel, the belt and pulley, are all agencies for augmenting force. At a certain marble ledge grooves are cut in the rock, at the top, of the proper thickness; in these grooves are driven small hardwood wedges; when the rain comes these wedges absorb the water, swell, and burst the ledge to the bottom. Gunpowder is stored power. It becomes force only when it lets go, when it changes relations. It is force that sends the bullet to the mark, but the death of the animal is phenomena.

The Holy Ghost is force; the Christian life is force. Christian growth and enterprise and achievement are phenomena. When the Holy Ghost enters a human soul there is a new class of emotions, a new series of phenomena, — conviction of sin accompanied with tears and prayers, cries for mercy, pardon, shouts of joy, and exhibitions of enthusiasm. All of these are legitimate Christian phenomena. But these are not all— they are only the beginning. Christian experience is an unfolding series, whose ultimate climax lies far in advance of present attainments. While there are only two crises in full salvation, religious experience has its epochs and goes on forever. Its full tide is reached in the Pentecostal baptism, but it does not cease there.

Religious experience is fellowship with God, and should continue without interruption.

No one was ever converted without the exerting of force, the manifestation of divine force. The gospel "is the power of God [exerted] unto salvation to every one that believeth." Not one soul was ever sanctified without force. Sanctification is not the influx of more life; it is not a process of enlargement; it is a refining process. "The Lord will sit as a refiner and purifier of silver, and he will purify the sons of Levi." Sanctification completes the salvation by eliminating the alloy of remaining impurity, and by this act the soul is prepared for greater utilization. One ounce of water converted into steam lifts one ton a foot high. The steam is force; the lifting is phenomena. In this case there is not any increase of water, but only a changed condition. When the conditions exist, the lifting is easy and natural.

The love of Christ shed abroad in the soul sublimates, refines, and energizes the entire church, and the phenomena appear. Sunday-schools, mission stations, institutions of Christian education, are all the product of force. The Christian civilization in which we live cannot exceed the force of Christian thought operative in it, and could not survive one decade the withdrawal of the Christian forces from the world. In the processes of nature, force is antecedent to and precedes all phenomena. The same is true in Christian achievement; and it is a felony on the resources of the church, and high treason against the gospel, to substitute a manufactured enthusiasm for the potentiality of the Holy Ghost. But we discover one more fact: in the physical world force is subject to the laws of environment. It is made efficient by good conditions. It is made available and powerful by carefully prepared adjustment.

My first observation of applied power was in a mill for cutting lumber. It was built on a small stream, and the saw was attached directly to the wheel. Each revolution of the wheel made two strokes of the saw, one up and one down. But a gentleman bought the mill, and removed all the machinery, put in an "overshot" wheel, and adjusted the power with proper gearing, so that with much less than one-half the quantity of water one revolution of the wheel produced two hundred and fifty strokes of the saw.

The same law is regnant in the realm of grace, and the success of the church and the salvation of the world turns on this fact. It is not more life the Christian needs, but better conditions, and the proper adjustment to the source of all power. All converted persons have life. The wholly sanctified Christian cannot have more life than the other; but the soul is refined, purified, the water of life is vaporized, the entire being is fused into steam.

This is God's method for the salvation of mankind; it involves the adjustment of the church to the source of all power. The divine command to "tarry" was as authoritative and as obligatory as the command to "go." It is because the personal Holy Ghost is the force back of all, and in all, religious enterprise, the force without which no success is possible, because he is the divine force, that failure characterizes all effort where he is ignored or misapprehended. Great enterprises are begotten of the Spirit. The baptism of the Holy Ghost came upon three women at a camp-meeting in Ohio. They were the representatives of different branches of the church. They obeyed the divine impulse, and in a short period of time ten thousand women were praying in the saloons of America, and out of this spontaneous movement grew the most potent organization in the history of reformations.

For twenty years an invalid girl lay helpless upon her couch; she had neither money nor scholastic attainments; God healed her malady, and gave her the Holy Ghost, and in ten years fifty thousand railroad men were converted to God through her labors.

For seven days Israel marched and blew their trumpets; then they shouted with a great shout, and God let slip one single pulsation of his power, and the walls of the besieged city fell flat to the ground. For seven days the one hundred and twenty tarried before God until the force came, and three thousand laid their honors at Jesus' feet in one day.

These principles are incontrovertible, and if the church will conform to the divine order, straightway something will transpire. Let all Protestantism conform to the divine plan, and there will be no need of "civic organizations," and the church will not need to abandon its legitimate work to lead the partisan hosts of the state in the enforcement of law. Let the baptism of the Holy Ghost come upon the pulpit, and ministers will not need to turn detectives, nor visit places of infamy to procure testimony against criminals. God calls to-day louder than thunder from the vaulted sky. It is criminal to disregard him. Get the force, and the phenomena will occur at once.

The force which gave the infant church the victory is an essential part of the gospel. It was a specific, definite manifestation of power. It was for a specific purpose; it was to cleanse and empower. This Pentecostal manifestation was years after most of them were converted. It was a second distinct crisis. I would not dare to assume that none of the three thousand converts were wholly sanctified the same day they were converted. That would have been the natural order of procedure; that was the proper time for such work; the tide was moving that way; that was a holiness meeting, a second crisis meeting; it was a live church waiting in holy expectation for the coming of the Holy Ghost. As the giving of the law was fifty days after the scenes of the Passover night and the tragedies of the Red Sea, and commemorated an event that transpired after the yoke of bondage was forever broken, it could not by any means be a part of the deliverance.

The name Pentecost fixes the date forever, and makes it a second event. The Hebrews kept it sacred, and celebrated it as a distinct event for fifteen hundred years. With them it was always an event that came fifty days after the Passover. Jesus observed carefully the same order.

At the Pentecostal feast the Jews offered the first- fruits of the wheat harvest, besides which they brought to the temple an offering entirely different from the Paschal Lamb. They presented seven lambs of that year, one calf, and two rams, for a burnt-offering, and a goat for a sin-offering. The record says, "It was a holy convocation, and a statute forever."

The inauguration of the gospel dispensation by the Pentecostal manifestation is an illustration of the universal fact that obedient waiting secures the divine fulfilment of the promise and the manifestation of the divine power. No individual, no church, ever did or ever will secure this power while antagonizing the divine order. Pentecost is for the church; and "ye must be born again" is still the voice of Jesus to sinners. It echoes down the ages, startling the legalist and the unregenerate from their sleep of death. But the same authoritative, "Tarry ye at Jerusalem," salutes the church. Wait until the fire falls from the divine altar.

It is as much the duty of the church to obey the divine command and receive the fiery baptism, as it is for sinners to repent and be converted; and it is treason against God, and conspiracy against the church, for men clad in sacerdotal authority to mislead and embarrass the multitude upon this subject.

The spiritual force of the church is the measure of its aggressive power in all fields; and an unbaptized church can never succeed against the combined oppositions of this age. Why should the church refuse the Pentecostal preparation? What substitute have these leaders for the fiery baptism? Is the Holy Ghost divorced from Christ?

Is the Pentecostal preparation which Jesus bade the infant church wait for of no avail now? Can the church hope for the divine favor while it disregards the divine method of procedure? Was there ever a true zeal that was not begotten of the Holy Ghost? Is there any other empowering agency? Can there be a well-directed effort that does not fully recognize the Holy Ghost in his divine personality and in his correct relations to his organic church? The lack of this recognition involves the absence of spiritual power. No person can consecrate his money or his time to God who does not first give himself to God. The giving of a pittance or of a large donation to relieve a troubled conscience is an offering made to self, a sweet sop to bribe the awakened conscience to rest. Even the devotion of the labors of a lifetime to the achievements of the church, without the surrender of the soul to God, is only a hecatomb upon the altar of personal ambition. It is only when a saved church, a spirit-baptized church, invades the world, that the victory of him who conquered the world and the devil two thousand years ago becomes an experimental fact in history and experience, and the world lays its honors at Jesus' feet.

What more can I say to inspire your courage or hasten your action? How swift the years are rolling! Soon the shades of night will gather darkly over the field, and shut out this generation of workers, and terminate their labors forever. The voices from the past, the echoing shouts from the Pentecostal chamber in the holy city, urge to better effort; the cry of despair from a thousand millions of lost souls appeals to the church to-day in the name of the world's Redeemer.

Go to the grave of Wesley and commune with his dust. Lay your hand on the hallowed urn that contains the ashes of the sainted Fletcher. Let them speak to you from the tomb. Listen to the sighing of the ocean, hear the spirit voices of Coke and Cookman wailing up from its myste-

rious depths. Uncover your heads and listen to the sough-
ing of the east wind, and catch the dying words of Bishop
Wiley from the Celestial Empire, or the eloquent periods
of Bishop Kingsley from the palm-groves of Syria. If we
could be still long enough in the mad strife for wealth
and position, we would hear the dying groan of the lost
millions of humanity, and feel the ebbing pulse of the
Nazarene as he poured his life-blood into the veins of an
expiring world; and we would start from our spell of self-
gratification as if touched by an electric battery.

XVI
CONDITIONS OF SPIRITUAL POWER

"And let it be, when thou hearest the sound of a going in the tops of the mulberry trees, that then thou shalt bestir thyself: for then shall the Lord go out before thee, to smite the host of the Philistines." —ii. SAMUEL v. 24.

"But ye shall receive power, after that the Holy Ghost is come upon thee." — ACTS i. 8.

THESE SCRIPTURES BOTH teach the same important truth; they reveal and emphasize the invisible spiritual force of the gospel, the supernatural element that always accompanies the word of God.

The spirit that disturbed the foliage of the mulberry trees, and led Israel to victory, was the same spirit that came like "a rushing mighty wind," which gave the tongues of fire and the Pentecostal anointing.

These texts both point to the one central source of all power, and indicate the conditions on which the individual and the whole church may obtain this power.

For the last two decades, the supreme question with

the church at large has been: "How shall we obtain power to do the work committed to our care? How shall we secure the end for which we labor." How shall we know and keep the conditions of power?"

In the course of our ministry we have come in contact with all classes of Christian workers, and with all classes of those who do absolutely nothing. We have clasped hands with those who are striving to do the whole and perfect will of God, and we have looked into the leaden eyes of the unsaved and perishing thousands who profess to be Christians but have no conception of obligation or privilege, who are drifting carelessly down the stream, or floating in the stagnant waters of indifference undisturbed by calm or storm, and will remain so until they suddenly plunge into the abyss of the lost, when their dying gurgle will become as audible as a peal of thunder from a clear sky.

If we are responsible beings, God cannot use us as a surgeon uses an instrument. We are volitional beings; we have jurisdiction over our selfhood; we decide all moral and religious questions; we determine all destinies; we are "co-workers with God" in the great enterprise of salvation. We grow weary of the perpetual imbecility that talks of Christians as "humble instruments." Christians are responsible factors in all the movements of the divine government. Christians are instrumentalities; they are agencies by which the Divine Father accomplishes his work among men. And it is because of this fact that God has made known and definitely specified the conditions upon which all necessary power may be obtained now, to give the victory to his people.

How shall we obtain power. What mysteries have been woven about this question by the multitude who serve at God's altar, with the veil still over their face, who profess to break the bread of life to the perishing, but have not yet eaten of it themselves!

We have heard men pray for power until they were completely exhausted, and it never dawned on their obtuse minds that power was contingent upon their personal relations to God, and that as responsible beings they had entire jurisdiction over their own personal relations to him.

The church in all its branches has not yet learned the significance of the Master's words: "All power is given unto me in heaven and in earth. Go ye therefore, and teach all nations… and, lo, I am with you alway, even unto the end of the world."

This scripture teaches us that the crucified Christ is the source of all power; that he who built the universe for his own glory, and organized the church as his own bride, — "Jesus Christ, the same yesterday, to-day, and forevermore," the personal Saviour, not dead, but alive from the dead, High Priest of humanity forever, — is in his church for grand achievement; and that where there is no supernatural power, and sinners are not saved, and believers are not sanctified, some doctrine or rite or theory has been substituted for the personal Christ, or the impersonal forces of nature have been substituted for the Holy Ghost, and enthroned upon its fireless altar.

When the church as a unit or in a large degree in the aggregate of its great membership shall accept the Holy Ghost, not merely as a doctrine, a theory, or an adjunct to their personal ambition, but as the source of all power, and receive power by accepting him, something will occur speedily. No church or person ever did, none ever will, receive the divine power, who does not with clean hands, and pure motives enter into fellowship with Christ.

Men affect humility and zeal, and entreat for the *influence* of the Holy Ghost. The Holy Ghost is promised in person only; we cannot expect his manifestation where we overlook his divine personality. No individual or church can obtain power, that is not willing to receive a personal Christ, and become subordinate to him. The church must conform to the divine order.

There are some primary facts that are essential to the proper understanding of this subject:—

1. God is always ready. There is no scripture nor reason, for the assumption that God is not now ready for a great manifestation of his power, that he has appointed a definite time far in advance of the present. It is our boast that the atonement is complete. We have for one hundred and fifty years emphasized the doctrine of the personality and presence of the Holy Ghost, and yet, so completely has the old dogma of "God's own good time" possessed the church, that every effort is paralyzed, and every purpose neutralized. We pray earnestly for power, but quiet our conscience and our energies by assuming, "that his own good time is not now." We assume a comatose state of indifference, and nothing is accomplished. We look down the dimly lighted but densely crowded, avenues of a thousand years, and see whole generations go down to ruin, and no effort made for their recovery on the assumption that "God's good time has not yet arrived. But the Book says, "This is the accepted time, and now is the day of salvation;" and humanity's only time is now, either for salvation or labor.

2. It is assumed that zeal is a condition of power. No greater delusion exists. Zeal is not a condition of power; zeal is not a primary condition of success. Again and again we are exhorted to "be in earnest," and are assured that earnestness is a condition of success.

The pseudo evangelist, with a limp Bible and a soul more limp than the flexible book in his hand, rants and attitudinizes and prates of "the influence of the Holy Ghost," while he has no knowledge whatever of his personality or deity. Zeal without power makes a bigot of one man and a fanatic of another.

3. Christian work is not a condition of power. Action,

whether in the domain of matter or spirit, is always one of the possibilities of antecedent power. Jesus always conformed to the divine order of things. He knew that power from on high was necessary to prepare the church for fruitful action.

We have listened again and again to the delusive utterances of the pulpit: "If you want the baptism with the Holy Ghost, go to work for God." But there is not an intimation in the Bible that God ever promised the Holy Ghost to any being in the world as a remuneration for toil, or for sacrifice, or in exchange for noble gifts for his treasury. But the divine order is the reverse of all these. Amid all the conflicting theories that have perplexed the church, we still hear the voice of the Master echoing down the centuries, rising above the din of error, above the clamor of compromise and concession. Clear and strong it salutes our ears, as distinctly as it fell upon the ears of the disciples at the first: "Tarry ye at Jerusalem, until ye be endued with power from on high." "But ye shall obtain power after that the Holy Ghost is come upon you."

4. God knows when the church is prepared for work. He will not trust a person or a church with power that will not comply with the divinely specified conditions of power.

5. Time given to the right kind of preparation, is gain in time and results. The command is twofold — "tarry," "go." The one is as obligatory as the other. God said to David, Wait yonder on your arms until the hoofs of God's cavalry disturb the foliage of the mulberry trees; but when the token comes, when the rustling foliage announces the presence of God, "Then shalt thou bestir thyself."

These divine commands are based on a true philosophy which is illustrated in every department of society. The student must master the primary lessons as the only passport to more mature scholarship. The incipient lawyer pores over the musty pages of Blackstone and the intricate processes of Greenleaf; he must master these or utterly fail of success.

The medical student is forbidden by penal statute from trifling with the life and health of the people. Weary months amid the odors of the dissecting-room, with knife and microscope, nightly vigils in the various wards of the great hospitals, fit him for his work, because obedience to law is the royal road to success.

It cost Herschel years of study and mints of money to construct his telescope; but when it was completed he walked like a native among the constellations, and was on speaking terms with the distant stars.

The Saviour of the world passed through thirty years of preparatory work before he could enter the priest's office; then followed three years of obedient work before he was prepared to die. And when he had done this, "He offered himself once for all;" and when the preparatory work was completed, he could save to the uttermost in a minute. And when he went back to the Father, he sent the Holy Ghost into the church to carry forward the work to the end of time; and the church is the responsible organic agency through which the world is to be saved.

The philosophy of religious power may be further illustrated by a familiar fact in nature. The water in a mountain stream, when raised by a dam to a proper height, is a source of power. Judiciously focalized and applied, it may whirl a thousand spindles, and drive an hundred looms, and make all the valley pulsate with industry and prosperity. The power is not in the machinery, it is not in the great wheel; the wheel is the point of contact where the power communicates its force to the machinery. The power is not primarily in the water; water is an agency of power. But power is always dependent upon the relation of things. There is no manifestation of power except when the dam is full; and the higher the water rises above the wheel, and the broader its surface and greater its volume, the greater will be its force upon the wheel. But the effect upon the machinery is always in proportion to the volume of water and the leverage of the wheel; and then, there can be no motion till the machinery is adjusted and the connection established at the proper point of contact.

The power that is to save this world is not in the church; it is not alone in the written Word; it is not in the ordinances nor ecclesiastical polity of the church, nor in the scholastic attainments, eloquence, or personal magnetism of the preacher. The power *is God*, — Father, Son, and Holy Ghost — and when the correct relations between God and the soul are established, full salvation is the result. Philosophers deify force; they make everything to depend on force. But force is only the outgoing of a personal God; the manifestation of himself in the realm of nature or of grace. Scientists speak of power, but cannot tell whence it cometh or whither it goeth. They speak of the power of cohesion, of attraction, of gravitation. What is cohesion or attraction, but matter obeying the fiat of Jehovah? And gravitation is nothing but the infinite God drawing all things toward himself.

Jesus said to the disciples, "All power in heaven and in earth is given unto me." If he told the truth, he upholds all things, sustains all things, embellishes all, beautifies all, adorns all, and saves to the uttermost every soul that submits to his authority.

For a thousand ages the stream rolled on quietly to the sea, rushed through the canyon, or lounged in the marshes and bayous to generate contagion. It was powerless for good until it was mastered and managed, till it was focalized, harnessed, and directed by man. The same law of focalization and direction applies to religious agencies. God has placed at the disposal of the church all power in heaven and in earth; but the church remains helpless in the presence of its foes, because it does not know and obey the law of the divine empowering. The great body of Protestantism is like Samson with his locks shaven, and his eyes punctured, and brazen manacles upon his limbs, grinding in the mills for the amusement of his foes, while the Niagaras of power are thundering all around. God not only demands obedience to the law of power in general terms, but he requires conformity to that particular law through which he communicates his power to the church — faith, obedience, purity, power. These are inseparable; they constitute a royal highway to victory. Our waiting is not for God to accumulate power; the divine Father is waiting for the church to separate itself from all impurity, from all deceitful and superficial methods, and submit to him completely. The degree of purity in the church is the measure of the divine indwelling, and constitutes the standard of spiritual power.

As the strength of the church is only the aggregate of individual power, in order to reach the grandest possible results, each individual member must so adjust himself to the divine personality that the life and energy which are in Christ, the vine, will permeate, vitalize, and make fruitful the individual branches. This willing, cheerful, unyielding obedience of the centres of influence in the church is the one grand essential to triumphant power.

The church as a body may have become feeble, but Christ has not abandoned the mediatorial throne. All that Christianity has ever done it can do now; all that was ever possible to it by divine affiliation is possible now. It is as absurd to think of omnipotence becoming feeble, as it is to dream of omnipotence being increased in power at some time in the distant future.

It is high time that we put away our statistics and ceased to comfort ourselves with the achievements of past ages. It is time the church ceased to strain its vision to catch the glory of celestial wonders, when the Saviour shall come again, and give honor to the Holy Ghost who is now here in the church, and only wants personal recognition, and the right of way, that he may turn loose upon the church and upon the world the full blaze of Pentecostal fire. All that Christianity needs now is a church that believes in the Holy Ghost, enjoys full salvation experimentally, and has the courage to push its triumphs everywhere. Douglas bore with him to the holy sepulchre, the heart of Bruce preserved in a golden casket; and when the strife was most severe, when the conflict was the hottest, when his wavering lines were breaking, and his soldiers were being overwhelmed by superior numbers, when the very stones seemed to turn into armed Mussulmans and cover all the mountain, he threw it forward with a shout. "Onward, heart of Bruce!" The effect was like magic; a new power possessed the heroic band; and with clash of steel and victor's song the crescent went down before the ensign of the cross.

We carry not the heart of a dead prince, but the person of a living king. To-day God bids the church advance. His voice rises distinctly above the confusion, above the strifes and conflicts, of this eventful period. Onward, ye victorious host!

If we succeed, we must obey God. If we are in the line of duty, the power may come upon us; but it is more probable, that it will fall upon the obstacles to be overcome, and remove them from the way. It may be twofold; it may come upon the laborers to empower them, and upon the foes to confound and destroy them.

When Gideon went out with his lamps and trumpets, God smote his foes. It was his part to obey God, to break the pitcher, to cry out, and sound the trumpet; all the rest of the victory belonged to God.

When God bade David fetch a compass, and by a strategic movement reach the mulberry-trees, he also bade him wait there, until the heliograph from the throne, should call to the battle.

David obeyed God; but those moments of waiting were moments of awful suspense. Indifference was an impossibility at that time. No committees were needed to plan amusements for the army. Every muscle and nerve trembled with intense expectancy. His hand grasped the cutlass and spear with sinews of steel. His ear was turned attent toward the mulberry-trees; and when the rustling foliage announced the presence of God he was ready to run; and the Lord smote the Philistine host, and their carcasses and the spoil, strewed all the plain from Geba to Gazer.

The week of prayer spent in the upper room was for human preparation. I have tried in vain to modernize that eventful period of waiting. As the prophetic moment drew near, every heart throbbed with the wildest anticipation of the coming glory. That was the pivotal moment of all the ages — the first prophetic promise pointed to that time. The scenes of Calvary and Olivet renewed the promise and pledged its fulfilment; and when the baptism came the infant church was at once prepared for victory over the hosts of sin; and now, —

> "The rolling year brings back the time.
> With blessed joys replete,
> When on the waiting Church came down
> The Holy Paraclete.
>
> The fire in quivering tongues of flame
> Descending sat on each;
> To fill with fervency of love
> And fluency of speech.
>
> Swiftly and straight each tongue of flame
> Through cloud and breeze unwavering came,
> And darted to its place of rest
> On some meek brow, of Jesus blest.

Nor fades it yet that living gleam,
And still those lambent lightnings stream.
Where'er the Lord is, there are they,
In every heart that gives him room;
They light his altar every day,
Zeal to inflame, and sin consume."

XVII
THE WHAT, THE WHEN, AND THE HOW OF HOLINESS

"Now ye are clean through the word which I have spoken unto you." —JOHN xv. 3.

"And God, which knoweth the hearts, bare them witness, giving them the Holy Ghost, even as he did unto us; and put no difference between us and them, purifying their hearts by faith." —ACTS xv. 8, 9.

THE DOCTRINE AND EXPERIENCE of heart purity are inseparable from the gospel. Holiness and heart purity are synonymous terms; they signify the same thing. Holiness lies back of all that is said or seen. It embraces the why of all doctrine and all theology. "Be ye holy, for the Lord your God am holy." God is holy; and man is his child, and can never be happy anywhere until he is made holy. God made man holy at the first, and he corrupted himself by sinning. After that, Jesus Christ "Redeemed him by his own blood," and provided for his complete restoration to the favor of God.

This complete renewal embraces three aspects or

phases: Pardon, life, and purity. The apostasy embraces guilt, spiritual death, and moral defilement.

These three aspects of experience, — pardon, life, and purity, — each perfect in itself, constitute the experience of full salvation as taught by the doctrinal standards of the Methodist Church.

These two texts of scripture are addressed exclusively to the church. They can have no primary application to unconverted persons. Jesus was talking to the disciples about purification; he said, "Now in the Christian dispensation ye are made clean by the word which I have spoken unto you." The subject of the conversation was, "How to cleanse converted persons from some element or quality of uncleanness remaining in them after their conversion."

We shall not be so bold as to call it "depravity," for some have recently discovered that there is no element of uncleanness in depravity. But I take sides with Jesus in this conflict. He says, "Blessed are the pure in heart." And then he says to the disciples, that as high priest of humanity he is the efficient and authoritative purifier.

The disciples were all Jews, and were familiar with the method of cleansing in the Jewish service. They knew also the difference between creating an object and the cleansing of the same object from any defilement it might contract.

In the old dispensation, purification was a rite performed by the high priest. He sprinkled the blood and the watery ablution, and then pronounced the defiled person clean. Jesus called their attention to the fact that the Aaronic priesthood was typical, and merged in him; that he was the end of the law for righteousness; that the whole Jewish economy merged in him; and he thereby became the high priest of humanity forever. And having shed his own blood, — sprinkled it once for all, — and having sent the Holy Ghost into the world, he now exer-

cised his kingly authority and bade the offending uncleanness depart from the soul; and, like Lazarus in the
grave, it hears and obeys. It appears to me that Jesus anticipated the issues of this hour. It is assumed by those
who are offended at the bare suggestion of a second crisis in full salvation, that there is no possibility for a second crisis, because there is nothing unclean in depravity.
Consequently there can be no crisis. Jesus did not call it
depravity, but called it uncleanness. And he affirms that
there are three stages of Christian life: (1) In Christ in a
fruitless condition; (2) in Christ in a fruit-bearing condition; (3) in Christ in a purified and more fruitful condition. Christ also said, "He that hath the Son hath life."
We find from the statement of Jesus, and from our own
personal experience, that life is found existing with a diseased condition of the soul as certainly as it is, with a
diseased condition of body.

Jesus plainly says there are three stages of spiritual
progress: Life without fruitage, life with fruitage, and a
purified life with a more abundant fruitfulness. Every
Christian occupies a place in one of these classes. Jesus
further says that the cleansing is essential to successful
fruitage. Luke was no fanatic. Next to Paul he was one of
the most excellent scholars of that period, and he supports all that I have said. Luke records the fact, that there
were certain conservative teachers at that date, and they
came down to Antioch, and declared their adherence to
Judaism, declaring it essential to salvation.

The conflict was on; the vital question had to be settled.
Jesus had said that Judaism was merged into him, that
he was high priest of the gospel dispensation; and purification was accomplished by the high priest of this dispensation, the same as the high priest of the old dispensation served for that purpose.

Luke says that when those disturbers of the church
came to Antioch and promulgated their heresy, the

apostles came together in convention to consider the
matter, — Paul and Barnabas and Peter and the lesser
lights of that brilliant constellation, — and when the subject was fully discussed, Peter arose, and said unto them,
"Men and brethren, ye know how that a good while ago
God made choice that the Gentiles by my mouth should
hear the word of the gospel, and believe. And God which
knoweth the hearts, bare them witness, giving them the
Holy Ghost, even as he did unto us; and put no difference between us and them, in that he purified their hearts
by faith. Now therefore why tempt ye God, by putting a
yoke on the necks of the disciples which neither our fathers nor we were able to bear?"

The subject embraced in the text is purity. How does a
believing soul become pure? The necessity of heart purity as the essential preparation for entering heaven, all
admit. It is alike apparent, from reason and scripture. It
is advocated by some of the civic organizations, and is
one of the tenets of the Universalist church; and backsliders and indifferent Christians of all denominations
expect to receive dying grace on their dying bed.

But holiness of heart is not a matter of taste or expediency; it is not optional with any man. God commands,
"Be ye holy;" and he accompanies the command with
the authoritative declaration, "For without holiness no
man shall see the Lord."

When we speak of purity, we do not mean pardon, nor
regeneration, nor maturity of Christian character; all of
these have their respective places in the Christian system. But we speak of cleanness; of the removal of some
defilement from converted persons, which Jesus said was
done by him, on account of his priestly merit, and in the
exercise of his divine authority.

This state of entire purity is a primary principle of
the gospel, and a fundamental tenet of Methodism. It
is this that distinguishes Wesleyanism from the

Antinomian doctrine. In the Augustinian system we are taught that the uncleanness remains regnant and co-operative till death; the two natures, sin and holiness, dwelling together, — divine twins, one with its origin in heaven, begotten of the Holy Ghost, the other arising from the other place, begotten of the adversary, and yet by divine arrangement co-workers, joint instrumentalities, in the achievement of human salvation. According to Methodist theology and the doctrine of Jesus, as stated in the text, purity should be one of the early stages in Christian experience.

This entire cleansing involves a second crisis.

Entire sanctification implies two features: —

(1) "To set apart for holy uses" — "To dedicate to a holy purpose." This embraces the human side of the work. It is all included in the term "Consecration." This is the work of the seeker after purity. It implies the surrender of the whole man to God. It is submission to the divine order of things, the proper direction of all the forces, powers, capabilities, passions, possessions, plans, purposes, and person, for his ownership and use.

(2) The second aspect of this work signifies "To make holy; "to purify and make clean something which is now in existence. It never signifies to create.

The cleansing is God's own specific work. No other being in the universe can make a human soul clean that has been defiled by sin. Three hundred years before Moses was born, the Patriarch declared that no being could bring a clean thing out of an unclean substance.

Thus we find that whatever may be the nature and extent of this impurity, it is overcome by the priestly merit of the Redeemer's blood, and the efficacious energy of the Holy Ghost.

The time for this experience we have said is soon after conversion. It is not intended for a death-bed experience, but for the fruitage of a successful life.

"Every branch in me that beareth fruit, he purifieth it that it may bring forth more fruit." This is God's time! Christ is at the right hand of the Father; the blood has been sprinkled; the Holy Ghost is here; all things are now ready. God commands, "Be ye holy;" and to refuse or neglect is to violate the divine command and incur the divine displeasure, and hinder the work of God, and imperil the future of the soul.

But there is one more feature of this subject we may not overlook. Holiness embraces more than actions, more than obedience to law. No act of the individual, no conformity to any ritualism or creed, or code of ethics, can efface or eliminate, an element of essential uncleanness from the soul. It is wicked to evade the issue, or pervert the facts, or resort to strategic interpretations; no sophism is of any avail. Jesus says there is uncleanness remaining even in a fruitful Christian, and that *he* is the purifier. We all concede that if the soul is defiled it must be cleansed or forever remain outside of heaven. Every scholar, every thoughtful person, knows that uncleanness cannot be pardoned. It is not within the realm of pardon, and is untouched by regeneration. The soul is regenerated, but the uncleanness is to be destroyed, or it will remain forever.

This state of holiness does not release its possessor from the liability to apostasy. The Antinomians, and all shades of necessitarian teachers who promulgate the doctrine of the imputed righteousness of Christ, insist upon the unconditional perseverance of Christians. But that which has distinguished Wesleyanism from every other doctrine is, that man volitionates his relation to every other being in the universe. All there is of Wesleyanism, of theology, experience, and economy was the product of the one supreme idea of responsible manhood. Apostasy, therefore, does not depend on any moral state, but on the unembarrassed action of the will.

The "angels that kept not their first estate, but left their own habitation," did so of their own free will. They were not unholy nor coerced, but, as being under the government of law, they chose to sin, and "left their own habitation."

Adam and Eve, surrounded with all the attractions of their Edenic home, in the exercise of their volitional freedom withdrew their confidence and fellowship from God, and transferred them to the adversary, obeyed him, and sinned, because as free beings they chose to do so; and no man or angel ever sinned, except they chose to do so.

Jesus, in his perfect unmixed humanity, was tempted, but did not sin; not because he could not sin, but because he chose to obey. He was born under the law; and as a perfect uncoerced human being under the environments of law, the motto of his life was, "Not as I will, but as thou wilt."

This holy state does not release its possessor from the liability and danger of temptation.

Temptation reaches a holy person from without. Temptation and apostasy are both possible; because both are independent of any moral state. Apostasy is predicated on the action of the will alone; but temptation may come from a variety of sources. The appetites, passions, the organs of sense, the consciousness, and the imagination, — all are seized at times by the tempter. In an unclean heart temptation may arise from within. But no temptation is sin; neither is it sin to be tempted *per se*. No being ever sinned until he chose to do so.

God deals with man on the plane of his moral agency on the fact of his final accountability to a just God under a wise administration by law.

Man, being a sinner by choice, the possibility of his salvation from sin is in the merit of Christ, as his vicarious substitute; but it is entirely under the control of his own will. It is not the example of Christ that saves from pollution; it is his sacrificial death. Many are eternally stranded upon this error. The work of Christ was not exemplary and ethical. He is the world's sacrifice for sin. It is his sacrificial death that opens the portals of glory to a lost humanity.

If the child born of Christian parents has any uncleanness at all from the Adamic fountain, it must remain forever untouched by any example. If such a child kept every precept of Jesus, and finally died a martyr to the truth, it would not bridge the bottomless chasm which sin cleft in the moral universe, nor eliminate the antecedent uncleanness from his moral nature. If there is uncleanness in man, it yields only to a cleansing process. "The blood of Jesus Christ his Son cleanseth us from all sin." We have boldness "to enter into the holiest by the blood." Hence, we continue to sing: —

"Thou dying lamb, thy precious blood
Shall never lose its power,
Till all the ransomed church of God
Are saved to sin no more."

There is one more primary fact. This cleansing always comes after regeneration. Jesus is speaking of the live, fruitful vine. The fruitless vine was removed. "The fruit-bearing vine" was cleansed. Luke tells of the Gentile converts who afterward received the cleansing by the agency of the Holy Ghost. This is the issue now. Our opponents have chosen their position; the battle is put in array; the mailed champions are in the field; from the centres of official power has gone forth the challenge that there is no uncleanness in man by nature. Methodism stands alone for the pure full salvation of man through the priestly merit of Jesus. Richard Watson says, "That a distinction exists between regeneration and entire sanctification will be generally allowed." He says that at that early date in the progress of Methodism no one called this in question. Methodism was a unit on that subject.

The Methodist Episcopal Church, in its incipiency and in its entire history and in all of its authoritative utterances of to-day, states it as the doctrine of the church that regeneration precedes the entire cleansing. A small number of chivalrous Bedouins from the Desert of Speculation have thought they had found the oasis of salvation where there was such vigor in the manifestations of the new life that no uncleanness remained in the converted heart. But neither the Discipline nor the doctrinal standards of the church have been changed so as to harmonize with their new discovery; and Jesus continues to declare that he purifies only the fruitful vine. So far as it relates to the divine method of cleansing, the text is very definite. The one issue must not be put aside, — "How is this uncleanness that Luke and Jesus speak of, that remains in the soul after conversion and hinders fruitage," — how is it removed?

Jesus speaks for the church of which he is the head — the intelligent, well-informed Head of the church. He says it is by priestly rite, by sacrificial merit, by the going forth of the divine word clothed in power. As the High Priest, he says, "Having shed my blood and sent the Spirit into the world… I now speak the omnific word, and the same divine power at whose command this universe arose in space goes forth of me in the purification of men from this uncleanness;" and Luke says, "God gave the Gentile converts the Holy Ghost after they were converted, and purified them from their residuary uncleanness," just as he did the disciples at the Pentecost.

Upon this universal testimony of the Scriptures, we affirm that this act of cleansing believers from this remaining impurity is God's own special work; that it is wrought by the Holy Ghost, and is an instantaneous event.

The candidate may be slow in his preparation, his approaches to this point may be very deliberate; but when he has complied with the divine requirements, God saves him at once, and the residuary defilement is expelled by the agency of the Holy Ghost.

Against the doctrine of heart purity as a second work of grace, distinct, but never separate from the other phases of experience, and constituting one "perfect salvation," many foolish objections have been urged. It is assumed by one class of teachers that *perfection* is always a product of forces that require time in which to complete their work.

This proposition is an evasion of the issue, and will not bear the test of logic. Purity is a part of the salvation, and is not a matter in which time can be a factor. Maturity is no part of salvation. All persons who receive this cleansing on their dying bed are simply saved; they have not and cannot have an experience of maturity. Purity and maturity are not the same; purity relates to the quality or condition of the party, maturity has regard to attainment to growth or to ripeness.

Aside from this fact, there is a fundamental error in the assumption that uncleanness could be grown out of the heart. Growth is enlargement; it is the accumulation of such particles or substances as compose the plant or animal when first formed. Growth, in whatever department of nature or being, is always by appropriation. That is the universal law of growth; it cannot be by any other process. Cleansing is always by elimination. That is the law of its being; it cannot be by any other process. Growth and purification are the opposites of each other; they never reach the same end. The grime and smut that accumulate upon the person and clothing of the child while at play, are not removed by the pardon of the childish offences, by the parent, neither does the fastidious mother wait for the visionary process of these Christian philosophers to "grow it away;" but with motherly skill in the use of suds and towel, she completes the work at once, and secures an enjoyable degree of purity. Purification has no relation to age or size. It is a change wrought in the nature or condition of some person or thing, and is always accomplished by some force from without. Growth is always performed by the life force operating from within; and growth never changes one animal or plant into one of another kind. A beech-tree never becomes a chestnut-tree. The ash is never changed so as to bear hickory nuts. A crab-apple tree cannot be grown into a *bellefleur*. A sheep never grows to be an ox, and a meadow-mole never could be grown into an elephant; even if it were to attain the size of the elephant it would still be a mole. If it should become as large as Jumbo or great Caesar, it would yet lack all the other qualities, for it requires more than size to make an elephant. There must be the organism, the life, and the nature to constitute an elephant, and size cannot enter into it; for the little calf that waltzes alongside of its mother is as emphatically an elephant in every regard, as the queen of the forest or jungle.

The same universal law of growth applies everywhere. It is by appropriation, and "everything after its kind."

Growth is accumulation. Purification is by elimination; it is by the removal of something. The very law that governs in the process of growth, makes the development of holiness impossible; furthermore, neither size nor maturity can by any means whatever enter into the fact or experience of salvation. Salvation is the deliverance of the individual from the guilt and dominion and impurity of the apostasy. It cannot involve any more than that; it cannot be secured with less. Nothing else can enter into the contract of salvation. Size, age, culture, wealth, intelligence, or social position, has no significance here. "Whosoever will, let him take the water of life freely."

Neither is it possible for this residuary uncleanness

to be removed by Christian work, or by conformity to an ethical code. The church at large is full of professors of religion who are offended at the testimony of the child of God to pardon or purity. Their boast is that "They do their religion, and are too modest to proclaim it from the housetops."

Suppose we apply this universal law of nature to this class of professors; and we perceive at once that a converted person cannot be cleansed by Christian work, nor made strong by work. Professors of holiness go astray at this point, and become formal, and backslide in spirit. Some of the most intensely selfish and bigoted persons in our acquaintance profess perfect love.

A river does not grow by running, nor does it become clear by running, when its waters have been polluted by the flood. It is cleansed by silting.

The river is made large by additions from its original source, by the flow of the tributaries from the mountains. The river loses while running; its enemies assail it continually. From its mountain home until it enters the ocean, it is exposed to continuous assault. The sunbeams scoop up tons of it, herds of cattle slake their thirst, and the irrigating syndicates fill their pools and ditches; so that if there was not a continuous re-enforcement from the hills, the flow would entirely disappear. Each rivulet from the mountainside swells the volume and increases the velocity and force of the current. The same law applies in the department of Christianity. Like as the heated iron placed in the frosty air gradually loses its heat until it becomes of the same temperature as the surrounding atmosphere, even so, the Christian separated from the fellowship of a personal Christ, loses all the time, and soon becomes of the same temperature of his religious surroundings; and he could neither retain his Christ-life, nor his moral purity, except by a perpetual contact, a personal fellowship, with a living Christ, who is the only fountain and source of all life and purity.

But it is assumed by others that death is a gospel agent, and is essential to the completeness of salvation; that the flesh, being the origin and seat of sin, cannot be subjugated to the law of purity.

A very little attention to the facts in the case will dispose of this error. Death is the result of some antecedent event; and because of that fact it cannot be an agent at all. It is the opposite of an agent. Death is the result of sin, therefore it can never become a gospel agent. Death is the ultimate end, the final climax, of Satanic effort; and because of that fact it cannot become co-operative with Christ, and become an adjunct of his blood.

Christ conquered death, but not in the sense that he utilized it, but that he utterly destroyed it.

Furthermore, death follows the universal law we have just been illustrating— "everything after its kind." Death begets death. One drop of blood taken from the veins of a dead man and injected into the veins of the healthiest man in the State, would result in death in an inconceivably short space of time; and there is no remedy for it. No antidote for this fatal poison exists anywhere. The skill of the most gifted sons of Esculapius are helpless at this juncture; here the flamboyant light of all genius goes out in eternal darkness, unable to enter this Plutonic portal. The blood of Jesus Christ never saw corruption. It is living and vital, efficient and available. It speaks for humanity in the High Priest's office at the right hand of God.

"He ever lives above,
For me to intercede;
His all-redeeming love,
His precious blood to plead.
His blood atoned for all our race,
And sprinkles now a throne of grace."

No business can be transacted with God, except in the High Priest's office. It is because we are under a priestly system of administration that man can be saved at all. Man had an ethical system in his Edenic life. So far as we can see, it was purely ethical, and man failed under its *regime*. But the gospel is remedial; it is purely a priestly system. The merit of Calvary's offering has opened the way to eternal life, and all the hosts of hell cannot close it. Sophists and sceptics, and ambiguous teachers and self-conceited ecclesiastics, may beguile men, may deceive themselves and others, and all perish together, but still, —
"The happy gates of gospel grace
Stand open night and day."

Suppose we put this heresy into a logical form. Sin corrupted man; corruption produced death; but death became a gospel agent and struck down his mother, corruption, and freed humanity from her foul embrace. *Similia similibus curantur.*

These delusive heresies are all fatal to a present experience of conscious salvation in any stage of its progress. Taken together they are the product of an idolatrous effort to rob Calvary of its sacrificial significance, and make it simply an emphatic incident in the march of events.

If we admit the fact of man's apostasy, we perceive that salvation in its entirety must be God's own work. No other being in the universe can remove Satanic impurity from the human soul. This residuary uncleanness cannot be removed by growth nor culture. Neither can this condition of purity be secured by Christian work, nor by obedience to any standard of Christian propriety. The uncleanness cannot be worn away by the attrition of pain and sorrow, nor can it be overcome by churchly rites. This kind yields only to the sacrificial blood of the Son of God. Christ is the only Saviour; there is no salvation but in him.

He whose holy tears fell in copious abundance at the grave of Lazarus when he called his dead friend from the embrace of death; he out of whose infinite heart went forth the virtue that healed the multitudes that touched him; he who when hanging on the cross rescued the dying malefactor; he who now from the throne of his omnipotence, from the High Priest's office at the right hand of God, lets slip portions of his merit, of his knowledge and wisdom and power to save the perishing, and when importuned looks in compassion upon the fetid leprous human soul and says, "Be thou clean" — he alone can save.

> "Thou dying Lamb, thy precious blood
> Shall never lose its power,
> Till all the ransomed church of God
> Are saved to sin no more."

XVIII
THE PHILOSOPHY OF
CHRISTIAN INFLUENCE

"For what is your life?" —JAMES iv. 14.

THERE ARE CERTAIN fundamental principles that lie at the bottom of every system of truth. There are certain primary laws of thought, affection, and influence from which all subordinate laws proceed and with which they must agree. There are laws that govern the relations of persons and things that are universal in their application. So far as these affect man in his relations to God and his fellow-man, they are formulated in one divine proposition: "No man liveth to himself."

As a subject of moral law, man is not only responsible for his belief and his conduct, but he is responsible for his influence over others— responsible up to the full measure of his ability to influence.

This principle is illustrated in the natural world. No atom of matter exists alone; no ray of light, no vesicle of air, is found in a state of isolation. Everything in the physical world belongs to some system of which it is a necessary part.

The same law is regnant in the moral and intellectual world. Every being, from the tallest archangel that flashes his golden plumage on the glittering air of heaven to the smallest child in the most obscure corner of the globe in its tiny craft just launched on the stream of time, belongs to some system of mutual dependencies. No human being comes into this world without increasing or diminishing the sum total of human happiness in its age, and in every subsequent age, and in eternity.

In view of these facts, we ask, "What is your life in its influence?"

This question involves more than profession, more than social position. It relates to character, and the influence of character on individuals and on society. It will not avail us anything in mitigation of the results if we shut our eyes against these facts, and deny the force of these primary truths. These are fundamental laws in the philosophy of the divine government, and are as unchangeable as the eternal God. We may change our relations to them; but they remain the same in all ages, and in all lands, and among all peoples.

Christians should study carefully the nature and the laws of influence. We have watched with intense interest and curiosity the expanding ripple set in motion by the falling pebble, and have seen it widen in every direction until it reached the outer edge of the pool. According to a law of natural philosophy, which says, "No two bodies can occupy the same space at the same time," if a marble, one-fourth of an inch in diameter, were dropped from a child's hand into the middle of the Atlantic Ocean, it would displace every drop of water in the ocean, and its vibrations would be felt in all seas, and grate upon all coasts, and swell against the rocky base of all islands, and heave the icebergs of the polar seas. On the same principle every human being sets in operation influences that continue forever— influences which he can neither arrest nor control. Paine and Volney, and Rousseau and Hume, set in motion influences which naturally increase forever; and Luther and Calvin and Wesley started a tidal wave of good influence that is still rising and sweeping toward the shore with ever-increasing power and majesty. Every rolling year places St. Paul and Moses still higher in the scale of advancing greatness. Less than two hundred years ago, Wesley began the revival work known as Methodism. He opened afresh to the perishing masses of humanity the fountain of salvation, through faith in Jesus Christ. Millions have already slaked their spiritual thirst in its healing waters; and the combined forces of earth and hell can never arrest the current of life that now flows through this channel to a lost world.

According to the truth of these principles, whether you go to heaven or hell you will see the finger-marks of your influence on the characters of those about you.

A traveller recently quarried a brick from the ancient tower of Babel. On one side it bore the perfect impress of a small hand. The boy had put his mark upon the brick while it was soft and yielding, and it remained forever. The moulder of the brick is unknown; the name and history of the carrier have not been written; but his mark remains upon his work till it shall return again to dust.

The impressions you make on mind, the fingerprints of your influence which you put on human character, will remain imperishable when the stars shall have gone out in darkness, and "the fashion of this world shall have passed away."

In my early boyhood I got possession of a volume of fables. One of them was illustrated, and it strangely and deeply impressed me, and is as fresh and clear in my memory as if it had been but yesterday. There was a broad plane slightly inclined, and at the upper edge there was a high mountain, whose summit was reached by a steep ascent, and on the crest was a beautiful plateau. At the lower edge of the plane was a vast multitude of people, all anxious to reach the height. They journeyed pleasantly together until they came to the abrupt ascent, when a fierce conflict ensued, and scores were crushed in the struggle. A very small number had succeeded in reaching the summit, and they amused themselves by throwing sand in the eyes of those near them, and in rolling rocks on those farther down the slope; but so soon as one of them succeeded in reaching the summit, he immediately joined the victors in their assault on the anxious multitude below.

This fable illustrates a fact in human experience. The road to success is all the way up hill, and when we reach the abrupt ascent of competition the real conflict begins, and those who succeed in getting to the front are jealous of all who come after them.

This fact is illustrated daily in professional life, and in business and social life. Authors and inventors, painters and artists, of all classes are infected with the deadly virus; and politicians and ambitious ecclesiastics spend the time between elections in disposing of their competitors. What shall Christians do? Shall they throw sand, or extend help? Shall they roll rocks, or lift up the bruised ones? Shall they be a benediction, or prove a curse to society?

Let me ask you, What is your life? Put the emphasis on the possessive pronoun, "your." What is your life in its relation to your responsibilities? "To be, or not to be?" is not the question. Life with its issues is upon you. You occupy probational ground. You are forming characters for eternity; not your own only, but you are influencing others for heaven or hell.

The people of this generation are giving direction to all the forces that shall come after them. The civilizations, the intellectual and religious institutions that shall dominate the future, are being shaped, and are receiving their momentum of this age.

It is in this momentous fact that the responsibility of existence is perceived. We misapprehend: responsibility does not begin at death; it culminates then. Whoever lives right dies a victor, though he perish alone amid Siberian snows or lie unburied on the torrid sands of the desert; but no man can undo the errors of a lifetime upon his dying bed.

> "The world can never give
>   The bliss for which we sigh;
> 'Tis not the whole of life to live,
>   Nor all of death to die.
>
> Beyond this vale of tears,
>   There is a life above,
> Unmeasured by the flight of years;
>   And all that life is love."

But it is equally true that—

> "There is a death whose pang
>   Outlasts the fleeting breath,
> And everlasting horrors hang
>   Around the second death."

The further development of this subject reveals to us the fact:—

(*a*) That the actions of men in this world affect them in the future life, whether they go to heaven or are assigned to hell. No individual can by any means escape his own personality, nor elude his own presence; and no human being can be happy anywhere, except he perfectly harmonizes with God in the domain of his law, and in the realm of his personality and essence. Man must not only be innocent, but he must be pure; for no man can be perfectly happy while he is consciously guilty or unclean.

Heaven embraces in its conception very much more than simply to escape hell. Heaven is not comprehended in the idea of elegantly upholstered seats with golden harps in luxurious palaces prepared for indolent and selfish dreamers. Heaven is remuneration for noble achievement; it is reward for grand and exalted effort. Heaven is moral and intellectual growth; it is the unfolding and development of unlimited possibility through everlasting ages. Heaven is perfect fellowship with God. Heaven is eternal progress in all that is pure.

(b) We also perceive that evil is cumulative. God may forgive the penitent offender and save him eternally in heaven, but the influence of his evil deeds, like a mountain torrent swollen by the summer rains, rushes on forever, unaffected by the penitence or death of the transgressor.

(c) Penalty and reward are always related to the law, but sequence is that which flows forth of the action alone. Law has no sequence. Divine forgiveness remits the penalty of the law, but cannot affect the sequences of human actions under the present constitution of nature. Penalty and sequence are not the same in nature nor origin. Penalty is that which the law affixes as punishment for an offence. Sequence is that which flows from the action or event alone.

A drunken husband in a paroxysm of frenzy smites his wife to the floor. When he becomes sober, he is heartily sorry; he signs the pledge; he truly repents, and is soundly converted. God freely forgives all the past, and his godly wife forgives him also. When he became a Christian, it took all the pain out of her heart; but the bruised and blackened face remain— the sequences of his act, the mute witness of his perfidy.

The profligate man when saved is not reinvested with his wasted substance. A sensualist may be washed whiter than the snow; but that divine act does not restore his wasted vitality, it does not reimburse his exhausted energy. No hygienic measures nor sanitary processes can build again the broken constitution, and fill it with its departed vigor.

The individual who consumes his manhood in the service of sin, who burns out his intellectual and moral nature in the indulgence of passion, and sacrifices his physical organism on the altar of unrestrained appetite, and by the mercy of God is saved on his death-bed, will be, by the force of eternal law, a pauper through everlasting ages. He can have no investments in heaven; he can have no treasure there. He has no growth of character in himself; he never did anything for God. No products of his business ever found their way into the treasury of the Lord, and no tissue of body or soul was consumed by labor in his vineyard. No weary heart was ever made glad by him, and no footsore pilgrim was ever helped on his journey by his effort. Because of his neglect by the sequences of his own life, he must remain a pensioner on the bounties of Jesus forever.

The significance of this life is comprehended in the fact that all its phenomena, its circle of activities, its opportunities and possibilities, everything in this life that is good — all are given as the necessary paraphernalia of a preparatory period; and the improvement of those privileges is essential to the best results in the more glorious life beyond.

Because this is so, the Christian worker has a joint interest with God in the development and extension of his kingdom. Christian life when unencumbered by mistakes and negligence is fruitful of grand results. It is like the pure light of the sun in the physical world; it is a potential force in the divine government. It has constructive power; it is a builder like the solar light in the leaves of the trees, combining the flowing sap and the atmospheric gases so that the entire forest and orchard feel its presence and its power, and twig and tree respond in their annual growth and fruitage. Even so Christian life builds, energizes, cements, and polishes the whole fabric of society.

To what else shall we resemble the influence of a real Christian life? Away off on the mountain-range, far up in its timbered solitudes, a small stream slides quietly out from the mossy crevasse in the gray old rock. The mountain partridge wets its beak in the tiny stream, and the chipmonk [sic] slakes its thirst in the purling water without fear of danger.

But that small beginning is re-enforced by kindred streams. It spreads out into a majestic river; and for more than a thousand miles the beautiful Ohio winds its course between the picturesque hills that rise grandly on either shore, as it rolls on to the sea, bearing on its bosom the commerce of a nation, its banks lined with farms and factories, with cities and villages, with Christian homes and Christian institutions thrilling and pulsating with the potencies and energies of a great people.

That stream is an emblem of the salutary forces that go forth of a Christian man— deepening, widening, rushing, rolling, sweeping in majesty ever onward. Receiving and pouring out, originating and dispensing, creating and disbursing, augmenting and giving direction to the religious forces of society, gathering the outcasts into the fold, training the youth to habits of intelligence and virtue, and laying all at the feet of Jesus.

Every Christian life is a fountain of blessing, making the waste places of society fruitful as Carmel, and as fragrant as a garden of spices.

No toiler in the Master's vineyard can measure the results of his own efforts. No act performed, no deed done, in the name of Jesus, but that will tell on the ultimate destiny of the world.

An obscure evangelist in the woods of Northern Ohio

preached the gospel of salvation to the pioneer settlers in a log schoolhouse. The heart of a rude, uncultured boy was touched by the story of the cross; some invisible power entered his soul, and possessed his entire being. He was transformed from the dull and sensual into the acute and spiritual. He was a new creature by a new creation. He was subject to the control of a new class of forces. He immediately left his old associations; the mules and the canal-boat were exchanged for the college campus and the forum. The years go by, and this young man is the pastor of a church. Afterward he is president of an institution of learning, then a member of the legislature of his native State. Again we find him at the head of an army, and then again we hear his voice in Congress. He is the leader of his party, the champion of universal liberty and progress. He is advanced to the Senate, and elected President of the United States. The lifeless form of the murdered hero sleeps undisturbed in its crypt in Lakeview Cemetery; but James A. Garfield lives in the history and literature of all the years— a star of the first magnitude in the constellation of Christian statesman— won to God, and restored to his proper orbit, by the fidelity of an unlettered pastor.

A mother in Israel found a white-haired lad in soiled garments and with grimy face and bare feet, outside the Sunday-school room, among the hills of Eastern Pennsylvania. With rare skill and persuasive power of Christian love, she brought him in; she won him to Christ. The Saviour was enthroned in his heart. He became a medical missionary; he flamed around the world as a living evangel. Bishop Wiley's ashes lie buried in heathen soil, but the radiance of his Christian life lingers in prophetic brightness above the Celestial Empire.

Standing in the golden sunset of this brilliant century, and looking back across the gulf of two thousand years, we see a student from Tarsus matriculated in the college of Gamaliel. He excels his teachers, and wins success at every stage of his progress. Now he is a rising young lawyer, a zealot, and a leader in the ranks of the persecutors. He is present at the death of Stephen. He holds the clothes, and directs the mob; and elated by his success, and flattered by the people, he started for Damascus to bind and imprison and put to death, the followers of the Nazarene.

But after the exciting scenes of that eventful journey, he became a Christian; became the standard bearer of the Lord in the West. After twenty-five years of incessant labor, he went to Rome as a prisoner; and after his conviction, he wrote his dying testimony from his gloomy cell, and the page carried it to the little group of Christians awaiting the issue. The sentence of death was pronounced upon him; and on a beautiful morning an officer of the Roman court, took him out on the Apian way, three miles from the city. At the Salvian brook, a cimeter flashed in the morning light, and the head of the great man rolled in the dust.

But Paul is not dead. He cannot be exterminated; he will live forever. The current of his influence now laves all shores, and the brightness of his rising illumines all lands.

XIX
PAUL'S VISIT TO PETER

"Then after three years I went up to Jerusalem to see Peter, and abode with him fifteen days." — GALATIANS i. 18.

THE TWO CHARACTERS of this text are among the most remarkable of all history. Peter had been with Jesus from the first organization of the apostles; and Paul had been arrested on his way to Damascus, had yielded to the Nazarene, and had been converted.

When the dispensation of the gospel came to him, he obeyed at once. He did not confer with flesh and blood. He did not go up to Jerusalem for the apostolic blessing and authority. His credentials were signed by the Holy Ghost. He went down to Arabia, then back to Damascus; and after three years he went up to Jerusalem to see Peter, and abode with him fifteen days.

Perhaps there never were two distinguished men engaged in the same work that were so completely the opposite in all the characteristics and qualities of their manhood.

Paul was a scholar— the most thorough, elaborate, and diversified scholar of that period. By nature, Paul was a genius; by training he was a poet, logician, and orator, and was called of God to the apostleship of the infant church.

Paul and Peter now had a common mission; and the meeting in Jerusalem had a world-wide significance. Peter, so unlike Paul,— who can analyze this unique combination of elements?— Peter was a strange combination of strength and weakness, genius and poetic warmth, blended with a childlike simplicity and an impulsive temperament. With his tremendous courage, there was mingled a degree of weakness; so that at intervals he would break down in times of difficulty. When he sinned, it was with a fervor and an emphasis that were overwhelming; but his perfect penitence was prompt, earnest, and genuine.

After his denial he responded at once, with a broken heart and overflowing eyes, to the sad, searching look of Jesus.

That solemn glance of the Master's eye pierced the great deep of his vehement soul, and opened an artesian fountain of penitential tears.

There is a legend that to the end of his life, whenever he heard a cock crow, the tears fell in copious showers.

There were two events in the history of Peter that wrought great changes in his character. As the scene on the Damascus road completely revolutionized Saul of Tarsus, those two events entirely changed the nature and spirit of Simon. One of these was the resurrection of Jesus; the other was the Pentecost. The development of Peter's character from the resurrection of Jesus to the time of the Pentecost is a study in itself. The intuitions of his nature responded to the affectionate breathings of the risen Christ, as orchard and forest open leaf and blossom to the April sun.

But the effect of the fiery baptism was so remarkable, his crude and impulsive nature was so modified by it, his whole being so sublimated and refined, so elevated and ennobled, that we can scarcely recognize in him the man "that blundered on the mountain of transfiguration." He is never again like the ambitious place-seeker at the supper, nor the weary sensualist that slept in Gethsemane, nor the one who so gravely rebuked his Master when he would wash the disciples' feet.

See him now as the dignified yet vehement president of the Pentecostal service. The weaknesses of his former life are all gone; the warmth and energy and poetic fire all remain. Or see him still later when, on his brow the glories of the sacred mountain meet and mingle with the halo of his approaching death, when he shall "depart in triumph to see and embrace his Lord." See him where you may now; he neither hesitates in his course nor swerves from his high and holy purpose. At the beautiful gate of the temple he heals in the name of Jesus. "Always the minister of mercy to the afflicted, while as the messenger of vengeance he stands with the javelin of death unsheathed above the heads of the dissembling Ananias and his guilty wife." Again we see him when his long evening shadow swept down the streets of Jerusalem, and healed all the sick that swarmed in its crowded and sultry thoroughfares. And again, when, with an angel for a harbinger, he quietly left his cell in the prison to attend a cottage prayer-meeting. Under all circumstances his Christian character is the very embodiment of sublimity. Peter, the impetuous and fluctuating, becomes the victorious and stable, winning for himself a martyr's crown.

But nowhere does Peter appear to better advantage than when he became the instructor of Paul the learned, in the things pertaining to the life and kingdom of Jesus Christ. Peter points out to Paul the places of historical interest, and recounts to him the doctrinal facts of the gospel, and mingles with this wonderful story sections of his own personal experience. I go back over the highway of history that spans the chasm of eighteen centuries; I visit Peter's house in the city of David. I am a silent spectator and an interested listener to the conversation of these two remarkable men. One was the acute and cultured disciple of Gamaliel, who held the clothes and urged on the brutal mob that murdered the sainted Stephen; and the other is the one who swore allegiance to Jesus even unto death, and in a little while quailed before the inquisitive glance of a waiting-maid.

The coming together of these two men would have been remarkable under any circumstances; but now the meeting assumes a universal interest, the whole world becomes absorbed and looks on in amazement. Paul, the philosopher, logician, and orator, the blaspheming persecutor, who surrendered to the Nazarene on the Damascus road without conditions, and became the standard-bearer of the cross in the Western kingdoms, comes to visit Peter, the large-hearted and restless son of the sea, who had been a disciple of Jesus from the first.

These two stalwart apostles come together to canvass the interesting events of the past, and to plan for the Christian campaign which was to continue till the whole world should lay down its honors at Jesus' feet. In my imagination I see the great-hearted genius of the early church receiving his distinguished guest with a genuine Oriental cordiality.

After the lapse of a few days, when this acquaintance had ripened into a real Christian friendship, Peter took his guest to visit some of the sacred resorts of the Master, and to look upon some of the Christian shrines. Passing on into one of the principal streets, they ascended a broad stairway, and passed through a narrow vestibule into a large and commodious chamber. Peter said: "Here is the place we ate the last supper with Jesus. Here Jesus cel-

ebrated his last Passover, and instituted the Holy Communion that commemorates his death. And here is where
we sat and argued the question as to who should 'be
greatest in the new kingdom.' It was here where Jesus
rebuked our selfishness by teaching us real humility. We
had come in from the street with soiled garments, travel-
stained, and begrimed with dust from the highway. The
Master took a basin and a towel, and girded himself and
washed our feet. He became a menial, performed the office of a servant, while we were planning for the gratification of our ambitious desires. It was out through that
door that Iscariot went with murder and treason in his
heart to betray him into the hands of a mob. It was right
here that Jesus sat when he took the bread and broke it,
and took the cup and blessed it, and gave it to us, saying:
'This is my blood of the New Testament shed for you.'
And there was a strange fire in his eye, and an unnatural
pathos in his voice, when he said: 'But, behold, the hand
of him that betrayeth me is with me on the table;' and we
all began to inquire which one it was that should do that
dreadful deed.

"After that, Jesus took three of us, and we went down
this street, and over the Kedron into Gethsemane, and he
began to be very sorrowful. We turned down this avenue,
and Jesus bade us tarry while he went alone to pray. It
was by that gnarled and knotted old olive-tree that he
kneeled down. The sad moon poured its full blaze of sorrowful light upon him. We saw that his visage was
marred, and his form distorted and unnatural, and while
we were talking we all fell asleep. After a while he came
and called us, and said: 'Could ye not watch with me one
hour?' Then he kneeled down and prayed: 'Father, if it
be possible, let this cup pass from me; nevertheless, not
as I will, but as thou wilt.' But still our eyes were heavy,
and we slept, leaving him alone in his agony.

"Then he came and touched us, and said: 'Sleep on

now, and take your rest.' The pained expression had passed away from his face, the storm had swept over him, his bowed form had regained its uprightness, he had been triumphant in the last struggle, and his soul was as calm as the Sea of Tiberias after the tempest had been stilled. Here is where we were when we saw the mob coming. The torches flashed through the thick foliage of the garden, and mingled with the receding moonbeams that struggled through the tangled boughs overhead. The noise of the rabble grew distinct, and scores of angry Jews, followed by the slums about the gates— an extemporized army supplied with the implements of war. Judas had betrayed him, and with a hypocritical kiss he pointed him out to the soldiers.

"I was angry. I could have killed Iscariot for his perfidy. I drew my cutlass, and began to smite right and left. The Master bade me put up my sword. My feelings were hurt. I was disconcerted. I would have died for him then; but before I could recover myself I began to tremble, and found my courage and purpose both gone.

"It was right here the crowd began to smite him. Then all of us but John deserted him, and fled for our lives. This is Pilate's judgment hall. I stood here when John came out and took me in. I sat there, filled with indignation, while the mob spit upon him in the presence of the officers, and struck him in the face. Then they brought the crown of thorns, and pressed it down upon his head till his temples and face were covered with blood. I was standing right here by the kettle of coals when *that girl* came and looked at me, and said I was one of his disciples. It almost crushes the life out of me now, whenever I think how mean I was. I cannot account for it. I shall never attempt to apologize for my conduct. I denied him with an oath, and repeated it over and over. I can never forget the look of the Master's face as he stood before Pilate, deserted of all his friends, 'treading the wine-press alone.'

"Now, let us go up to Calvary. Here is where they nailed him to the cross. Those great, rough, cruel soldiers with relentless stroke drove the copper spikes, crushing through the flesh and bones into the hard cedar wood. Right here is where they planted the cross. There was an acute pain stung through my soul as they lifted him above the surging crowd, and thrust the upright beam down into the rocky soil. I stood down by that rock when it began to be dark. I felt the earth tremble. I saw the awakened dead slide out from their musty crypts, and look on the tragic scene in amazement. I heard the crash in the temple when the veil was rent. Amid the darkness and confusion I heard the voice of one of the malefactors pleading for mercy; and above the din of the tumult I heard Jesus say distinctly, 'This day thou shalt be with me in Paradise.' And yet, after all this, when Jesus was taken down from the cross, not one of his disciples was there to care for the body.

"Here is the sepulchre. It was Joseph's new tomb, hewed out of the solid rock. In front of this the soldiers walked back and forth with haughty air for three days. There is where the Mighty-to-save conquered death in his own dominions, cleft his helmet, wrested his sceptre, and 'brought life and immortality to light.'

"This is the path we came down as we went out to Olivet on the day of the ascension. As we came along, the Master repeated to us the promise of the Comforter. He assured us that he would come as he had said before; that he would reveal all things to us, and bring to our recollection the things we had forgotten. He said, 'All power in heaven and in earth is given unto me. Go ye therefore, into all the world, and preach the gospel to every creature. Lo, I am with you alway, even unto the end of the world.' Then he began to ascend. He did not appear to step upon the air as if it were a stairway. He seemed rather to rise above it, higher and still higher, as if impelled by an inherent force, till he floated away as a mere speck in the sky. Then there was a bright cloud luminous with ten thousand rainbow glories, which opened to our vision ranks on ranks of shining seraphs. Line upon line the serried hosts parted to the right and left. File on file the heavenly escort opened wide its van, and received him out of sight.

"We were standing there yet, when two angels in shining habit said, 'Why stand ye here gazing up into heaven? This same Jesus that ye have seen ascend up into heaven shall in like manner descend again.'

"When we had seen the Lord ascend and had heard the testimony of the angels, we knew that it was all right, and that the Holy Ghost would come in due time. So we all went up to that sacred upper chamber where Jesus had shown himself to us after his resurrection, and where we had held our meetings. There we remained in prayer and consultation from nine o'clock in the morning till three o'clock in the afternoon of each day, 'looking for the promise of the Father.'"

It was on the seventh day[1] after the Lord's ascension; we were all in a state of serene expectancy. We were all early. We all knew it was the fiftieth day from the crucifixion, and we all felt that he would come at that time. And as we kneeled for the opening prayer, we heard the rustle of wings; then there was a rushing and roaring sound like the noise of a tempest, but there was no wind, it was only the sound. The house was filled with the noise. He sat on our heads in liquid flame, and in the sublimity of that hour we were swallowed up in God.

"Dear Paul, these are all facts in my own personal experience. I was with him in the holy mount. I heard the

---

1. I count the three days that Jesus was in the grave added to the forty that followed his resurrection make forty-three. We must count fifty from the crucifixion, and no more; and we only have seven days for the prayer-meeting-days, or days of waiting.)

voice from the excellent glory that proclaimed him the Son of God. I was familiar with the scenes of his life and death. I witnessed his triumphant reception back to his Father's house. Now, right here where his victorious feet left their last hallowed impress upon the earth, let us pledge ourselves to stand together and carry on this work till he shall call us from labor to reward."

XX
Antitheses of the Gospel

"For the wages of sin is death, but the gift of God is eternal life through Jesus Christ our Lord." —Romans vi. 23.

T HE BIBLE IS a volume of antitheses; strong and terrible contrasts greet the eye on every page. The dual idea of possibility is inseparable from the Bible record of humanity.

The Bible states it as a fundamental fact, and repeats it in almost endless variety of promise and prophecy, that a life of sinfulness culminates in eternal disaster, while a life of holiness ultimates in a condition of everlasting felicity.

We find the fact of alternative destiny emphasized and conspicuous in the simple style of Moses. It shines out distinctly in the gorgeous imagery of Ezekiel, and is interwoven with the story of Isaiah, as he points to the babe in the manger, or welcomes the Christ as a victor from the grave.

It comes to us clothed with authority from the lips of him "who spake as never man spake," and burns and blazes amid the tangled tragedies of the Apocalypse—wages for sin, life eternal, the gift of the infinite God.

No person can construct a theodicy on the basis of necessity. Theories have been formed and creeds piled mountain high, but they do not vindicate the divine character; but the reviews and religious papers continue to support their creeds by affirming "that there are no alternatives with God," that by the nature of his being he can act but one way.

But if the text is true, their statements are deficient in both logic and fact, and perish for lack of support.

If for a moment you will place yourself outside of all the past controversies, if you will for the time omit all reference to the Bible, and stand all alone in the sacred precinct of the human consciousness, and make a complete inventory of the soul— of its own natural possibilities, of its possessions and furnishings— you will discover that there is that which we call virtue, and there is that which we call vice. These are not the same, and they do not exist by the arbitrary will of God.

These antagonistic aspects of human experience are not sentiments evolved from the Bible; they exist as possibilities in the constitution of nature, and would remain forever under the present form of government even if God were eliminated from the universe.

These two unavoidable possibilities of the text lie back of all human activities; they exist in the constitution of the universe.

So far as they relate to man as a subject of law, they have their origin and application in that department of his being over which the will presides; in his moral nature.

On this fact the text is predicated: "The wages of sin is death." That is all any one can get, as hire for doing sin; "but the gift of God is eternal life through Jesus Christ our Lord."

Two courses in life open equally before every human being. Two classes of actions directly the opposite of each other in their moral character, challenge the purposes and energies and final choices, of every child of Adam.

Suppose you go with me and stand beside the crib where the little babe nestling in its flannels lies so softly in its first earthly sleep. This morning that child commenced a career that shall never end. From that crib, stretching away across the field of human adventure are two divergent paths, which by the very nature of things do not reach the same station. They are as distinct in their termination as they are in the angle of their divergence. The one passes out through the open portals of worldliness on through the gilded halls of sinful pleasure, or winds its tortuous course amid the charmed haunts of indolence and petty vices, or turns abruptly down the steeps of sensuality into the abyss where death has his eternal abode.

The other leads up through the narrow gateway of a life of self-denial, along the quiet pathway of earnest consecration and personal purity, along the pathway of obedience to law, overhung with the foliage and fragrant with the flora and fruitage of Christian fidelity and achievement, up to the abode of the blest, to the home of the saved of all ages, to the fountain and fruition of eternal life.

There are two possible destinies for every human soul, only one of which can be accomplished, and one of which awaits every member of the human family,— wages for sin, eternal life a divine gift.

This text is a definite authoritative declaration of a great fact,— a fact inseparable from the constitution of man. There is a peculiar emphasis placed upon the text by its author. Wages is the pivotal word; for the practice of sin you get "wages." You get something that is not yours until you earn it. It is not yours by nature nor by administration. It is *hire*; it is the price paid for service rendered. Do sin, and get death as hire, as wages — for what you have done. The individual sinner gets something as a remuneration for doing something. It is not a gift; it is not the sequent of former actions; it is not the penalty of violated law alone. It is that which is paid for service rendered. For the "doing of sin" humanity gets death. "Lust when it hath conceived bringeth forth sin; and sin when it is executed, or performed, bringeth forth death." There is no escape from the fundamental fact that what God calls death is a product of sin, — the first born of sin is death. Death was no part of man's Edenic experience. Death existed only as a possibility; but it could not take place inside the garden. Death had no claim on man, and had no access to him under the environment of his Edenic home.

Death is not a normal experience. It is this fact that gives significance to the words of the text: "Death, the wages of sin." If man had not sinned, death could never have been known, except as an unfulfilled possibility, known only as a grisly terror, that looked out on man through the law which guarded his pathway through this world. Death! do you know what death is? No one can know, for it is not revealed. You cannot see death. You have seen his shadow; that is all humanity can see. You tremble when his shadow falls across your pathway. You have walked in the gloom of his presence. You have felt the chill of his breath upon the current of your life; but you could not see nor touch the invisible foe of God and man. No one living ever saw death. Often we have stood by the highways of his kingdom, over which he continually travels, but he has carefully eluded our sight.

With microscope and scalpel we have gone carefully through every organ of the body; but no glass ever was constructed with focus strong enough to reveal this grim-visaged destroyer.

We have met and interviewed many of the servants of death; but they do not reveal their master. Through all the rolling centuries they have kept the secret of their princely proprietor.

We have gone back along the pathway of man, and amid the dim centuries that converge about the early home, just outside the broken walls of Eden, we find the bloody club, and the mutilated form of the first victim. That is not death. That is the first agent pressed into the service of death. That is— murder— the first soldier mustered into the service; the red-handed leader of the marshalled host of the great destroyer. But murder was too slow for the arch enemy, and he hissed to the four winds and grim-visaged war, reared his hydra-head, and beneath his gory hoof the nations perished; and a thousand battlefields proclaim his victories to the ends of the earth.

He hissed again and pestilence responded; and from his shrivelled lips he blew the mildews of death, and in one single night the city was tenantless and still. Contagion obeyed his call, and still sweeps down the ages. Death waved his magic wand, and fire and flood joined the army he called, and excess responded, disease obeyed his voice, and the earth was full of the odors of decay. Consumption, spasm, epilepsy, and cancer, malaria, pyemia, and the long list of fevers that lurk in the shadow of the hospital and the home, entered the ranks and put on the armor to fight the battles of death.

But none of these is death. If we regard death as the penalty of violated law, or as the ultimate sequence of wrong action, or if we regard it as penalty and sequence combined, these all taken together do not meet the requirements of the text. There is still to be added the positive statement of the text— wages, something paid for service rendered.

Revelation and mythology each gives us some idea of this universal foe; but Death himself, the grisled king of terrors, remains untouched, and from his invisible throne directs the forces of his empire.

In the unexplored regions of Tartarus there are many weird and statuesque forms of death, dimly visible from the earthly shore in the leaden mists of that eternal gloom. There you see the unfortunate and famishing Tantalus forever submerged in the abundance of all things, but dying of hunger. There you see the dripping sweat of the toiling Sisyphus falling forever on the burning stone.

The monkish age of Christianity represented death as a huge skeleton with an hour-glass in one hand and a javelin in the other, while from amid the rhapsodies of apocalyptic vision we hear the apostle say, "I looked, and behold a pale horse: and his name that sat on him was Death, and Hell followed with him." Hell is the servant of death. But none of these, not even all of them combined, give you the true significance of the text. But science comes to the aid of theology at this point. Science assures us that death, *per se*, is a destroyer. Death forever stands over against life. The antithesis is complete. Death a destroyer. Life a builder. Death disintegrates, perverts, pollutes, destroys, but cannot annihilate.

There is no function that death can perform for any being or anything except as a destroyer. Hear it, O ye deluded ones, who expect some service from your arch foe in the moment of your dissolution to prepare you for heaven. Death is a destroyer. In whatever field death operates, the result is always the same. He touches the great city, the centre of the world's commerce, the centre of military power and political control, and immediately satyrs dance in the homes of elegance and culture, and monkeys rear their young in the deserted halls of affluence where once rippled the laughter of childish mirth. He breathes in the face of kings and princes, and worms revel in the abode of genius and statesmanship. Death puts his polluting touch on the intellect, and the loftiest soul lies in ruins at his feet, and the maniac howls in glee, from the blighted throne of reason. He smiles at virtue, and it perishes forever in his foul embrace.

Death is never a blessing; never is a gospel agent. Death is a curse. Death is a disaster. Death is the sum total of the catastrophe in Eden.

Death is king in the department of adversity. All the destructive elements of nature, and the destroying agencies of the universe meet in death.

When death takes possession of an organism, he separates it into its original elements; he puts it to other uses, but he cannot annihilate one single atom.

In man's present probational state he can never see death; he can only see his shadow. Death is a conquered foe. His shadow falls across the path of man, and is all that can touch man without his consent and co-operation. The blood of Christ stands forever between death and humanity. He died for man, and the light from his empty grave makes death invisible here.

But the disclosure will come to those who "yield themselves servants of uncleanness, and of iniquity unto iniquity."

In the administration of this government, the wages will always be equal to the labor performed, and inevitable doom makes the payment sure. When the sea gives up its dead; when the myriad graves shall open; when the battlefield no longer conceals the slain; when the desert shall uncover the vast caravans that lie under its drifting sands; when the shrouds of snow shall unwind, and the frozen generations shall arise from their beds of ice; when the wilderness shall surrender its garnered store; when death and hell shall no longer imprison— then shall every servant of sin receive his reward; then the glittering shekels, long due, — death, the current money of hell, — shall be the eternal reward of those who "do iniquity unto iniquity."

Then "death and hell" with the multitude of their followers and adherents shall be cast into the lake of fire which is the second (instalment of) death.

Then the "fearful and unbelieving, and the abominable and murderers, and whoremongers and sorcerers, and idolaters and all liars, shall have their portion, the wages for which they toiled, in the lake which burneth with fire and brimstone, which is the second death."

That is death, still invisible to mortal eyes, still pushed back into the shadows by the light of the gospel. That is the wages of a sinful life; that is all that sin can do for humanity; that is all that death can do, the only service it can render to man.

But the other branch of the text is true also. The free gift of God which is in Jesus Christ is eternal life. This gift is not wages; the antithesis exists in every aspect of the text. This gift is the opposite of wages; it is not reward; it is not the sequence of wise choices, nor the fruitage of exalted behavior, it is a gift.

The most influential heresy of the centuries assails the Redeemer at this point — a heresy rank with the odors of death — it is that sickly poisonous flower of pseudo ecclesiasticism that still affirms that life is the product of development, and that salvation is the fruitage of character. But the text says, "It is the gift of God, through Jesus Christ our Lord."

But this eternal life is not given for something done or suffered. It is not wages. It is not reward for labor, nor for meritorious conduct. It is not a state of the soul wrought by the impersonal forces of nature. It is not a product of growth; no element of culture enters into it. It is not the fruitage of any disciplinary process, nor of churchly rites.

It is the free, unmerited gift of God, and is bestowed

upon man in order that he may be, and do, and have, and achieve, all that is embraced in redemption.

This eternal life cannot become an experience in the human soul except it be received as a gift. "The gift of God which is in Jesus Christ is eternal life." God gave his Son to the world that he might in him restore humanity to its forfeited holiness and fellowship with deity, which is eternal life.

This text is in the past perfect tense. It declares an act and an event perfectly accomplished. The gift in its completeness is made. "God gave his Son." There can be nothing added to the gift. God gave his Son to be the life of the world, and it is only by the reception of him that man can receive the life. And dwelling in his fellowship, and abiding in him, the life remains; and "He of God is made unto us wisdom, righteousness, sanctification, and redemption."

Two great facts are stated in the text: death, the indescribable climax and culmination of the fatal catastrophe in Eden, as the "wages for sin;" eternal life in Jesus Christ as a divine gift.

In this text two tremendous possibilities turn on the volitional act of the human soul, and the individual, uncoerced, makes the final choice.

The Father has gone to the outer verge of possibility to recover man from the disaster of sin. Hear his own declaration: "What more can I do to my vineyard that I have not already done to it?"

Jesus came to the world clothed in human flesh. He preached his own gospel without money and without price. Far and wide the great gift was proclaimed throughout all the land. In the valleys and on the mountain heights, in the privacy of domestic seclusion and in the marketplaces, in public on the feast-days and in the presence of thousands of people in the wilderness, and by the sea-side, he proclaimed his mission, and confirmed it by the manifestation of miraculous power.

Four great mountains stand as perpetual witnesses to the divine effort to save humanity. Standing far back of the centuries, shadowed by the eternal gloom of the desert, is Sinai, the mountain of God. Bare, dark, and cragged, it rises in awful majesty, pushed up by an infinite force from the burning sands of the desert, chasmed and seamed and thundersplit by the storms of ages, fit pedestal from which Jehovah should speak. As we look, behold, God has wrapped his mantle about it; a thick cloud, fire girt, has suddenly invested it; and amid pealing thunders and clanging trumpets molten as the livid lightning, issued the fiery law that echoes down the centuries.

Sinai is the symbol of authority; it represents the law. It speaks of judgment, while from the sombre shadows of Calvary proceeds the voice of mercy. For four thousand years Sinai has smoked and thundered; for four thousand years the clanging trumpet's startling blast has echoed down the corridors of time; for four thousand years the fiery law, lurid with eternal vengeance, has proclaimed the fact that the "soul that sinneth, it shall die." For two thousand years Calvary has looked down on the broken walls of the desolated city, and proclaimed its great sacrifice above the empty altars of Judah.

Calvary pleads to-day as in the past. From amid the gloom that shrouds Golgotha issues the voice of mercy.

We listen at this time to the rending rocks and crashing veil in the temple. We feel the trembling rolling earth as it rocks like a toy above the earthquake's shock. We look upon the bursting graves, and behold with amazement the ghastly promenading of the awakened dead; and above all the confusion is distinctly heard the dying cry of the Nazarene, "It is finished," and the tragedy is ended; mercy has prevailed; love is triumphant; the world is redeemed; humanity is free. There are two other mountains that testify of the divine interest in man— the mountain of instruction, and the mountain of victory.

We go back along the pathway of history, across the centuries. We stand on the sunny slopes of the mountain of blessing. We listen to the words of wisdom as they flow up from the fountain of truth, and drop down from the lips of the great Teacher: "Blessed are the poor in spirit; theirs is the kingdom of heaven." "Blessed are they which do hunger and thirst after righteousness; they shall be filled." "Blessed are the pure in heart; they shall see God." "Or what man is there of you, whom if his son ask bread, will he give him a stone? Or if he ask a fish, will he give him a serpent? If ye then, being evil, know how to give good gifts unto your children, how much more will your Father in heaven give good things to them that ask him?" Thus stands the mountain of instruction at the very threshold of the new era, and on it rests forever the glory of his benediction.

And we love the name and history of Olivet. What sacred memories gather about it! What triumphs it records! We love to linger on Olivet, where the risen Christ left the last impress of his victorious feet on the plastic soil of the world he had redeemed.

Often on other occasions the Saviour had wearily climbed the western slope of this mountain, as he went out to Bethany for a season of rest; but on this occasion his step is as elastic as youth, he has the air of a conqueror. After he had repeated and emphasized the great commission, after he had given special instruction about the Pentecost, when the company had come to where he had raised Lazarus from the dead, standing beside his empty grave, he began to ascend. With an inherent force he walked the ethereal stairway and took his seat on the mediatorial throne, crowned and sceptred Prophet, Priest, and King of the new dispensation.

God did all of this that he might give eternal life to all who would receive his Son.

But this life is called a gift; it is the opposite of wages. It is that which belonged to man in his Edenic state. It was his by creation, and not by endowment. It embraces all that was lost in the fall, and is the sum total of the redeemed estate which the Saviour now holds in trust for humanity. It is the forfeited life, redeemed and held for man. It comes by gift, and can be obtained in no other way. Every effort to obtain eternal life by any other way than by divine gift, is theft or idolatry. "This is the record, that God hath given unto us eternal life, and that life is in his Son."

Life is no more mysterious than death. Life is the opposite of death in every regard. The antithesis is perfect. Life is a builder; life is an architect, a constructor; life is an organizer, a director of forces. Life has been the mystery of all the past ages; more than a score of theories have been projected and abandoned. The professional scientist has made test after test; the physiologist has gone out through every open door, with knife and glass; but he has not discovered life, nor revealed its origin.

Until recently it was assumed that life was the product of organization, that "given an organism we must have life as a result." But the theory was reversed by scientific test. No one can know what life is in itself. But the discovery has been recently made by scientists that life always comes from antecedent life. And when science stood at the altar of progress and proclaimed the fact that there "was no life except from antecedent life," Jesus stood by the other side and, smiling, said, "I am glad you have made the discovery. For six thousand years I have proclaimed the fact, and science refused to accept the truth. I now announce to the world that 'I am that antecedent life.' I am not simply the life giver, nor the revealer of life. I am not the λογος, alone, nor the βιος, alone; I am the

Zon, the life itself. The force that reared and animates this universe flows out from me. I am the life which is the light of men." "He that hath the Son hath life;" and "This is eternal life, that they might know Thee the only true God, and Jesus Christ, whom thou hast sent." And standing on the borderland of two worlds, God continues to announce in the text that "the gift of God is eternal life through Jesus Christ our Lord."

Eternal life is eternal and perfect fellowship with the Father and with the Son and with the Holy Ghost. "And truly our fellowship now is with the Father and with his Son Jesus Christ." Do you ask me what this eternal life is? Suppose that to-day I could draw aside the veil that separates between the two worlds; suppose you go with me as I approach that little child that two weeks ago fluttered out of its mother's arms and passed up the shining way and took its place amid the holy throng. I ask it to suspend its flight, to lay aside its harp, and tell me what it has learned of the great problem of life. I think its answer would be: "I cannot tell; I have had so many surprises; there has been so much to see and to learn, I had not thought of that; but it occurs to me that the white-robed messengers that met me in the valley of shadows said in the raptures of holy song, 'The gift of God is eternal life through Jesus Christ our Lord.'

And if I should pass on to where that sainted father stands, far up among the blood-washed company that encircles the throne, and should ask him to define and analyze the term, he could not excel the emphasis of the text. Suppose I should say to him, "Father, you have now been here for more than twenty years. Tell me the story of eternal life. I heard you speak of it in the earliest period of my earthly existence, when I first learned to lisp my evening prayer at your knees; and in later years we discussed it in the Sabbath-school lesson; and in the love feast, you spoke of it as a conscious experience; and on that bright and beautiful morning when we stood about your bed, while your launched bark lingered a moment on the crystal wave, your departing soul whispered of eternal life. Tell me now, after these years of citizenship with the saints, what you know of this mysterious gift. I think his answer would be: "It is the Christian's perfect, unembarrassed fellowship with the Father through Jesus Christ our Lord." And if I should still press my way onward amid the throng, past the serried ranks of holy angels that guard the pathway, to the inner court, onward to where the martyred Stephen in white apparel wearing the first crown of the new order of saints, leads the seraphic hosts, and make my request of him, the answer would be the same: "It is the gift of God through Jesus Christ our Lord."

And if passing by Daniel and Micah and Isaiah and the long list of ancient worthies I should come to Abel, whose voice uttered the first note of triumph over sin and death and hell; to him who is the first redeemed spirit that thrilled the heavenly courts with the song of salvation; to him who holds the special service and directs the worship of the martyrs of all the ages; to Abel, who for six thousand years has sung his hallelujahs and poured his praises into the ear of Jehovah, and ask him to solve the mystery of the text, the answer would still be the same: "It is the gift of God through Jesus Christ our Lord." And while we linger in the divine presence, the words of Jesus still echo down the centuries: "This is life eternal, that they might know Thee the only true God, and Jesus Christ, whom thou hast sent." And in this perfect knowledge and fellowship the saved of all lands, the redeemed ones of all nations, of every kindred and tribe, shall bathe in the ocean of infinite love, and from the perennial fountain of eternal life quaff the pure nectar of unbounded joy.

XXI
THE CHRISTIAN'S OUTLOOK FROM CARMEL

"Beloved, now are we the sons of God, and it doth not yet appear what we shall be: but we know that, when we shall appear, we shall be like him; for we shall see him as he is." —JOHN iii. 2.

THIS TEXT EMBRACES the present condition and the future outlook and possibilities of the Christian— now sons of God, children of one Father. It doth not yet appear what we shall be. But we know that we shall be like Jesus in his glorified human nature.

Jesus, as he now is in his glorified state, is the model of all manhood under the ultimate power of the gospel.

But the future possibilities of manhood are not conceivable except the present possibilities are secured. Sonship is the childhood state of Christian experience, and in the natural order of things must precede the bloom and fruitage of an advanced Christian state in this life; and both are essential to the best results in the life to come.

Sonship is likeness; nothing less than perfect likeness

constitutes sonship. The child has every element, every constituent quality of the parent— intellectual, moral, and physical. The slightest peculiarity of color, form, or mental idiosyncrasy that exists in the parent is also visible in the child; not as endowments after birth, but as original elements, pre-natal qualities of constituent being. Adam was a son of God by creation. He only of all the created beings was a son, because he alone possessed in his unfallen state every constituent quality and attribute of the Deity. This is what he lost in the apostasy. Hence, the sons of Adam, being alien from God by the fall, are made sons of God by regeneration. None but the truly regenerate are children of God.

Adam was a son by creation; he was God's child; he possessed by virtue of his sonship every quality of his Father. These were all original and natural qualities of his manhood.

Every Christian is a child of God by regeneration, and possesses in himself in a finite degree every quality and attribute of deity. Nothing less than this can constitute sonship.

The text says we who are now regenerate, who are now Christians, are sons of God, have become partakers of the divine nature, and have now in a finite sense all the qualities of the Father, Son, and Holy Ghost. Nothing less than this is regeneration.

God made man for his own companionship; made him for himself; made him like himself.

When man sinned, these qualities were not withdrawn nor superseded by evil attributes; but these were corrupted and perverted. Salvation is the recovery of man from the disaster of sin, the reconstruction of the fallen fabric of manhood. It is the elimination of all the impure elements from man, and his re-establishment in his perfect healthful relations with God.

Manhood is the highest and grandest and most sublime idea that God ever had or ever can have. All his other works were made to this end.

God built the universe that he might make man. He worked up through all the ages to this supreme thought. Manhood was the climax of the divine effort. So far as we can now know God is still "resting from all his creative acts." His purpose now is to provide as elaborately and as magnificently for the saved ones as he did at the first for the whole race.

When God began to create, he made the heavens and the earth; made everything from original elements. He began at the lowest type. He first made the atom, then he constructed the universe.

Then he began again. He made the lowest form of living thing. As light was the first in the divine order of the inanimate creation, life is the first in the living kingdom. God began with the lowest form of living organism, and up through almost an unlimited series he marched to his creative climax in manhood.

It was after the sea swarmed with living things, and the earth and air echoed with the beat of hoof and wing, after angel and seraph and archangel had compassed the eternal throne and laid their tribute of praise on God's altar, that he said, "Let us make man." "Let us make him after our likeness and in our image." "So God created man in his own image; in the image of God created he him." That little word "so" is a descriptive term. It emphasizes the manner of the creation— "In the image of God."

As the physical man was made out of the original elements of matter, of such as he made the earth at the first, it was natural that man should draw his sustenance from the earth and the air.

God formed the organism, created the living soul and spirit,— "breathed into his nostrils the breath of life,"— made him tripartite,— body, soul, and spirit,— possessing in himself, not as an endowment, but as his own nature, all the constituent qualities of deity. Man is at the head of the column; he is above the angels. Jesus is the model of humanity. Children of God are all one with him. Man was made lower than the angels for a little while, during the period of his probation, just as Jesus was made "lower than the angels for the suffering of death."

But man's place in the scale of being is at the head. Man is a regal gentleman. He was crowned and sceptred at the first; and though fallen, he comes back to his supremacy through the redemption that is in Christ, and takes his place by him on a throne of power, who is now "crowned with glory and honor because he hath tasted death for every man." The achievements of Jesus Christ in the arena of redemption are all in the past perfect tense. It is all finished in that field of effort; and saved manhood joins him in his victory.

"For unto the angels he hath not put in subjection the world to come." But one has testified of man, saying: "Thou madest him lower than the angels for a little while; thou crownedst him with glory and honor, and didst set him over the works of thy hands; thou didst put all things in subjection under his feet." "For in that thou hast put all in subjection under him, there is nothing left that is not put under him. But now we see not yet all things put under him, but we see Jesus, who was made lower than the angels for a little while for the suffering of death." We see him "crowned with glory and honor because he hath tasted death for every man." Our Christian progress all depends upon our conceptions of Jesus and our personal relations to him. "Beloved, *now* are we the children of God." This is a present relation. It does not say shall be. We now are children of the Divine Father. It is a great thing to have a good father— to be a member of a noble household. Every child has a natural and inalienable right to be well born, and that father is a murderer who stabs his child in its embryonic state with hereditary poison of soul or body.

This text is addressed to children, not to aliens: "Brethren, now are we the sons of God." In the family there is advancement for all. There is education; there are growth and culture. These are the privileges of children only. The future possibilities are all connected with the present facts: "It doth not yet appear what we shall be."

God hath not revealed to us all the possibilities of redeemed manhood. "All things are created anew in Christ Jesus." Salvation becomes an experimental fact in the human soul by the agency of the Holy Ghost. But "it doth not yet appear what we shall be."

John had been the confidant of Jesus during the period of earthly ministry. He had listened to him when he unfolded to his disciples the mysteries of nature and of grace. He had gone with him on the mountain of transfiguration, entered the gilded pavilion of Jehovah; had heard the Father's voice and seen his glory. He had leaned on Jesus' breast at the supper, and stood near his cross on Calvary; had walked by his side to Olivet; had gazed upon his vanishing form as his victorious feet walked the ambient stairway of the skies, and had looked in prophetic vision upon the panorama of the gospel as its mailed contestants advanced to the final victory; but still greater developments were foreshadowed in the realm of redeemed manhood. More chivalrous deeds and nobler achievements await every one along the line of Christian adventure.

It doth not yet appear what we shall be in our physical organism. "We believe in the resurrection of the body and everlasting life after death." God made man immortal— tripartite— body, soul, spirit. So far as science can prove anything, matter is proved to be immortal. It does get out of place, but does not lose its identity. This bodily organism may be dissolved, but it will never perish; it cannot be annihilated. We do not clearly perceive what constitutes bodily identity. Three-fourths of what we call the body is aqueous matter; it is no part of the body. It is the running force of the organism. One-half the solid matter that remains is there, only as a contingent of waste and supply; it is part of the running force; it is the power which, acting with the life, propels the organism.

Thus, suppose the body weighs one hundred and sixty pounds; three-fourths off leaves forty pounds, and one-half of that leaves only twenty pounds of real identity — that is what shall be raised from the dead, for nothing else died. The identity will be raised and glorified. There is no significance to the gospel if the resurrection be emasculated therefrom.

The New Testament stands and shines in the brightness of this expectation. The gospel as a remedial system is the supremest farce without the resurrection. If you eliminate this fact from the Bible, it reads like the ravings of a maniac. But in the light of a *bona fide* resurrection the gospel gleams and flashes with auroral brightness, and declares a complete victory over the farthest reaching sequence of the fall.

This body shall be raised, and "it doth not yet appear what we shall be; but we shall be like him."

The curse of labor will be removed. The heavenly body will not be callous and stiff with unreasonable toil. Sorrow and care will not sit on the shoulders bowing them to the earth. Loathsome diseases will not feed upon gland and tissue of the heavenly body. He who "is the resurrection and the life" "will change our vile bodies and fashion them like unto his own glorious body," for we shall see him as he is, and "be like him" — glorified in immortality.

It doth not yet appear what we shall be intellectually. The joys of heaven, the employments and pleasures of the heavenly state, will be chiefly of an intellectual character. God has put a premium on this feature of manhood, because it is in the realm of intellect and spirit that man more especially resembles the Divine Father.

But in the heavenly state these intellectual powers will be greatly enlarged. The embargo of sin will be taken off, and the soul will be free. The toilsome process of primary lessons will never embarrass the soul in the heavenly state.

While it will always be true that man will gain knowledge by the exercise of the same faculties he now possesses, yet the effort will be natural, and will not weary him; the energies will not become exhausted; the stream of knowledge will not become muddy; facts will never become confused; the imagination will never falter in its flight. Natural historians assert that the white albatross of the Southern Pacific Ocean can float on the air for one whole week without perceptibly moving a wing. Poised on her broad pinions, she sails the upper deep. She moves ever on as if impelled by a force within.

This is to my mind a symbol of the human intellect, when the faculties shall be liberated from the bondage of sin, and readjusted in their immortal state. Supplied with new organs, and impelled by new forces, the mind of man will out-soar the mistress of the seas.

It doth not yet appear what we shall be in our moral nature.

The moral nature embraces that department of man's being over which the will has jurisdiction. It includes the realm of perception, conscience, and motive. In the future life, the moral perceptions will be different from what they are now. All things will then appear in their right relation to each other. There is a great change to be wrought in some professed Christians. No unsanctified person will ever pass through the gates of eternal glory. In this life man is dependent. He lives moment by moment on the merit of Christ. The virtue that makes man holy, that makes and keeps him alive from the dead, flows forth from Jesus Christ. It is received by faith. But in heaven man's exercise of morality will be in some measure independent.

We will not only be pure and developed, but we will have passed the limits of probational being and be in some real sense free. Individuality will always be under the dominion of law, but it will have no other limitations. Being the sons of God, we shall see our elder brother as he is, and be like him — know as he knows by intuition, and be like him in our moral nature. Jesus Christ is God's Son. We are the sons of God in him. We are as close to the Father on the human side as he is, and we are as close to Jesus on the human side as the Father is on the divine side. We meet our Father in him, and are made one with the Father by the Holy Ghost in him. The law of man's being is eternal progress. God created him under the dominion of that law, but sin precipitated man into ruin by antagonizing him with the law. Where law is violated, the forfeited perfection of man cannot be secured by a recurrence to the original condition in Eden. It is by the redemption that is in Christ Jesus the Lord, that he comes to his estate. The beautiful garden, man's Edenic home, was spoiled by sin; but it is rebuilt by the Saviour of men. We turn back the pages of history; we linger in dreamy reverence beneath the faded bowers of Eden; we sigh for its wasted fragrance; we wander along the banks of the four sacred rivers, and listen to their murmuring music as they roll on in gladness to the sea. But coming down from the prophetic heights, perfumed with more fragrant odors than Eden ever knew, is the Word of God — "Behold I make all things new." Satan spoiled Eden, and if Christ cannot give us something better, Satan is still the victor. Christ's victory does not imply a restoration to Adamic manhood. It is more than that. It is what Adam would have been after his probation was ended. It is the perfection of all his powers, energies and faculties in a state of immortality.

For centuries the Parthenon stood on the Acropolis, a monument to the genius of Pericles and Phidias. The temple of Solomon and its beautiful successor were the admiration of the ages; but the New Jerusalem, as seen in the vision of St. John, excels them all. So our redeemed and perfected manhood excels our highest conceptions of all its past stages— no dwarfish materialism crushing forever those godlike powers. The broken columns and crumbling walls of that divine structure set up in Eden have been rebuilt and cemented by the blood of Christ, to stand forever as a monument of his love.

Brethren, it doth not yet appear what we shall be. Every child of God will be like him. It is in our essential nature rather than in our actions that we are to be like Christ. Beloved, you are to see Christ as he is. Not as he was in his humiliation, fleeing from Herod to-day and escaping the murderous Jews to-morrow; shall see him as he is; not as a poor, homeless tramp, followed by a band of ignorant plebeians, doing the country on foot. Not as he appeared in Gethsemane, nor on Calvary, nor in the grave; these are the phenomena of his humiliation. Do not linger to-day at his empty tomb, nor seek again the transfiguring glories of Tabor— that was an official event. It came only once, and is but a faint shadow of the glory that is perpetual.

Everything depends on the view you have of Christ; on the conception you have of his character and office. The thought you have of Jesus assimilates you into the likeness of your thought; but the Holy Ghost transmutes you into his likeness and image.

It is a low, base, sensual conception of the God-man that always associates him with the fish stalls and oyster booths of Judea. Jesus is not there; he is exalted. Let us pass by Gethsemane and Pilate's Hall, and the tragic scenes of Golgotha, and the empty tomb in the garden of Arimathea, past Olivet where his victorious feet left their last hallowed impress on the world he redeemed, and see him as he is, with the rainbow glories of eternal victory about his brow.

That which transpires when we see Jesus is always in harmony with our thought of him.

The penitent sinner sees Jesus as his sacrifice, as his advocate with the Father; and peace fills his soul. The contrite believer sees Jesus as his purifier; the purple current passes over him, and he is made whiter than snow.

The bereaved ones in the midnight of their sorrow see Jesus as the comforter, and "there is light at eventide;" and eternity unfolds its beatific vision through everlasting years.

The dying Christian sees Jesus as the conqueror of death, and victory fills his soul and he joins the triumphant procession before the throne.

When you see Jesus as the conqueror, you enter into his victory, and share in his triumph.

John saw Jesus when he had been greatly depressed. It was Sabbath afternoon when John, brooding over the adverse influences about him, fearing the utter overthrow of the church, sought the solitudes of the mountain on the west side of Patmos, to lay his burden down at the Mercy-seat.

While he prayed, the prophetic vision was opened to him. He saw Jesus on a white horse; and the armies of heaven followed him on white horses; and the kingdoms of the world laid their honors at his feet; and the glory of the millennial day made the darkest corner of the earth bright as celestial noon.

When the stones were flying about the head of Stephen, when the angry mob gnashed on him with their teeth, and hissed and stamped in their rage, "he being full of the Holy Ghost, looked up steadfastly into heaven, and saw the glory of God, and Jesus standing on the right hand of God;" and he went up to pillow his bleeding head on the bosom of the world's Redeemer.

"Beloved, now are we the sons of God." And standing in this sacred presence to-day the outlook is glorious. "It doth not yet appear what we shall be," but we shall be like the glorified Master.

How the years speed away! The scenes of this life are soon to be exchanged for the eternal.

Beloved, when these weary feet no longer press the burning sands of life's pathway, from the summit of some Tabor in the Beulah Land, wrapped about with the divine glory, or from some high eminence on the western slope of Carmel where the unrimmed sea of full salvation stretches outward forever, the purple clouds shall part, and I shall join the blood-washed multitude before the throne.

Members of Schmul's Wesleyan Book Club buy these outstanding books at 40% off the retail price.

Join Schmul's Wesleyan Book Club by calling toll-free:
800-S$_7$P$_7$B$_2$O$_6$O$_6$K$_5$S$_7$
Put a discount Christian bookstore in your own mailbox.

**Visit us on the Internet at
www.wesleyanbooks.com**

You may also order direct from the publisher by writing:
**Schmul Publishing Company
PO Box 776
Nicholasville, KY 40340**

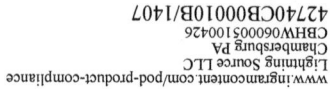